Endorsements

Hector Ortiz has once again shown that visualization and positive thinking are the keys to happiness. Dr. Ortiz articulates within his own life how positive motivation can change a community and even the world. This book is a good read for anyone seeking a successful life for themselves or others.

Graham S. Hetrick, MS, FD, B.C.F.E.

The power of positive thinking cannot be overstated. Hector Ortiz has masterfully captured the essence of this transforming force. Anyone looking to improve his or her personal and professional life can benefit from Dr. Ortiz's insightful guidance.

Pedro A. Cortés
Pennsylvania Secretary of the Commonwealth
Past President of the US National Association of Secretaries of State

Dr. Hector Ortiz has written a book that has taken the commonly heard topic of "positive thinking" and elevated it into a deeper discussion that is both educational and inspirational. This book captivated me because Dr. Ortiz writes with the mind of a scholar as well as the heart of a poet. His research on the topic is impressive, and his bibliography lists books that should be in every thinking person's library. But Dr. Ortiz goes beyond textbook-style thinking as he uses stories, examples, and quotes that illuminate his ideas and make them very applicable to readers, whatever their stage of life. This book will occupy an honored place on my bookshelf and is one that I heartily recommend to anyone who wants to live a positive, happy, and fulfilled life.

Dr. Dilip R. Abayasekara
President, Speaker Services Unlimited
Toastmasters International President, 2005–2006
Author, *The Path of the Genie—*
Your Journey to Your Heart's Desire

Hector Ortiz has written a thought-provoking and inspiring piece that all of us can use in our daily walk through life's journey. I applaud his commitment and passion for positive thinking.

Patricia Gadsden
President & CEO Life Esteem Inc.
Founder and Editor-In-Chief of
***Women-CONNECT* magazine**

Hector is a community leader and an exceptional person. He approaches everything with energy and positivity. I believe his book will help both individuals and corporations to take a positive approach to creating an environment of ongoing and unlimited success.

Amma Johnson
Singer, Songwriter, and Entrepreneur

Table of Contents

Foreword ix

Acknowledgments xi

Introduction xv

Chapter 1   **Knowing and Respecting Yourself** 1
- Knowing and Understanding Yourself 8
- From Mental Commitments to Concrete Achievement . .17
- Respect: The Foundation of Knowing Ourselves 24

Chapter 2   **Affirmative, Critical, and Creative Thinking** 29
- The Merit of Checking the Mind-set Influence in
  Allowing Positive Thinking 39
- Personal Management: A Key Element in
  Organizing Your World 42
- Personal Management and Its Relationship With
  Life's Cycle 44
- Applying Personal Organization and Time
  Management Skills 49
- Planning Skills: An Aptitude and an Attitude
  to Be Developed 51

- The Importance of Leadership in Creating and
  Executing a Plan 57
- Physical Organization: An Asset in Personal and
  Professional Growth 63
- Time Managing: An Invaluable Source in Achieving Plans . .66

Chapter 3 **Positive Attitude** 73
- Natural Human Abilities 91
- Guidelines in Applying Emotional Intelligence 94
- Positive Thoughts Are All About Controlling
  Your Emotions 109
- Positive Emotions 117
- Motivation and Intuition, the Greatest Assets in
  Maintaining Positive Attitude .125
- Proactive Decision-making Is Not Just Inherited,
  but Learned 131

Chapter 4 **Predisposition to Change** .143
- Components of Change 148
- Steps of Change 150
- Dimensions or Aspects of Change 153
- Stages of Change 157
- Phases of Change 160
- The Cycle of Change 165
- The Sequence of Change 166

Chapter 5 **Faith to Believe** 169
- Religious Diversity and the Analysis of Doubts in
  Dealing With Spiritual Resources 181
- The Spiritual Transcendence of Praying 189

Chapter 6 **Practice What You Preach** .195
- Positive Thinking, a Key Element in Facing Challenges . .200
- The Circular, Linear, and Dimensional Approaches in
  Dealing With Challenges 205

- The Importance of Praising People Instead of Merely
Criticizing Them 209
- Consistency and Determination: Skills Needed
to Achieve 212

Chapter 7   **Humility to Understand Differences** **217**
- Understanding and Accepting Diversity 230
- Understanding Poverty 237

Chapter 8   **Solidarity to Share** **249**

Chapter 9   **Positive Relationships** **263**
- Communication: An Invaluable Asset to Maintain
Healthy Relationships 269
- Relationships of Mutual Respect: An Approach in
Creating Healthy Relationships 275
- Emotional Investment: A Key to Maintain Loyal and
Healthy Relationships 283

Chapter 10   **A Genuine Approach to the Pursuit of Happiness** ..**293**

Conclusion **315**

Bibliography **331**

About the Author **337**

Foreword

———◦◦◦———

I enthusiastically endorse Dr. Ortiz's book, *The Creative Energy of Positive Thinking: A Basic Approach to the Genuine Concept of Happiness*. Readers will relate readily to the concepts presented and find immediate applicability to their personal situations, regardless of where they are in their lives. Recognizing the interconnectedness of mind, body, and spirit is, indeed, the foundation for understanding oneself and being able to build positive steps to genuine happiness. Readers will learn to accept that the genesis of our happiness rests inside us, and that once we discover that we were born with that "integrity," the journey of self-discovery becomes a joyous journey toward self-realization.

Edna V. Baehre, Ph.D.
President, HACC
Central Pennsylvania's Community College

Acknowledgments

———◆———

I would like to express my gratitude to my parents, Hector A. Ortiz and Digna Revelo de Ortiz, for teaching me the value of personal responsibility and making me aware of the countless opportunities that come from visualizing the future, not just in my mind, but also in my heart. I thank them also for teaching me the value of education, the significance of self-determination, and the priceless advantage of faith and self-confidence. I no longer have the good fortune of their physical presence but I have been blessed with their spiritual support and the pleasure of following their inspiration and teachings.

When young I had the privilege of learning the implications of balancing rights and responsibilities. As John D. Rockefeller said, "Every right implies a responsibility; every opportunity, an obligation; and every possession, a duty." That is why I also extend my gratitude to the teachers who helped me change my way of thinking so I could build a different future. In addition, I express my gratitude to the fortune of remaining conscious of the blessings that we receive on a daily basis even as I live in the middle of worldwide consternations. I am thankful for having the courage to accept the obstacles that we face on earth as normal tests of life and I understand that they represent the experiences we need to acquire true knowledge and a significant life purpose.

Thank you to my siblings and my extended family, because familial roots show us the essence of who we are. I would like to express special thankfulness to my wife, Marisol, and my two wonderful children, Cristhian Ricardo and Bonnie Zenobia, for their inspiration. Marisol, thanks for your support, comprehension, love, and friendship. Marisol, Cristhian, and Bonnie: When I see your faces and contemplate your kindness I discover that life is a beautiful journey.

More importantly, I have gained the understanding that whatever we think, say, and do should be linked to the premise that our conscious minds have no limits. We can achieve whatever we conceive and we can make dreams become real. We have the power to use the gifts of mind that have been graciously given to us and we should be thankful for those emotional and spiritual resources that can help us overcome difficulties, and for the physical and rational assets that help us understand that there is a higher purpose and meaning in our lives.

I would also like to express my deepest gratitude to my extended family, which includes not only those related by blood, but also by heart. I must thank my friends, colleagues and coworkers, mentors, and team members for their fellowship and for sharing dreams and values to improve our life on earth. It is a pleasure to express thanks to all who have contributed ideas, thoughts, and comments as I wrote this book. Special thanks to Antonio Karantonis, Stephenie Strayer, Camille Bigles, David Ritter, and Graham Hetrick for taking their time to revise and pre-edit several chapters. This book would not be possible without their help, patience, and advice. I extend my gratitude to Marsha Blessing and her publishing team for giving me the confidence and the opportunity to start this journey. Thanks to talented illustrator Mikell Worley for her commitment and inspiration in transforming abstract words into sensitive expression in forms.

Special thanks to Graham Hetrick and his wonderful wife, Esmeralda, for their sincere friendship. You have been invaluable. Thanks for your friendship and your solidarity. Graham, I consider you a true friend and a personal mentor. Graham was the first person who inspired me to write these modest comments about the mystery and rewards of life and the ways we become aware of our own resources and privileges, the best avenues of opportunity and the different routes to happiness. Once you accept that everything is about choices, you will understand that, "No mountain is too high, no river too wide, no foe too large for the person who will choose to live his dreams."

Friends are fundamental for a happy life. If I don't name more here, it's simply to avoid the unpleasant circumstance of leaving somebody out. Nevertheless, you know who you are and how much I understand the important role you play in my life. All of you have a space in my heart because, in one way or another, I have learned from you.

I would like to express my gratitude to all the philosophical resources and bibliographic support I mention in this book. I have cited, quoted, and paraphrased many wonderful thoughts that can help people improve their lives and get a true sense of purpose.

Thank you, dear readers, for giving a portion of your precious time to read these words and invest in your self growth. I trust that this reading exercise will reward you with social, economic, and educational returns. I myself have benefited by practicing the ideas in this book. Be positive and stay positive. That is the best way to enjoy life and confront challenges on earth. When you give love, you generate love; that is the key element for creating a successful and rewarding life. As Dr. John Demartini says, "Love and gratitude will dissolve all negativity in our lives" (Byrne 2006, 128).

My final heartfelt acknowledgment and gratitude goes to God for His inspiration. I owe Him my sincere and deep thankfulness for all the blessings granted to me during my wonderful life experience.

I hope you find the value in these concepts and accept the challenge to make your own journey. Apply these principles and become aware of the wonderful opportunities you have to enjoy a better life right here and right now. It does not matter what your circumstances are now; enjoy what you are doing in the present and improve the perception of your future. God bless you and your intentions.

Introduction

———◦•◦———

It is a great privilege to write a book whose primary aspiration is to create a positive-thinking mind-set in our conscious and unconscious judgments. Every day offers opportunities to create whatever you want from life. The power of your thoughts makes you capable of anything. Once you decide what you would like to see, create it in your mind and recreate it in your actions.

As William Arthur Ward said, "If you can imagine it, you can achieve it; if you can dream it, you can become it." Similarly, if you have life, you have vision. If you can envision, you can conceive. If you can conceive, you can believe. If you can believe, you can achieve. If you can achieve, you can be happy. The way we act is directly related to how we feel emotionally, which is a direct result of our thoughts. In the first four chapters of this book, I will show you how to respect your own self, create affirmative and critical thinking, maintain a continuous positive attitude, and cultivate a predisposition to change.

This requires personal determination from each individual. In chapters 5 and 6 I introduce another element that comes from our inner self—our internal definition of faith. The faith to believe provides the spiritual foundation we need to ensure we will practice what we preach. The last chapters discuss the role of the individual's commitment to society. We need one another. Life cannot be approached solely from an individualistic perspective. In order to practice ongoing positive thinking, we require the humility to understand our differences. You must practice solidarity and improve your relationships to gain a genuine approach to the pursuit of happiness.

We all see the world from different angles—physically, mentally, emotionally, and spiritually—and we contemplate success, happiness, and achievement through different parameters and from multidimensional perspectives. As a result, you may consider yourself inferior to some or superior to others. It depends on how you measure your realizations. However, on a fundamental level, you are neither inferior nor superior to anyone. We are all just different.

My hope is that this book will help you find the opportunity to become conscious of the multiple blessings that are present within and between us. Please share these ideas with others, especially to those in need. I do not mean just those deprived of material assets, but those who are needy in spirit. As Seneca said, "It is not the man who has too little, but the man who craves more, that is poor."

There is a substantial difference between wants and needs as well as needs and desires, which I will address in this book. As Ernie Zelinski says, "It is important not to mix necessities with desires [neither success with happiness] [...] Success is to get what you love; happiness is to love what you get" (Zelinski 2001, 227). Furthermore, happiness and sadness are both just mental states. They cannot be ruled or imposed on us because they depend on our power of choice. We cannot spend our whole lives preparing to find happiness. We have to act to discover the magic in ordinary things and find the vital elements of life's meaning. "There are many things in life that will capture your eyes," says an old proverb, "but very few will capture your heart."

When you discover your life's purpose or simply reaffirm it, your final goal is to solidify your character, the base of your internal and external interface. Internal peace comes mainly from the perfect interaction of physical, intellectual, emotional, and spiritual perspectives. Your character arises from the correlation of these elements, while your behavior evolves from the social and emotional dimensions that come from your ways of thinking.

Character provides the basis for a person's virtues, while skills are the foundation of an individual's talents. Any commitment to maintain character depends on the power of your mind. There's an old saying that goes, "Life's battles don't always go to the stronger or faster man, but sooner or later the man who wins is the man who thinks he can!" Your thoughts guide your choices, and therefore optimistic thinking can help turn a visionary dream into a precious reality.

The people who can see their dream transformed into reality are those who can utilize positive imaging and then act in the present the way they would like to perform in the future. They endorse an optimistic mind-set and view life from that viewpoint. Remember: it is through the appreciation of differences that people can reach collective consciousness and make inclusion an automatic choice.

The pursuit of happiness is a reasonable motivation, but the acquisition of peace of mind is even more important than happiness. A peaceful mind manifests itself in a physical body invigorated by the conscious awareness of the soul. Such a spiritual approach suggests countless new ways of enjoying the great adventure of life. Therefore, you should not necessarily seek happiness. Instead, create it. Seek it not outside, but create it inside. Perhaps happiness should be awarded, not hunted.

God bless you in your journey! "The best is always yet to come!"

Knowing and Respecting Yourself

"You do not become good by trying to be good, but by finding the goodness that is already in you, and allowing that goodness to emerge."

Eckhart Tolle

Chapter 1

Knowing and Respecting Yourself

In order to gain clarity in your life, order in your objectives, measurement in your commitments, responsibility for your family and peers, accomplishments in your career, and respect for yourself and others, you must balance your decisions and actions. More importantly, you must harmonize your physical, mental, emotional, and spiritual health. This is necessary to preserve welfare, peace of mind, love, and the pursuit of happiness. One of the main responsibilities of human beings is to take care of all the assets granted to them. We have life and we have the power to shape it for good or ill.

We are physical beings but we also have intangible qualities of emotions and spirituality. Emotional resources are positive thoughts that stimulate your mind and intellect. It is important to maintain humility during times of triumph and fortitude to endure life's difficulties, and healthy emotions give us the ability to feel comfortable and accept situations and conditions as a normal part of life. The transitory feelings of sadness or happiness, anger or peace of mind, are temporary conditions that usually flow from the power of our choices.

To maintain healthy thoughts, positive attitude, and high self-esteem, we must evaluate our internal assets as well as our external influences. In addition to the emotional responses we make in reply to the barriers we face or successes we achieve, we need spiritual commitment, persistence, emotional control, and patience to keep dreams alive and objectives clear. Spiritual support provides the knowledge to understand and the confidence to make your beliefs a way of life; it creates consistency, understanding, and purpose for your existence.

On the other hand, persistence will stimulate you to keep going no matter the odds, and patience plays an important role by keeping goals and objectives alive. It can also generate the environment of positive thinking you will need to achieve and enjoy the beauty of life. When people are able to balance rational, emotional, and spiritual assets, their physical resources help complement the cycle of life. In fact, you achieve wholeness when the body becomes intrinsically connected with the mind. The key to creating a healthy environment is to combine the capability to move, the ability to become self-sufficient, and the skills to exercise your body and mind.

The body represents your physical resources. It provides the foundation and structure of any human being. Taking care of your physical assets is a basic responsibility that starts at an early age. The human body is an amazing combination of hundreds of systems, cycles, airways, and organs. Its design allows for the automatic generation and regeneration of cells that work under a natural immune system that allows the body to take care of itself. However, there are no guarantees that our bodies can withstand the years of hard work, stress, depression, fears, and concerns that we confront almost every day. A positive attitude becomes a mandatory part of the personal responsibility to nurture your body, as much as a balanced diet and regular exercise.

A healthy body and a bright mind can take care of each other. Our emotions and spirit work in a similar way, and people should remember the essential responsibility of taking care of them. One way to do that is by nurturing, consistently and constantly, the four basics elements of our structure: brain, spirit, emotions, and body. Merely accomplishing these natural responsibilities is not enough to excel. You must get these elements to permanently interact if you want to go the extra miles you need to succeed.

Consequently, you should keep an elemental balance in place that will create harmony between hard work and wisdom. In other words, you should work to live, not live to work. Do not abuse or exhaust the life given to you. On the contrary, you must respect and take care of your body if you want to get more than you expect from it.

We need both a healthy mind as well as a vigorous body to pursue our mission on earth. All of us are born with the extraordinary ability to discover our personal legend and create a meaningful and purposeful life. If you have not discovered yours yet, I hope this book may help you along the way so you can start enjoying the true happiness of life. Take those things you see as routine and convert them into emotional habits that allow you to enjoy the details of life. This will help you identify your main mission so you can accomplish it during your presence on earth.

Let us start by counting our blessings, quantifying our assets, and making an inventory of our invaluable possessions. More importantly, use, feed, maintain, and utilize these resources in such a way that you are prepared to confront difficulties and balance them with the enjoyment of pleasant things. As you may know, our mind generates our rational actions while our emotions call the tune of our bodies' responses, "When we accept our bodies and use them they become gifts," stated Bernie Siegel. "When we resent them or hate them they become burdens" (Siegel 1998, 165).

Like our bodies, our minds also need nutrients, which so often come from our emotional responses. Consequently, proactive thinking and positive energy provide balance to our emotions, peace to our mind, and positive feelings to our senses. Furthermore, to tune body and mind, it is important to link them to the third element of this unbreakable relationship, our soul, which is cultivated by our internal values. Spiritual resources are fundamental to stimulate our positive thoughts and spiritual beliefs.

Our mind operates under these two basic influences: intellectual considerations and emotional approaches. To guide our actions under the principles of faith, solidarity, peace, and love, we must possess a high spiritual conception of the real purpose of life and a clear understanding of sharing and giving. These are two true avenues to discover the secrets of joy, peace, and happiness. The emotional segment of our body makes it possible to experience the sensations of sadness or happiness and becomes a key component in delivering positive thinking. It interacts directly or indirectly with all our possessions and responses.

I started this chapter by explaining that every person is unique. All of us are gifted and possess numerous talents and virtues. Some individuals have not developed or even discovered their assets. The dilemma is that most of the time our assets remain hidden because of our intolerable ways of thinking or from obsessive conformism when dealing with change, advantages, and opportunities.

I do not mean to imply that those who supposedly do not possess some of these assets cannot succeed. I merely mean that those who possess all these connected components—physical skills, mental abilities, proactive emotional resources, and spiritual beliefs—are in the perfect position to achieve peace. Even better, they also have the basic conditions for the pursuit of happiness. Of course, accomplishments are still in proportion to attitude, choices, and way of thinking. On the other hand, individuals who have not connected these four components still have choices to make and an attitude to select.

The real difference between those who possess all the assets to be happy but do not use them and those who confront their future without consideration of their physical, mental, or spiritual challenges is attitude. As John Maxwell mentioned, "Success depends not merely on how well you do the things you enjoy, but how conscientiously you perform those duties you don't" (Maxwell 1993, 176). Remember that motivation and stimulation are powerful forces that transcend limitations and physical and mental barriers.

Homer and Milton, those two extraordinary poets, were blind. Beethoven, one of our most brilliant composers, was deaf. As a child Einstein was considered a slow learner and diagnosed with learning disabilities at the age of six. Julius Caesar suffered from epilepsy, and Plato was a hunchback. Resources are important and necessary, but these examples show that an apparent lack of them should never become an excuse to give up. Positive outcomes take place even in the midst of supposed failure. Tolstoy abandoned high school; the famous sculptor Rodin failed entry to the School of Arts three times; Winston Churchill repeated sixth grade; while 18 editors initially rejected Richard Bach's famous tale of *Jonathan Livingston Seagull.*

Some people become consumed by initial mistakes and spend their lifetimes blaming others for their misfortunes. Others, even those with disabilities or limited resources, choose wisely to improve their lives. They possess the determination and courage necessary to build the solid foundation of a perfect life. The first step on such a path is to count your blessings and analyze your assets. When you value what you have and make your maximum effort to succeed, you will produce the desired results. Remember the wisdom of an anonymous saying: "The happiest people don't have the best of everything. They just make the best of everything that they have."

You must know yourself and work hard with the assets you have. Do not waste the opportunity to embark on your own journey of self-discovery. Make wise use of any opportunity to recognize the little things that create self-awareness and make life meaningful. For instance, when an unexpected setback occurs, a pessimistic view usually tends to reject what happened or blame others. A positive outlook accepts the situation as a temporary condition, learns from the experience, and uses it as a lesson to gain knowledge and understanding.

In summary, establishing the foundation of positive thinking requires the development of and interaction with the basic elements of life's success. Both intuition and informed decision come from mind and intellect; commitment and compassion take place with the heart and emotions; faith and confidence derive from your inner-self and spiritual orientation; and finally, action and mobility emerge from your body and physical resources.

Knowing and Understanding Yourself

It is amazing to what extent outside factors can alter a person's attitude, perceptions, and ways of thinking. I know individuals who are depressed by situations that arise due to unexpected circumstances. On such occasions we may not be able to change the facts, but we can alter the outcome by selecting our attitude and choosing our responses. Remember that life itself is a balance between beauty and challenges. That is what makes it so thrilling.

On the other hand, thousands of unimaginable events occur every day as a routine part of our daily life and that tends to make us lose consciousness of its greatness. We take for granted such things as a rainy day in spring, a snowy night in winter, or even a bright, hot summer's day. Too often we complain about things without considering the benefits of challenging our assumptions and conquering our fears. It is all about attitude. A positive mind is power; a negative one is weakness. Sadly, the most common approach is to reject and react instead of dealing with an issue. When faced with a setback, we might look for a person or situation to blame so we can satisfy our ego, hide our lack of self-esteem, and eliminate a basic sense of responsibility. To respect yourself you must begin by taking responsibility for your ways of thinking and acting. If you want to discover the kindness, virtues, and talents that all human beings possess, you must stop pointing fingers and blaming others for your bad mood, clumsiness, or laziness.

Keep in mind that "every adversity brings with it the seed of an equivalent advantage" (Hill 1983, 24). Often we initiate some negative scenarios through our own erroneous mind-set or when we fall under the influence of acquaintances who impose their bad habits on us. Generational negativity is a terrible disease, one that is very difficult to confront solely by one person involved in a cycle of pessimism. It may require an extra charge of energy combined with true positive relationships to break the circle of negative influences.

However, asking for help does not mean you must always rely on others. In fact, dependency on others is the first sign of a life of routine, one where you are not entirely living, but merely existing. People have a tendency in such situations to give up and conform or embrace a negative attitude. When addressing these kinds of self-defeating people, Napoleon Hill said, "They are the creators of their own misfortunes because of this negative belief, which is picked up by the subconscious mind, and translated into its psychological equivalent" (Hill 1983, 33).

The problems of the body are often easy to detect. Tribulations of the mind are more difficult to address. The germ of negativity that causes mental lethargy is invisible but it can kill all vestiges of positivism. It is similar to a mortal sickness that cannot be cured if it is not treated quickly.

Everything starts with your frame of reference. In his book, *Untapped Potential,* Jack Lannom says, "Mind-set precedes skill-set, belief precedes behavior, philosophy precedes performance, and theory precedes practice" (Lannom 1998, 162). When plagued by poor self-esteem or hopelessness, it is easy to fall under the sway of others and lose perspective, purpose, mission, and control of your own life. This is the factor behind the proliferation of gangs, substance abuse, and all forms of delinquency and crime. In such cases the closest influence wins, not necessarily the best one.

Several authors affirm that a person's behaviors, attitudes, ways of thinking, and typical responses are generally absorbed from the people with whom they associate. We are all products of our own environment and we collate an average of what we find around us. The great news is that we have the option to select and the opportunity to choose. Consequently, revise your acquaintances, count your friends, and evaluate your relationships. You need positive and proactive thinkers around you in order to generate optimistic energy. Of course, it is not my intention to create stereotypes around cultural, economic, ethnic, political, or social differences. The core criteria for selecting your friends should be exclusive in content, but inclusive in essence. Do not allow negative thinking to contaminate your thoughts or take away your dreams solely because that mind-set fits with your environment.

I support the principle that "no one can control your attitude, but you." Unfortunately, the influence of others can be tenacious. Positive or negative friends may influence the choices you make and the actions you take. Your obligation is to choose wisely whom you want around you. Helping yourself is a mandatory duty of your conscious self. However, you should also help others embrace the importance of social competence by advocating the spiritual rewards of solidarity.

This is not just a discretionary attitude; it is also a civic and fraternal duty. But spiritual responsibility begins at home. It starts with you and your commitment to take care of yourself. Your first task is to maintain a positive spirit and invigorate your enthusiasm in any given circumstance. Analyzing all the obstacles that we may face will help us become proactive and assume ownership of our responsibilities instead of crying over the "bad" things that occur. There is always a lesson to be learned, even from the most terrible circumstances. "If you want to be happy, the key is learning from your problems rather than walking away from them," says Dr. Bernie Siegel.

Positive thinking means you can allow the release of pain by permitting your feelings and even your body to express their affliction in terrible times. That can also apply to your logical reasoning as well as your spiritual concerns. Find the balance you need to gain confidence and pursue your goals without letting momentary episodes or past oppressions affect you. This is important for maintaining focus and acting accordingly without losing sight of your mission and purpose in life. It is why the essence of kindness assumes importance. It brings an opportunity to help others, discover their hidden virtues, and affirm them.

Of course, we should do it with ourselves before handing it to others. Any circumstance is a new opportunity to learn if we make a commitment to counting the blessings and the marvelous things that are hidden from us. The more challenges you face, the better your rewards. We can achieve whatever we conceive; the bigger the effort, the greater the outcome; the higher the obstacles, the larger the satisfactions.

Sometimes we cannot control events. But we can change the way we confront them. It is all about positive attitude and unconventional choices. Consequently, it would help to remember that several researchers say that facts dictate just a small part (10%) of our decisions while the biggest portion (90%) comes from our reactions. That's why it is important to take a couple seconds and meditate about your responses to extreme circumstances. Consider the power and influence of your responses and the effects of your decisions, because your attitude when facing a situation will have more impact than the situation itself. Your attitude promotes actions, and your choices embrace consequences. It is up to you to find the alternatives to deal with problems. Calm, meditated, and informed decisions are crucial when addressing issues and concerns.

Winston Churchill said, "A pessimist sees the difficulty in every opportunity; an optimist sees the opportunity in every difficulty." Since opportunities and struggles are really in the eye of the beholder, make a point to learn from your experiences. When facing obstacles in the future, keep in mind the difference between concerns and worries. Concerns imply a proactive approach while worries lend themselves to pessimism. According to Dale Carnegie, "Concern means realizing what the problems are and calmly taking steps to meet them. Worrying means going around in maddening, futile circles" (Carnegie 1981, 350).

That is one reason why people at all times must value the splendid torch of life that has been granted to them. Keep it bright so you can see the beauty around you. Our perceptions relate directly to the way we see life experiences—as opportunities and challenges. Use the power of your imagination to picture the best instead of concentrating on the worst.

Success comes easier to those who explore choices and opportunities without fear. It is natural to be anxious or nervous when taking new risks, but you are not being fair to yourself if you quit or become negative at the start of a new dream, goal, or commitment. Create a positive way of living instead of blindly following the apparent fatality of circumstances. Don't let yourself be driven by fate, but by choices. When you exercise the power of choice, you avoid the trap of focusing on faults, defects, or weaknesses.

Therefore, inventory your assets and be thankful for your privileges. Showing appreciation for what we have encourages us to understand the real meaning of life and enjoy each second of our short existence. Says Piero Ferrucci, "If we recognize the value of what we have, we feel rich and fortunate. If we do not recognize it, we feel poor and unhappy" (Ferrucci 2006, 174). I realize, of course, that not even our contemporary scientific discoveries can prevent us from dying. Death is a common destiny for all. Life on earth is finite. It is granted exclusively to you. It is your time. Use it! Live it! Enjoy it!

When the creator of the Nobel Prize, Alfred Nobel, read a premature announcement of his death, he was shocked by the terrible appraisals people made of him, the man who invented dynamite. This experience transformed his life. After seeing what people thought about his life, Nobel established the Nobel Prize to clear his name and recognize scientific advancement. We, too, should consider how others would perceive us if we died at this moment. Such a thought might compel us to reappraise our mistakes and accomplishments, or, better yet, appreciate the advantages we have, such as life, love, wisdom, intelligence, aptitude, friends, peace, health, home, a career, dreams, plans, skills, talents, hope, family, and relatives. Such a list will bring appreciation to your soul and spiritual comfort to your inner self. It will remind you that you are unique; you are the greatness of life's conception.

We need to stop repeating traditional mistakes, such as fooling ourselves or complaining about financial hardships. It will always be better to enjoy a few pleasant hours gained through effort and sacrifice than to collect many fruits without right or due to the labor of others. Sometimes we need help and must ask for assistance. At such times of need we should always welcome an expression of solidarity. All people should have access to solidarity and the common good, especially the weakest among us, those with disabilities, the poor, segregated, and marginalized. The basic mission of any government agency or individual is to respect the dignity of all human beings and faithfully discharge their institutional or personal responsibilities. That is why one of government's fundamental tasks is to institutionalize social justice and accessibility of services for all, without considerations of creed, culture, or differences among its constituents.

Some cultures promote individualism and others collectivism. I respect both viewpoints but I believe interdependence provides one of the best ways to create active and productive citizens. If an individual, family, or community needs assistance, there is nothing wrong with their accepting help— provided they use the assistance for the purpose it was conceived and accept it as temporary. A permanent reliance on others can stunt natural abilities, increase anxiety, and prevent independence. A Chinese proverb says, "Give a man a fish and you feed him for a day. Teach a man to fish and you feed him for a lifetime."

Everything in life has a price, and every right implies a responsibility. However, there are so many poor people in the world, most of them suffering from generational poverty, whose potential for optimism seems blocked by the desperation of the moment. The fact is that in most of these cases the lack of resources has forced them to the edge of the mainstream. They become marginalized and suffer from the silence of an unyielding and unfair system. However, even for people in these cases I recommend that they make an inventory of their values and possessions so they can better appreciate their talents and gifts before they treat themselves badly.

There is a question I ask of people who consider themselves poor or underprivileged. I ask how much money they would accept in exchange for their organs. Would they sell their eyes for fifty thousand dollars? Would they allow somebody to take out their ears or tongue for seventy thousand? Would they give up their legs and arms for ninety or even two-hundred thousand dollars? Can you even set a price for these organs? Obviously not! Therefore, you must accept that you have your own kind of wealth. If we are alive, we have hope. If there is hope, then there are desires, and if we have desires we must assert ourselves to the maximum to achieve them.

I am trying to demonstrate the necessity of becoming aware of what we already have. Sometimes we possess assets without being conscious of them, or we diminish their value and lessen our own capability. Conscious awareness is the fundamental factor of a life focused in the present.

What I am advocating here is the necessity to take action and become aware of what is going on in our society as a matter of personal and collective intervention. On the communal level, the need for the intervention of charitable and/or professional institutions is obvious. People who are mentally ill may need behavioral health assistance or medical intervention instead of prison sentences. In my view, it is just another way to show compassion and avoid excluding people from social interactions. Some people may require medical treatment. Some might be trapped beneath a heavy burden of traumatic episodes from the past, where a healing process would help. The main point is that with kindness and solidarity, we can help people master their circumstances with love, patience, sacrifice, commitment, and passion.

In other cases, some people may choose the commodity of waiting for divine help or the occurrence of a celestial miracle to solve their problems. Neither living permanently from the charity of others nor praying in a pew without demonstrating commitment to action is the answer to promote positive thinking. As the saying goes, "God gives every bird its worm but He does not throw it into its nest." Come on! Wake up! Today is the most important day of your life. The creation of your destiny is only yours. You have been granted talents and gifts that should be shared and expressed so you can discover the necessity that brought you here.

You have to do it now. What would you do if you knew that today was your last day on this planet? I assume you would like to be close to your loved ones. Many people would ask their divine or spiritual guide for another opportunity, another chance to remain longer with loved ones. Almost no one would be thinking of what he/she should have done better with their business or careers.

We did not bring anything with us when we were born and we will not take anything when we die. At the beginning and end of life, the only concern is our spiritual and emotional relationships. Then why not dedicate more time to build what is really important for your life's journey? We should not need the threat of non-existence to live as we should. We are already wealthy. We possess our bodies, at least temporarily. That alone should feed our self-esteem and reaffirm our confidence.

I have mentioned our physical possessions but have not said much about the mind and the incredible things it can produce. I am not even talking about the intelligence or abilities that make you a truly unique and gifted human being. Keep in mind that "riches begin in the form of thought! The amount is limited only by the person in whose mind the thought is put into motion" (Hill 1983, 47). If we have life, then we have been granted many gifts that we should be using and enjoying right now.

Every day provides an opportunity to achieve. If you can see, hear, speak, feel, and think, then you have no excuse. It is time to get up and live intensely. Take a sum of your blessings. Make an inventory of your greatest gifts. Count all the blessings that flow around you. The only response can be to proclaim gratitude and thankfulness for the gifts you have received.

Some of you are probably creating assumptions and perceptions about me. Maybe you think that self-help authors like me have not experienced your problems. That makes no difference. All people have their own unique problems and circumstances. However, the rule of positive thinking applies to everyone in all circumstances. Just see all the marvelous things that take place around you. Too often we fail to do that. We all have gifts and talents. We receive them every day. We must become aware of and acknowledge our gifts and the invaluable value of life. Such awareness becomes a predisposition to live the present entirely. Acknowledgment is a conscious commitment to find the wholeness without losing the details, and to constantly approach the perception of happiness. Sometimes we do not accept that because our worst enemy may be inside us. Then, we must take steps to eliminate one of our most perverse enemies, the "inferiority complex." It is an enemy that distorts self-esteem and hides self-confidence.

This is why it is so important for you to make a periodical inventory of your talents. The spirit of positive thinking is attitude; the heart of consciousness is awareness; and the soul of happiness is peace of mind. Without peace of mind, the approach to contentment becomes vain and the real meaning of pleasure turns futile. Peace of mind results from inner equanimity and positive thinking and leads to the harmonious interaction of thoughts, emotions, and beliefs.

From Mental Commitments to Concrete Achievement

The willingness to experience joy is a mental commitment that comes from your attitude to see, hear, perceive, feel, and digest the beauty of life. The real spirit of joy allows you to get pleasure from both the greatest miracles of the world and the simplest things that take place every second in our own backyard. When the spirit of joy flows, it produces a more successful goal-setting approach, a less stressful problem-solving outlook, and a more fulfilling life. One of the ways to find it is by using mental models, tools that can help you visualize the desired future.

Mental models can help you make abstract dreams become reality once you accept and understand your power of choice. Mental models are alternative ways to simplify and conceptualize ideas so that anything you think and dream is possible. It is all in the power of your imagination. A mental model is a concept you pick from your intellect and place inside the mind's emotional site so it appears concrete and feasible.

In effect, a mental model is a transfiguration between mental imagination and concrete realization; a psychological ability that can be symbolized by a drawing, diagram, or solid idealization of a dream. In order to clearly identify a mental commitment, you must accept that in addition to making the basic connections between body, soul, and spirit, people must assume personal responsibility for their actions and choices. Everything starts with a proactive attitude. As Buddha wrote, "All that we are is the result of what we have thought. The mind is everything. What we think, we become" (Mandino 1991, 68).

Imagination gives us an ability to visualize the future by moving ideas until they become reachable realities. It is also a powerful demonstration of the intellect, which invigorates our emotional strengths and its spiritual components. As Wally Amos states, "Imagination is the power of the mind to form a mental image of something neither real nor present [...] whatever you materialize in your life must first be pictured in your mind by your imagination" (Amos & Amos 1988, 137). Imagination is creativity strengthened by passion and shaped with patience to create a proactive attitude to change. The power of imagination helps us form mental pictures so we can visualize a positive future. While it takes time to develop this tactic, it is one of the easiest ways to tap into the power of realization. When you see something in the mental model structure, it turns into your truth.

Imagination crystallizes the things that others cannot see, but it also gives us the ability to enjoy those things before they become realities. Walt Disney provides one example of the power of visualization. When Disney's Epcot Center opened in Florida, a reporter commented that it was too bad Disney was not alive to see the beauty of his creation. "I guess you are wrong!" replied the president of the Disney Corporation. "Epcot Center exists precisely because Mr. Walt Disney saw this place in his mind before anybody also could even image it" (Bolet 2001, 198).

The power of visualization usually brings ideas in a mental picture and/or in the way of a spiritual revelation. Norman Vincent Peale said that visualization means, "Holding the image of yourself succeeding, visualizing it so vividly that when the desired success comes, it seems to be merely echoing a reality that has already existed in your mind" (Peale 1982, 29). Why waste time with worries, anxieties, and fears on your way to succeed? They drain our time, but also attract pessimism and negative thoughts. To paraphrase Silvia Bolet, 40 percent of our worries never happen, 30 percent are part of the past and beyond change, and 12 percent relates to our health. Ten percent represents insignificant things, leaving just eight percent of our worries that need our attention (Bolet 2001, 215).

Consequently, some of our self-imposed warnings may be for things that won't even occur. Being aware, planning accordingly, and taking action may be necessary; but too much worrying just intensifies stress, nervousness, uneasiness, depression, and emotional challenges. That's why two very important elements for positive thinking are enthusiasm and hope.

A permanent approach to positive thinking takes place when you develop spiritual and emotional character to harmonize body, soul, and spirit. Remember that "everything that ever was, that is, and that ever will be started with an idea" (Amos & Amos 1988, 150). So exercise your mind and energize your emotions; use the power of your intellect by imagining the pleasure of living your dreams and achieving your goals. More importantly, fill your life, on daily basis, with positive experiences by exercising your brain and igniting your mind with positive thoughts.

You are the only one who can determine what your day will look like. You are in charge of your present, and therefore your immediate future. Leave the things you cannot manage or understand in the hands of your religious or higher spiritual guide. Perhaps your faith will help defeat your own self-imposed limitations and get you thinking and acting in a positive way so that the light of hope will brighten the course of your thoughts.

You will be surprised at the changes that occur every day of your new, revitalized life. This way of thinking fills your days with pleasure as you become the architect of your own destiny. Your old role, the one where you became accustomed to complaining and asking for almost everything, will vanish. In addition, you will take responsibility for your actions as part of the auto-imposed self-commitment to rebuild your life.

True, sometimes simply accepting responsibility is not enough. From time to time, we may need the joint efforts of the whole society, a public and private exercise of solidarity that helps people fulfill their responsibilities. Remember, it is fair to ask for help when you need it, in order to fulfill the basic needs that any human being has. Nevertheless, I really believe that once you affirm your assets, change your attitude, and think in a positive way, you will experience the transformation that will bring about desired outcomes on a continuing basis.

Once we believe in ourselves, we can fulfill our immediate needs and maximize our well-being. Positive thinking will inspire you to accept the responsibility of being in charge of your life and helping others find the real purpose of theirs. You can start by enjoying the greatness of life every day. Your attitude is what really counts. If you have found the treasure of your blessings, enjoy them—but don't forget to extend your solidarity to others. When somebody less fortunate requests our assistance, our human responsibility is to help. The Bible says: "Rejoice with those who rejoice, and weep with those who weep" (Romans 12:15 NKJV). It is not just an act of fairness, but of solidarity. I encourage individual responsibility, but we also must understand our collective responsibility. It is a duty for all of us to implement a fair system of equality, equity, and opportunities. It is what I call a mandatory duty for serving others. It perfectly matches what Eldon Tanner said: "Service is the rent we pay for the privilege of living on this earth" (Covey 1989, 299).

Scholars refer to "contested ideas" because they may hold different meanings depending on the background of the beholders. The real meaning of social justice must include a balance between conservative, and liberal views. In my opinion, moderate, conservative, and progressive values can coexist if they avoid radical postures and extreme viewpoints. We can redistribute justice and wealth not only according to merit, but also to provide for the needs of the less fortunate. Consequently, we should remain accountable for our acts and contribute responsibly to the social and economic debates about injustice, discrimination, and segregation.

The fact is that our core values are tested and our sense of community is built when it comes time to spread brotherly love, compassion, and hospitality among those in need. I value the individualities of the few without sacrificing the public needs of the many. In fact, instead of constantly pressuring people to compete or merely succeed, we should praise cooperation and collaboration. More importantly, we should resolve our differences with sensitivity and not demean people's affiliations with liberal or conservative approaches or religious or spiritual preferences.

The main purpose of living in community is to build relationships of mutual respect and human dignity. Therefore, it is right to advocate for fairness, social justice, and equal opportunity to achieve personal development and self-fulfillment. It is all about praising and following values that are essential for social interaction. Some values may be similar and some different. In fact, people with similar values may differ in their interpretation of them.

For instance, the concepts of freedom and equality can be seen from different viewpoints. This presents an opportunity to learn and make informed decisions. Establish a commitment to open your mind and become sensitive and flexible. Accept that nothing is absolute. In the political, economic, social, or religious environment, any extreme viewpoint may become contentious because there is no absolute truth. Consequently, we should be cautious when we weigh our values. Buddha called it "The middle way," which is interpreted as the harmony needed to avoid extremes and to balance all sides.

Our values are very important resources even if they come from different perspectives. Values so often manifest themselves in behavior, beliefs, and judgment. They influence our actions and our interpretations of principles such as honesty, integrity, discipline, and moral and ethical standards. They also represent our beliefs about people and of the purpose of life, including concepts of freedom, equality, religion, spirituality, fraternity, and solidarity. Finally, values influence the way we judge, act, create, and develop our relationships.

Your values are important components for building credibility, acquiring trust, and gaining confidence. Behaviors, values, and judgments become important components in your distinctiveness as a human being. They influence who you are and they help determine who you will become. Our core values can prevent us from becoming self-centered and show us the necessity for solidarity, understanding differences, and accepting the benefit of the whole over the delight of the few.

THE CREATIVE ENERGY OF POSITIVE THINKING

Proactive thinking takes place when people assume total responsibility for their acts by prioritizing values and following principles. Rationality precedes feelings, beliefs surpass dogmas, and change overcomes paradigms. The right to act in a responsible way is a moral and ethical commitment that all human beings must pursue. If we have identified our gifts and recognized our assets, then we should change our attitude and move from the side of the simple observer to that of the active doer.

One of the principles of solidarity is that we have a personal and community obligation to assist those in need in a timely and proportional manner. The decision to assist others comes from our spiritual commitment to compassion; it affirms our pledge for moral justice and reaffirms the necessity of compassion and solidarity. These legal and moral philosophies come from the main principles adopted by international laws from institutions such as the United Nations. For example, most democratic nations accept the Universal Human Rights Act, established in 1948. Respecting the dignity and rights of others is not just a legal action, but an engagement in social justice and a spiritual approach to commonality and respect for others.

I accept that these ideas may not represent the teachings of all faiths but I have included them with deepest respect for other religious and spiritual insights. The underlying principle is the predominance of love and compassion. To love one another means you should love your neighbor as yourself. However, it must not be limited to your neighbor, but extended to all. It is our sense of duty to give those in need a hand, embrace their talents, advocate for their rights, and help them take care of themselves and achieve their dreams.

When you encourage self-sufficiency in others, ask for action and participation and look for affirmation of values and reaffirmation of identity. Affirmation of values gives people courage. Reaffirmation of identity gives them confidence. If we want to change the world, we should start by changing ourselves. I am challenging you to start promoting goodwill, peace, and fellowship by offering true love, at least to those who are around you.

Does that sound idealistic? I would like to remind you of an anonymous saying that goes, "Don't limit your challenges; challenge your limits." To love each other does not mean merely to express it, but to demonstrate it with actions. I accept that any extreme is negative, even in charity. Problems start when we become accustomed to living off the charity of others, when we receive things without effort and replace begging for working or pity for solidarity. We are fortunate to have many people and thousands of philanthropists and charitable organizations who help the underprivileged. We thank them for their kindness; however, we should accept material or financial help only as a temporary condition.

On the other hand, the giver must provide help in the spirit of solidarity instead of solely as a gesture of charity. Solidarity is the magic word that allows the people who receive the benefit to conserve the dignity that all human beings possess. Jose Ingenieros pointed out the difference between charity and solidarity by saying, "Solidarity allows that generosity becomes rights while charity offers it as a favor." The intention of solidarity is to help today with the goal of eventual independence and acquired self-sufficiency.

We all know that financial independence is not merely the accumulation of wealth, but having the power to produce wealth. We should give life skills, affirmation, and encouragement while we should expect courage, commitment, enthusiasm, and purpose of life. We can receive monetary fulfillment and still feel empty or depressed. It is all about attitude and commitment. As an old saying reminds us, "We can buy a bed, but not a dream, books, but not knowledge, food, but not appetite, a house, but not a home, prescriptions, but not health, diversion, but not happiness."

So change your way of thinking now. It does not matter if you are a father, mother, grandfather, grandmother, sister, brother, teacher, elected official, or pastor. You are unique! Enjoy every second of this beautiful world. Do not condemn yourself to an existence restricted by your own self-imposed limitations. Make the decision today that will change your life forever. Maintain positivism and allow yourself a pathway of critical thinking. Then redirect your mind and thoughts by knowing your assets and respecting yourself. Live the joy of the moment and prepare the pathway of the future.

On the other hand, there is no reason for being unprepared for those things that may not happen the way we hope. Not that you should display negativism, but be prepared for any challenge without affecting your predisposition to positive thinking. Value what you have instead of complaining about those things that you do not possess. Praise your present commitments and future plans without losing the occasion to discover the marvelous occurrences that take place every day. Appreciate nature and respect yourself. This is fundamental for the pursuit of physical, mental, and spiritual health.

Respect: The Foundation of Knowing Ourselves

Knowing and respecting yourself means you recognize and accept who you are. That requires awareness of everything you think and do. Attentiveness is where motivation, stimulus, and consciousness appear. It brings respect, value, and worth to whatever we plan and execute. When you know yourself, you become aware of the tangible and intangible elements of your external and internal being.

As Eckhart Tolle says, "Most humans see only the outer form, unaware of the inner essence, just as they are unaware of their own essence and identify only with their own physical and psychological form" (Tolle 2005, 4). Only when we acknowledge ourselves and others do we find reverence for the dignity of humankind. Respect is the foundation of social skills. "Treat others exactly as you would like to be treated yourself," says the Book of Matthew. Respect is the foundation of any healthy association. Interacting with peers without judging them is the healthiest way to keep and maintain positive connections with people.

Respecting others is a useful tool for creating long-lasting relations. It cultivates manners, politeness, and sociability. Mutual respect allows people to maintain proper and strong relationships. It begins when you respect yourself. If you do not respect yourself, no one else will. It does not matter if you are a leader or follower. Show sympathy and kindness to others just as you would expect deference for yourself. It is always better to solicit than order; to be polite instead of rude; to use sensitivity instead of tolerance; to be involved than to be merely interested. Respect, however, does not mean tolerating atrocities or supporting injustice.

Respect for others builds the groundwork for a civil society, but respect for ourselves helps lead to success. Praising yourself promotes positivism, self-confidence, hope, and optimism. Of course, I recommend keeping it inside in order to avoid narcissism. Self-recognition is an opportunity to value yourself and a tool to keep your attitude up and self-esteem animated. Self-talking is a technique that serves to create an invisible compatriot in both difficult and favorable circumstances. Sometimes we talk to blame ourselves or complain, in silence, against somebody who has created problems or concerns. Self-talking is an internal communication with your private self, an inner voice that usually provides support and confidence.

Introspection helps you find support in your own strengths at those times when your self-esteem has been hurt. For this reason, it is a good idea to perform periodically a proactive self-talking practice to value your own assets. It will also help to feed your spirit the same way that food feeds your body.

Self-talking is also a method to control your anger and/or irritability and release it slowly instead of exploding emotionally. A dialogue with your inner self is a tool to gain confidence and self-respect, so do not confuse pride with arrogance or assurance with narcissism. There is a big difference between self-encouragement and vanity. Self-support increases confidence and self-esteem. Vanity, or egocentrism, can destroy you and your relationships.

The first step in feeding your self-esteem is to recognize the value of your accomplishments. Do not confuse exaltation of virtues with egotism. Lack of humility can become vanity, but self-recognition is a conversation between your conscious and subconscious as well as your mind and your soul. Do it when you are alone to reinforce your strengths so you become proactive instead of reactive. But make sure you use self-recognition to develop self-confidence instead of arrogance or, even worse, self-centeredness.

By praising yourself you will understand what you have achieved and recognize the power of thankfulness. In fact, gratitude is one of the greatest assets of praise people. Begin with yourself and pass it to others. Do it kindly and sincerely. Start by recognizing the greatest talents you already have. Admire your own life. Build your attitude based on your strengths. Use bad situations as ways to gain knowledge instead of recriminating yourself or others.

Appreciation for life is something we may not even consider because we take it for granted. Our freedom, opportunities, and resources tend to lose their real value when we get them without effort or grant them without sacrifice. Gratitude helps us recognize our necessities and become aware of the needs of others. This state of thankfulness allows us to show gratefulness and appreciation not just for the great things provided to us, but also for the challenges and difficulties that we face. Respect includes revering your way of thinking, but fundamentally it means preserving the art of living.

Respecting yourself and others is one step to improving your personality and your relationships. Respect is the foundation of life. It includes, but it is not limited to, material and sociological things, reverence for the elderly, and consideration for justice, equality, and equity for all, especially for the marginal and more vulnerable individuals. One way to offer respect for life comes from Gandhi, who warned of what he called the seven deadly social sins: "Politics without principle; wealth without work; commerce without morality; pleasure without conscience; science without humanity; [and] worship without sacrifice."

To summarize, respecting and knowing yourself are fundamental virtues if you want to embrace affirmative and creative thinking. Respect and follow values and principles. They acquire even more significance when they are connected to moral and ethical values and a respect for human dignity above material goods, pleasure, and spiritual delight. Respect is fundamental to create understanding and promote acceptance. It expresses the most reverential way to appreciate the elemental foundation of morality, social interaction, and mutual coexistence.

Affirmative, Critical, and Creative Thinking

—————◆—————

"We all live under the same sky. But we don't all have the same horizon."
John Maxwell

Chapter 2

Affirmative, Critical, and Creative Thinking

———◆◆———

True positive thinking requires a strong connection between body, mind, soul, and emotions. Our mind is the conscious and analytical part of our body. It promotes the reasonable responses that come from our intellect. The soul is the living spirit that nurtures our faith and finds significance in the purpose and destiny of our life. Emotions are the circumstantial expression of our feelings based on the perceptions our senses generate, while the body is the receptor and interpreter of our rational, emotional, and spiritual considerations.

One of the routes to positive thoughts can be found by establishing a solid connection among the mental, emotional, spiritual, and physical centers of the body. This creates reciprocal feedback from each part of our structure that becomes necessary to maintain a connection between the internal assets (mind and soul) and the external physical and emotional resources (corporal responses and feelings).

I will start analyzing the physical, mental, emotional, and spiritual methods of maintaining positive thinking by exploring their components individually and collectively. Let us concentrate first on our rational and intelligent approach. Clearly there is a difference between the brain and the mind. The brain is the soft tissue that functions as the center of our nervous system, while the mind is the person's intellectual ability, memory capacity, and free will. The mind combines two basic components: rational and emotional responses. Feuerstein said, "It is possible to have a brain and not have a mind. A brain is inherited; a mind is developed." It is my understanding that in referring to mind, he means intelligence or intellectual potential.

Our minds and feelings are affected by the positive and negative energy that flows in the environment. Both people and nature influence thinking and therefore decision making. A person uses internal and external responses to assimilate the effects of their desires. Since this is a choice, you have the option to seed your mind with positive thoughts and allow it to frequent environments charged with positive energy and proactive interactions. Critical thinking is a rational concept that usually filters our emotional components as well as the interference of patterns or paradigms. Sometimes, that helps us reaffirm principles or confront diverse realities that we may encounter in our search of truth.

It is not my intention to create uncertainty or challenge your beliefs. My purpose is to make you aware of the existence, influence, and transmission of negative thinking. There is no doubt that positive and negative energy exist. In fact, there is no intermediate level in the energy field. It is either positive or negative. You have the choice of accepting the positive influence or, even better, generating an affirmative chain reaction of positive thinking instead of being trapped by negativism. I understand that the dimension of both positive and negative influences relates directly to the structure of your personality. One approach to personality, the DISC theory, introduces four basic people personality types: Dominance, Influence, Steadiness, and Conscientiousness.

Your personality type certainly influences your way of thinking and acting. The bottom line is that your personality is shaped by the effect you have on others and the impression that others make on you. People sometimes erroneously accept negative influences as an inevitable human situation. However, it is merely one option. You can live prostrated by the disguised choice of others or grow up under the intelligent design of your own positive perspective. A fresh approach can help you consciously reevaluate the current present and prepare for an optimistic future.

Positive energy is a series of impulses that influence your mood, character, temperament, and predisposition to act without being affected by external impediments. Positive energy makes everything possible. In addition, it is necessary to present ideas to ourselves with curiosity, a little bit of knowledge, unlimited enthusiasm, rational considerations, and auto-controlled emotional commitments. Being able to balance heart and intellect is one of the basic responsibilities of our spirit.

A dream is an opportunity your mind creates, your intellect develops, and your heart supports. Therefore, a dream represents the interconnectedness within our holistic self. It converts a visionary premise into pragmatic reality. Negativism is an extreme viewpoint based exclusively in unbalanced pessimistic responses. Skepticism is a little different. It still lies on the pessimistic side because it embraces doubt, uncertainties, and reservations. I will call it the moderate side of negativism. From time to time, it is wise to remain uncertain of some statements or beliefs. At such times you may require more information or accurate self-analysis before you can make a rational response.

I accept that we cannot maintain an absolute and invariable positive mood, but a conditioned and positive realistic one is possible. One way to find balance and harmony is by applying the "middle way" approach or the "middle fair" technique when measuring your actions. This helps you maintain a positive attitude by balancing skeptical inputs and optimistic views. Sometimes that comes from inside. At times, it may emerge from the outside. "Concepts are not things that can be changed just by someone telling us a fact," George Lakoff said. "We may be pervaded with facts, but for us to make sense of them, they have to fit what is already in the synapses of the brain" (Lakoff 2004, 17).

Your frame of reference depends on your attitude. Allowing different opinions will help you affirm the advantage of creating critical and positive thinking. There are many reasons to open our minds to different opinions. For example, it allows us to refresh our apparent objectivity by interpreting facts that may have different meanings for others. Keep in mind that we have the free will to choose and the responsibility to accept the consequences of our choices. Those choices are based in our core values but they mold perceptions and reduce conditioned assumptions. This is the first step toward understanding that any theory or axiom needs to be tested before you accept it as true. We should be cautious because in reality, anything in life is relative.

It is also helpful to be aware that there are different ways to interpret the same situations or conditions. The way we accept or reject people's interpretations can cause bitterness, altercations, and negative outcomes. Such conflict can arise from an intolerable way of thinking, a rude tone of voice, inconsistent body language, and/or a preconceived attitude. Whatever the situation may be, there are always a way to deal positively with any issue. The focus should be on solutions and opportunities and not merely difficulties and failures. Realistic, positive, and critical thinking comes from a practical, affirmative, and enthusiastic approach. Be predisposed to apply positive thinking when difficulties arise in order to handle them in a proactive manner. Attitude is a key element in generating positive thinking.

Wally Amos, in *The Power in You*, asserts, "Attitudes are never a result of circumstances. Circumstances are the result of attitudes" (Amos & Amos 1988, 36). Most of the time, you determine the way you respond to the challenges of every new day. If you are in charge, then you lead your life. It is your responsibility to choose how to act and think, and that is determined by your attitude, stimulus, and motivations. Keep in mind that you must control your attitudes or, inevitably, they will unconsciously control you.

A positive attitude opens you up to options and choices. It can lead to un-expected streams of positive energy as well as creative approaches to life. Positive attitude is all about affirmative thinking. But attitude is more than merely thinking; attitude is a response invigorated by the rationality impregnated in your ways of thought and the confidence of your emotional responses.

Your attitude derives from conscious discernment and emotive feelings. Positive attitude allows you to focus on those little details that so often bring happiness when you're not focusing your attention on the places where you would like to be. To paraphrase John Maxwell, positive attitude is the internal force that maintains the clarity of your future commitments without losing the opportunity to enjoy where you are and where you are going (Maxwell 1998, 53). You must seed and reseed positive thinking in your soul and intellect. It is a course you must take even if others cannot understand it. Attitude is a choice and an internal decision; positive thinking is a lifestyle and an external way of thinking. Positive thinking can interpret feelings, reorder priorities, and attract positive energy. Positive thinking characterizes us; positive attitude defines us.

When you think positively, you accept the result of your choices and learn from the outcomes instead of complaining about them. Positive thinking provides a clear way to understand that the only pathway to achievement is by creating opportunities and being prepared to utilize all possibilities to accomplish your dreams. With positive thinking, success becomes just a matter of time, hard work, and perseverance. Positivism brings options and helps you determine opportunities to reach success.

In addition to the opportunities it offers, positive thinking is a necessary part of critical thinking that sets goals, clarifies objectives, and creates concrete action plans. Critical thinking, as Terry and Stuart Hirschberg write in *Every Day, Everywhere,* is "The process of asking questions, forming and supporting opinions, evaluating evidence and placing issues in a broader context" (Hirschberg & Hirschberg 2002, 12). Critical thinking is necessary for developing plans, but not choosing your dreams. It transforms wishes into goals and desires into realities.

When you practice critical thinking you must identify all of the elements of your dream, evaluate all the resources available, and analyze all the evidence. Positive thinking is the roadway that transports us from the mere conception of ideas to clear probabilities. Critical thinking is the highway that moves us from probabilities to possibilities. However, critical thinking alone is not enough to get your goal. Critical thinking will help you maintain a proactive attitude, defend your thesis, interpret resources, and evaluate your personal beliefs and habits. A critical and positive attitude facilitates the conception of plans, and helps us make predictions of those circumstances that we can manage and accept those things that we cannot control. Critical thinking and a positive approach works to prevent reactions and uncontrolled emotions that may arise due to adversity.

In fact, the best way to solve a problem is to accept it as a fact, identify the symptoms, define and process the situation, and then confront the causes with alternative solutions. Remain aware of the presence of consistent negative patterns whose influence can be expressed in the context of critical thinking. Be critical, logical, and rational when you approach dreaming, planning, thinking, and acting. That is why reflection, evaluation, and reaffirmation are recommended procedures to improve and transform a good thing into a great one.

These concepts empower positivism and encourage the application of critical approaches to any adverse circumstances you encounter. They are also fundamental tools for discovering truth and consolidating your confidence. Critical thinking tests your own truth and explores factual alternatives. It confronts criticism and controversies without losing perspective or self-reliance. Keep in mind that perception is based on the lenses we use.

As Stephen Covey says, "Others can see things differently from their apparently equally clear and objective point of view...When we stand depends on where we sit... [Mainly because] We see the world, not as it is, but as we are" (Covey 1989, 28). That is why I recommend self-evaluation and critical analyses of our own virtues and weaknesses. After all, we learn more when we listen than when we talk. Listening is one of the most direct routes to understanding and improved relationships. It is better to value different opinions instead being absorbed by the exclusivity of our own. In fact, one path to wisdom is to obtain feedback, and reaffirm your convictions and aspirations by listening to others as well as yourself.

Respectful communication is fundamentally important when interacting with others. I encourage you to apply attentive listening skills and learning strategies so you can appreciate the intellectual value of the people with whom you interact. We will address this topic in depth later. In the meantime, I just would like to mention that intuition is also important for distinguishing positive advice from negative direction.

Active listening skills, intuition, and enthusiasm are extremely important for maintaining positive thoughts. They also help people be attentive so they can recognize those slight negative influences that so often convince individuals to abandon dreams, goals, or objectives. The intuition to discern your thoughts and critical thinking to evaluate the views of others become crucial before you seek advice from those who probably never tried for their own dreams.

It is better to live your own experience than to rely on unhappy episodes of other people. Go ahead! Make your own decisions instead of living under the influence of past negative practices made by others. God and your spiritual intuition will prevent you from becoming afraid of reliving the failures of others or facing the incomprehension of those who have not even thought about the pleasure of success.

The following tale reminds us of the importance of following your instincts and leaving the pessimism of others behind. It goes as follows:

Several frogs held a competition to see which one could reach the top of a very high tower. A big crowd gathered to cheer the contestants, but no one believed any of the tiny frogs could reach the top. "Too difficult," they said.

"They will never make it." "The tower is too high." "Not a chance that they will succeed." "Silly frogs, they will kill themselves."

The frogs began climbing. As they ascended, they began falling one by one. Several others, though, kept a steady tempo and climbed higher and higher. The crowd shouted out the same pessimistic statements. "Come down or you will die." "Crazy frogs! Nobody has made it before." The crowd repeated itself over and over.

More frogs grew tired and, influenced by the crowd, they finally gave up. Only one remained. This frog looked like it would not give up and he finally made it to the top. When he returned to the ground, all the other frogs and the members of the crowd wanted to know how he had found the strength to succeed. It turned out that the winner was deaf!

The lesson is clear: never listen to other people's negativism. Look at the positive side instead. "As you focus on the negative events of the world, you not only add to them, but you bring more negative things into your own life at the same time," says Hale Dowskin (Byrne 2006, 144). Remain graciously deaf when people tell you that you cannot fulfill your dream.

Never permit anyone else to determine the size of your dreams, deter your mission, or limit your potential. "Life's battles don't always go to the stronger or faster man; but sooner or later who wins is the man who thinks he can," as an old saying puts it. Our personal philosophy and positive thinking provide the internal strength that influences our environment and leads us into a better future. Positive thinking generates conscious awareness and it will always remind us to see the current situation as well as the visionary future as pleasant and vivid.

"Imagining helps [...] because if you imagine a desired goal vividly enough, if you visualize the rewards of patience and self-discipline clearly enough, you can often supply the motivation that otherwise might be missing," wrote Norman Vincent Peale (Peale 1982, 216). A critical approach will always work if you have faith and confidence in your talents and potential. However, it helps if you pay a little more attention to those positive voices and omens that you can usually find around you so you can contrast those who prevent your failure with those who impede your success.

Uncertainties are part of any beginning, but once you make a decision to start you must stop doubting or procrastinating. The decision-making process is over. It is time to move forward instead of becoming trapped by fear. It will always be better to make the attempt than to remain in a comfort zone. Caution and prudence can be your allies, but you should not allow your uncertainties to feed pessimism or transmit negativism. A positive attitude separates those who decide to live their lives fully and those who merely exist. Keep this poem in mind: "There was a very cautious man who never laughed or played. He never risked; he never tried. He never sang or prayed. And when he one day passed away, his insurance was denied. For since he never really lived, they claimed he never really died."

Life brings mobility when you embrace action; activity promotes commitment; passion creates continuity; and challenge endorses devotion and the persistence you need to achieve. The capability to make balanced and informed decisions comes from the ability to recognize the value of your holistic self. You always hold the possibility of entering the doorway to opportunity. One of the greatest pleasures is to take the initiative to overcome barriers. The reward is not just provisions for your mind, but food for your soul. Consequently, take the risk, test yourself, challenge your self-imposed limits, and examine your capacities to enjoy the unlimited possibilities that come from the power of decision.

The Merit of Checking the Mind-set Influence in Allowing Positive Thinking

Critical thinking is fundamental. It helps identify those who compel you to fail. On the other hand, affirmative thoughts help us identify those who encourage us. The same energy may also defend you against the negativism of those who, based on past episodes or procrastinating behaviors, may transform your initial commitments to procrastinating worries. Any decision implies both risks and opportunities. The point is to avoid letting the negative hold you back. Keep going by maintaining a positive attitude and confront any adversity as an incidental condition. Sometimes, intentions alone are not enough. Your intellectual mind-set or internal frame of reference plays its own fundamental role in critical thinking. The confluence of mind and spirit is necessary if you want to gain the fortitude needed to confront uncertainty.

Our frame of reference becomes of transcendental importance in our social interactions. It dictates the framework for understanding respect and acknowledging differences in our circle of influence as we confront the facts and ideas offered by others. It is as we frame our values that we develop an attitude of positive thinking and gain confidence. The challenge is to confront and manage troubles with informed intuition and in a timely manner to avoid turning concerns into problems.

"A test of a leader is the ability to recognize a problem before it becomes an emergency," wrote John Maxwell (Maxwell 1993, 81). Problems can cause confusion, and uncertainties can generate a lack of confidence that leads to pessimism and negative responses. Yet even confusion and skepticism may become resources instead of exclusively bad omens. In fact, when Jose Ortega and Gasset defined the term confusion, it was as "an initial phase of all knowledge, without which one cannot progress to clarity." In other words, do not let contested questions frustrate you if your only intention is to reaffirm what you consider truth. It is a basic test in applying critical and positive thinking.

That is why we must not become blinded by our own mental barriers when confronting hostilities or complaints. An open mind requires a proactive approach to different ways of thinking. A predisposition to positive thinking requires you to modify your own thoughts, habits, and behavior and gain total control over your feelings and emotions. A mind controlled by positive, rational, and emotional responses can transform habits and attitudes by filling the environment with positive and proactive reflections. If we control our attitude, then we have the power of choosing how to handle whatever we face.

More importantly, we have the power to select our responses by carefully and intelligently selecting our replies. The accuracy of our frame of reference becomes a critical element for overcoming pessimism and accepting pragmatic realities. For example, if our rational intention is to arrive on time to any selected place, the priority should be to analyze the accuracy of the point of reference. If our maps or directions are wrong, then our outcome may not be what we desire.

When dealing with topics such as negativism, accepting differences, understanding poverty, and/or promoting positivism and proactive ways of thinking, we must remain open to different viewpoints or we may become reactive instead of proactive. The problem is that we may not be prepared to rationally and emotionally accept differences in our inner self. Changing a frame of reference is a process of challenge and opportunity that may affect the essence of your life purposes.

Personal change is an internal commitment that you should evaluate sufficiently so you can cultivate an open mind instead of destroying the foundation of your own values. Transformation starts with your own self. It is always preferable to meditate on your decisions to avoid the intransigency and intolerance of an inflexible way of thinking. If your feelings control your actions, it may be because you have abdicated your responsibility and empowered them to do so. Instead, favor rationality and apply a constant evaluation to deter the expansion of uncontrolled emotions. As Stephen Covey wrote, "It is not what happens to us, but our response to what happens to us that hurts us" (Covey 1989, 73).

To periodically reevaluate your frame of reference you must be willing to change and you must be committed to reframing your current way of thinking. Such a reframing may require the resetting of core values and the belief that you can improve, enhance, or refine your ways of thinking. When reframing or reevaluating, attentive communication allows important elements to shift so you can make assertive decisions. Proactive communication and active listening skills become essential when you want to identify the variables involved in the different ways people interact. Is someone merely chatting or engaging in a deeper conversation? Instinct is one element that may help you determine the difference between gossip and informed research. In other words, intuition is the ability to find the difference between an emotional comment and a conscientious analytical analysis.

Serious consideration of issues helps people avoid acting on impulse. Critical thinking can help you predict future scenarios and prevent undesired consequences. Applying critical thinking is your best ally when you take responsibility for your actions. Critical thinking and conscious self-analysis of your talents are fundamental for promoting strategic thinking, which is a basic approach to create proactive ways of managing your life.

Personal Management: A Key Element in Organizing Your World

The way that you manage your personal activities is crucial if you want to identify what's important to you—the elements that create your identity and form your personality. That includes, but it is not limited to, character, integrity, honesty, courage, and moral and ethical standards that exist independently of the circumstance you confront through life. Personal management skills are tied to the ongoing process of dreaming, planning, and achieving. It is our responsibility to learn, evaluate, and apply the techniques or strategies we can implement to accomplish a simple task or a whole-life commitment.

The main point is to establish a preconditioned discipline that follows self-defined values, principles, policies, and procedures that help us pursue strategic goals and objectives. The first rule for applying a standardized personal management system is to define your own mission. In order to succeed you need a clear vision and a consistent mission statement. That's also true for any organization. The mission plan allows a leadership team to follow directions, assess actions, and rationalize their efforts and resources as they promote the organization's vision, mission, and purpose.

The same thing applies to your own life. There is no excuse for people living lives without sense or having an earthly presence without meaning. Start planning your vision and assimilating your mission of life. It is never too late to start, and you will see that such a vision will be an asset that will transform your life and provide meaning to your presence on earth.

A positive-thinking mind-set will help you identify your true mission on earth. Personal management will keep you on track so you can put whatever you conceive into action. Personal management starts with your internal commitments. Your mission is a unique statement. It may share elements with those of others, but its authenticity derives from your uniqueness. It is a perspective enriched by stimulus and enhanced by motivations whose energy will help you identify your own concepts of truth, values, and beliefs.

To be effective, a planned and organized purpose needs order and a sense of coordinated effort. Start by ordering and recognizing your values, talents, and objectives. Assemble them in an appropriate order so you can manage your personal, professional, family, and social life. Managing your life in this way leads to involvement, trust, stimulus, and motivation that fill your mind with courage and your spirit with the tenacity you need to achieve. However, as John Maxwell wrote, "Motivation comes not by activity alone, but by the [strong] desire to reach the end result [...] People are motivated when they know exactly what they are to do and have the confidence that they can do it successfully" (Maxwell 1993, 122).

A life mission statement gives you balance and harmony. It helps you differentiate living from merely existing. It provides a guide that reveals how you cannot waste any more of your time in worthless activities that hold no purpose or connection with your mission in life. A personal mission gives you the conviction of utilizing all your mental, emotional, and spiritual resources in confident and conscientious ways.

You serve as the administrator, manager, and chief of your life. If doubts or uncertainties appear, ask for help, pray, or request spiritual guidance. You can also use self-talking and self-help techniques to diminish pessimism, laziness, or discomfort and find direction in your life.

When life challenges and unexpected adversities come to us, we must be prepared to accept life's tests. A personal mission gives you another advantage for dealing with different environments, both present and future. A personal mission statement provides an avenue to life's purpose and becomes an asset that helps you balance your assignments, commitments, and responsibilities with your values and ethical paradigms.

Personal Management and its Relationship With Life's Cycle

As individuals, we should take care of our mission and vision for our time on earth and administer everything granted directly and indirectly to us. We can find the real meaning of life's purpose in the responsible acceptance and conscious understanding of our roles as human beings. To do that we all need a mission to pursue and a purpose to follow. Such a personal management system includes, but it is not limited to, managing our body, mind, emotions, environment, family, and community.

Life is short, and we should live it intensely. For instance, our childhood is the time when we make discoveries and develop desires to become "somebody." It is the time when we wake up our talents, aspirations, and dreams. We have not reached our potential. Perhaps we have not even enjoyed life's beauty, yet as children and young adults we become independent and cross the line to adulthood.

When we reach the prime of life we tend to become aware of all the changes that are constantly taking place in our minds and environment. Later on, you may start a family and add to life's continuity. That provides another opportunity to count your blessings, enjoy your present, and prepare the future for your families and communities.

The important point is that if you determine your actions, your choices will measure your outcomes. That may lead to an exciting career, a well-established legacy, a new economic empire, or simply survival among the world's social and economic injustices. As the years pass you will confront the changes that are all around us. Remember, what you think is what you do; and what you do is what you get. Life affects all of us differently. The phases of life offer constant challenges that you should address accordingly. These challenges influence who you are or who you will become.

So be careful how you think and act. Remain cautious in how you present yourself to others. "Your appearance reflects and affects your image of yourself [...] what is imaged in your mind tends to actualize itself in fact," wrote Norman Vincent Peale (Peale 1982, 183). We can be miserable or fortunate; happy or sad; optimistic or pessimistic. Pay attention to the details of the aging process and take conscious responsibility for the short life granted to us on earth. An enjoyable life is possible through purposes, motives, meaning, and objectives. Most of the time, people reach this awareness in their years of maturity—not necessarily in biological years, but a mixture of the spiritual and psychological ones.

The next period in life's sequence is the elderly state. As you age, your mind tends to reduce its limitless aptitude and your emotions become more controlled by your feelings. It is all in relationship with the conscious care that you dedicate to your body, mind, and spirit. Everything in the universe ages, so we must accept the progression of life. Acceptance will help us focus our attention on what we can produce in our mature years and in those phases of reflection and moral contemplation we experience while growing up. It is the period when wisdom becomes clear. As people age, their maturity becomes experience and the knowledge they have acquired transforms into expertise. The concerns of life tend to change as they shift their focus from gaining possessions and knowledge to creating peace and leaving resources to those they will leave behind. That does not mean just material possessions, but also the intangible and invaluable legacy of values and principles we acquire and develop during our life. This is the age when love again becomes a priority, the time when life starts its regression, and we become, at least in our hearts, the children we left behind. It is the period when our memory looks back to our youth and reexperiences the splendid cycle of life.

In the history of humanity, all phases of life have created exceptional individuals who have left legacies to humanity. Nevertheless, it is in the senior age that many people express the purest love, sincere appreciation, undisguised opinions, and fair judgment. Unfortunately, we often waste this invaluable social capital and abandon the elderly after they have given the best of themselves to us. As Dr. Andrew Weil pointed out, we value older trees, wines, cheeses, and antiquities because their age increases their value. The same is true with people. The elderly should not be a cause of shame, but pride. Remember that Moses led the Jewish Exodus when he was in his eighties, and Arthur Rubinstein did his best performances when he was in his nineties.

Positive thinking and peace of mind may come after we realize that we all follow the same life road. If we lament the way we will be treated, we should note how we care for others. What we do is what we get. It is not just a call for solidarity or compassion that moves me to include this essential topic in this book. I am also prompted by the conviction that each human being is unique and that all phases of life offer great opportunities to change and transform your current way of thinking.

So take your time to appreciate all the phases that make life amazing, and consider that what we seed is what we harvest. Start preparing today for what you would like to become tomorrow.

We cannot influence or change what our parents made, but we can determine what we will do for our kids and for our grandparents. We can nurture our kids and care for them to ensure they become productive citizens. We can love and protect our grandparents by forgiving their mistakes and watching them become venerable elders. Positive thinking means completely assuming our life roles in the different phases of life. Responsible adults love the elderly and nurture and empower the little ones.

When parenting, a man and a woman exercise one of the sacred missions of life. Therefore, if we educate our children correctly and prioritize respect, self-confidence, love, and solidarity, then we will not have to worry about how they will perform as the parents and grandparents of tomorrow. A positive attitude, high self-esteem, physical activity, and an environment filled with love and social interaction are vital for children so they can grow up healthy and in peace. Physical activity, body flexibility, a relaxed mind, and spiritual engagement filled with pleasure and peace are among plausible desires of any living person.

Growing older and staying productive translates into invaluable social capital. It is also an advantage for those who have the privilege to share in the wisdom, experience, and maturity of their elders. As I've said before, in order to respect others, we should primarily start respecting ourselves. We should also have respect and reverence for the elders so we can inspire respect when we reach the same condition. Therefore, all that we need is to find in our core values the character to fully understand our life's mission and to stand for it until the last second of our earthly presence.

Aging is a natural progression and an uncontrollable part of life's cycle. Nevertheless, it is equally clear that prevention and adequate treatment of sickness is a necessity for a healthy lifestyle. Exercise, periodical relaxation, and regular flexibility are also important. Don't neglect your mind either. You must take care of it in order to control your body, feed your thoughts, and nurture your attitude. If you can maintain positive thinking with a mission of life and the visualization of a life purpose, then you can celebrate the outcomes of your choices and rejoice in the greatness of your accomplishments.

One problem people have is that instead of prioritizing their objectives based on the tangible resources granted to them, they live in fantasies of acquiring everything without paying anything. That is not possible. There is an order in the universe as well as in our bodies. The natural process of life may modify our expectations, but it is not possible to play God's role without receiving a deserved punishment for our boldness. We can enjoy and accomplish our mission if we approach it in easy stages. I assume that many of us would like to enjoy life forever. However, the wise desire is to live whatever years our God allows us to live, by conserving and connecting our mind, body, and spirit.

It is normal to desire an everlasting life, but I am sure that no one would like to live forever with a body wracked by serious diseases, terrible pain, and a mind plagued by loneliness. A life with health, joy, and companionship is the best gift that we can desire for our old age. Earthly life does not last forever. It is our responsibility to seed and harvest it during our lifetime. Start today so you can live in the present and prepare for the future.

Life is a journey where everything is possible and anything can happen. Some people try to include everything in their objectives without prioritizing the things that really matter. As you plan a trip, so should you manage your life. Concentrate on those things that give sense to your existence. Clean your mind of dark thoughts, and stay away from negativism and uncertainties that spring from past distresses and future anxieties. Be grateful that you have and can use your talents to fill your mind and thoughts with clean ideas, imaginative objectives, and positive feelings. Our time is now. Make your decisions today to provide meaningful experiences and satisfaction along your life's journey. Prioritize your time and activities by organizing and enjoying them accordingly. As John Maxwell said, "A life in which anything goes will ultimately be a life in which nothing goes" (Maxwell 1993, 23).

Applying Personal Organization and Time Management Skills

How you handle an issue is usually determined by three basic elements: your emotional ability in coping with the topic (feelings), the willingness of your mind in creating proactive alternatives (will), and the wisdom and confidence of your spirit (hope). This mental approach, supported by your personalized methods and strategic skills, becomes crucial for generating creative solutions and upbeat thoughts. Organization is essential as you arrange your thoughts, emotions, and abilities.

Since the real task is learning how to deal with life's daily tasks, you need adequate managerial skills for handling any short or life-long assignment. Correct decision-making lets you act appropriately when dealing with unexpected obstacles. However, the main predisposition to understand and take proactive action comes from the strong relationship between mind (rational approach) and emotions (feelings correlation).

Norman Vincent Peale reaffirms this when he writes, "Positive thinking is how you think about a problem. Enthusiasm is how you feel about the problem. The two together determine what you do about the problem" (Peale 1967, 237). We should express our emotions prudently, in collaboration with our mind. The combination of mind and emotions is what characterizes us as sensible human beings.

When applying personal organizational skills, keep in mind that the basic steps of management structure are planning, organizing, executing, and evaluating. The ability to plan is one fundamental requirement for setting goals based on measurable outcomes and deadlines. Organization provides the groundwork for implementing and executing action plans. It is also a vital tool for evaluating and redesigning the avenues toward the final goal. Planning and organizing are essentially interdependent and interconnected with each other.

Organization comprises the set of faculties, capabilities, and strategies intended to accomplish your intentions. Execution is the step that translates the ideas into practical phases. The most important thing to consider when choosing priorities is to emphasize the things that are really important. As the Pareto's principle teaches us, 20 percent of your priorities will typically give you 80 percent of your production. It's interesting that research also indicates that 20 percent of people are responsible for 80 percent of world success (Maxwell 1993, 20).

Planning prepares the foundation while organization synthesizes the accomplishment. Planning is necessary for confronting the unknown future. As John Maxwell pointed out, "Major barriers to successful planning are fear of change, ignorance, uncertainty about the future, and lack of imagination" (Maxwell 1998, 41). The most valuable characteristic for good planning is a predisposition to change, an attitude that makes it possible to open your mind as you apply your planning skills and deter ignorance and hesitation. The situation improves when your planning basis lies in demonstrable facts so you can measure accomplishments and set progressive and measurable outcomes. Having a positive attitude and the motivation to change is a plus—it becomes easier to spark the imagination and develop intuition.

Organization plays a fundamental role for achieving results and transforming plans into realities. It is crucial for passing from planning to execution. Organization becomes part of the plan as well as a portion of the execution. As Christopher Robin says, "Organizing is what you do before you do something, so that when you do it's not all mixed up" (Maxwell 1993, 166).

You can learn and develop organization skills at any time. However, it is better when we acquire them in our early years so they can become sustainable habits. Both physical and mental organization are tools that help us establish a sequence in what we think, say, and do. Organization allows us to better utilize our daily activities, confront time constraints, and prioritize our tasks in a systematic and coordinated way, which leads to improved productivity.

An organized person tends to be more patient, consistent, and in control. In addition, an organized person usually finds more creative solutions to solve problems and meet expectations. More importantly, organization deters reactive inclinations, reduces impulsivity, and helps with prioritization of needs. Proper organizing helps you prepare yourself physically and mentally for whatever you may face.

An important step for acquiring managerial skills is evaluation. This is where you must analyze processes to reach goals and redefine objectives. Evaluation is the phase where perfection becomes possible because you have clearly identified the vision, mission, strengths, weaknesses, opportunities, and threats. Professional management principles are also applicable to personal affairs. Apply these skills and your dreams may pass from a mental picture to a concrete realization. Make sure you pay attention to the outcomes without forgetting the details, a rule of positive thinking and an important aspect in organizing resources. One of the most valuable talents for leadership and management abilities is the ability to establish order, organize tasks, and master details.

Planning Skills: An Aptitude and an Attitude to Be Developed

An aptitude is an ability or dexterity we exercise through our talents. Attitude is the commitment and determination to pursue a dream, plan, or goal. Any dream is a pathway for discovering opportunities and something that appears in the mind as a mere idea or visualization. A plan is the first step that allows us to attain our dreams without losing perspective of the work's reality. An action plan may be considered complete once it incorporates pragmatic ideas, credible resources, supporting evidences, and a clear assessment of how to transform probability into possibility.

You can imagine a plan as a mental model so it can come initially from any of your four basic resources—physical ability, mental initiative, spiritual connection, or emotional commitment. Planning is the phase where you measure the willingness of your rationality, evaluate the hope of your spirituality, and test the enthusiastic feelings of your emotions. A plan usually starts with a mental picture, a rational diagram, or a blueprint of your ideas, which should be transformed from the initial abstract vision to a concrete strategy or scheme. A well-organized action plan exists when you assign procedural structure, phases of development, span of action, and a cross-action time frame.

A plan outlines the tactics, strategies, and procedures you will implement over a predetermined period. Its structure should help you foresee events and assure sustainability. A well-developed plan should offer the capability of keeping focus, applying strategic stratagems, and assessing performance when determining and achieving goals. Once you've conceived a plan, the next step is to get organized so you can execute it. Planning is important, but you should support any action with a preconceived design and strategy. However, don't waste your time by waiting for the "perfect time" when all the necessary conditions align in your favor.

Any dream needs a leader to plan and execute it and followers to organize and process it. To paraphrase John Maxwell, a successful leader is a person who can acquire a clear and realistic objective by discerning and guessing the probability of accomplishing expectations (Maxwell 1993, 149). A leadership figure is necessary for any personal, family, or community project. In fact, one of the basic duties of the commander-in-chief of a project is to plan and organize facts as well as imagining the results. A leader must provide the followers with a clear vision and concrete mission in order to transform dreams into realities.

Since we can be either leaders or followers as well as managers or team members, it is indispensable to prepare ourselves physically, mentally, and spiritually to overcome challenges by applying the basic rules of goal setting, planning, organizing, and executing private and public goals. Effective planning linked with action makes it possible to reach a goal in a specific time and space of reference.

There is a clear difference between managing and leading. Managing means administrating processes and things. Leadership means organizing and directing people. "Management is doing things right," wrote Warren Bennis; "leadership is doing the right things" (Covey 1989, 101). Nevertheless, leading and managing are both driven by knowledge (information and administrative skills) and motivations (enthusiasm and conviction) and guided by a positive attitude. The most difficult time for transforming desires into plans and intentions into actions is the first step, when you must make the firm decision to look forward.

However, beginning is just one of three basic elements of any match or competition. The second part is the competition itself—the courage, energy and commitment to face and address challenges. In this phase we acknowledge our responsibilities and prepare our body and mind for a continuous acquisition of knowledge, training, and accumulated learning experiences. Sometimes delaying action may be the right decision if an action plan and an organized blueprint is not in place. On the other hand, suspending action may just represent a self-imposed limitation intended to hide fear and procrastination.

Once you've made a decision, preparation and self-control become necessary so you can apply the action plan and follow the steps of the process to conquer the goals you've already visualized and planned. People often hear a calling but deny it due to the lack of planning and organizing skills. They let opportunities pass by. As an example, here's an old tale that reminds us how circumstances can appear differently from optimistic and pessimistic viewpoints:

Two shoe salesmen went to Africa to look for new markets of their products. The first thing that impressed them was that most of the people they saw did not wear shoes. This discovery affected them in opposite ways.

The pessimistic salesman made a phone call to his company and said he was returning home. "I have wasted my time," he said, "because nobody wears shoes here." The optimistic salesman called his company, too, but he said, "Please quadruple the original order. Everybody here needs shoes!"

Some people, from mental blindness or spiritual negativism, see failures where others observe opportunities. We can shape events not just through open proactive perceptions but also with enthusiastic, positive attitudes.

The ability to plan depends on informed decisions based on facts, resources, realistic deadlines, and a chronological order of steps for achieving desired results. Consequently, when you plan you should consider your allies, strategies, and opportunities. Make a mental picture of the final destination and place a psychological ladder in your mind that will let you reach it, whatever the height may be. That's not to say you should dismiss other views or potential critics, barriers, and unexpected challenges.

You want to keep going forward. Once you've made a decision and a plan, you don't want to move backwards or quit on your own preselected commitments. Doubts and uncertainties may arise, and you will have to evaluate them and make any necessary revisions in your plan. However, when you have a firm predisposition to pursue your dream, nothing should keep you from moving forward. You might have to slow down, revise your objectives, or balance your resources, but you can do that without limiting your enthusiasm.

There is a time to lead and a time to manage. There is a time to plan and a time to execute. There is a time to order and a time to organize, and there is a time to meditate and a time to perform. However, when it is the time for action, it is not time to revive fears or find reasons to procrastinate. That is why Homer Croy wrote, "When little worries and anxieties and uncertainties try to disturb me [...] I banish them by reminding myself...'I've hit bottom and I've stood it. This is no place to go now but up' " (Carnegie 1981, 526).

The decisions you make according to a plan and in an organized manner are the choices that lead to predictable circumstances. There are times, however, when those well-intentioned choices may lead to bad results. That is just part of life. Positive thinking will help you accept all results, learn from your experiences, and take the next steps. Then, once you make a firm choice, do not embark on a regressive contemplation of past or future constraints. "Once you have made a careful decision based on fact, go into action," Dale Carnegie wrote. "Don't stop to consider. Don't begin to hesitate, worry and retrace your steps [...] there comes a time when any more investigation and thinking are harmful" (Carnegie 1981, 288).

A plan should be your stratagem, your guidelines, and a consolidated process along the way to your aspirations. Of course, one of the basic goals of the evaluation process is to assure that your tactics and strategies will keep your attitude and execution unaltered. An open mind while working with constructive critics and a predisposition to change will let you conceive, execute, supervise, and evaluate a plan. Of course, any plan needs a set of measurable outcomes and a time frame.

A well-organized plan will give you the opportunity to succeed. It does not matter if it is a plan for your life, family, or work. It applies everywhere. But any plan requires self-control and personal commitment. You must follow regulations and assure compliance with policies and procedures. That is why administrative skills balanced with emotional release are fundamental for the construction of our dreams.

Since the motivation to change and the opportunities to learn are so important for shaping and planning a successful life, I have to agree with John Maxwell when he says, "Major barriers to successful planning are fear of change, ignorance, uncertainty about the future, and lack of imagination" (Maxwell 1998, 41). We can build a pathway to success with planned objectives, strong beliefs, hard work, and uncountable sacrifices.

Discipline is necessary in order to pursue any successful plan. The concept of self-discipline is linked with the principle of self-determination. As Og Mandino says, "Self-discipline means being in charge of yourself [...] An important part of our personal development is learning to take responsibility for ourselves" (Mandino 1991, 116-117). The progression of a plan is usually a task overseen by leaders and partially delegated to managers, although it is best when managers also possess leadership skills so they can lead and execute what has been planned.

Any serious plan or meditated strategy requires a critical analysis of four basic characteristics: strengths, weaknesses, opportunities, and threats. This analysis will become essential for overcoming barriers and maintaining positive thinking. Keep in mind, though, that there's a clear difference between being positive and staying optimistic. The first is an ideal frame of reference while optimism represents a way of accepting any event without bias, but keeping a proactive attitude to balance the results in a harmonious manner. Being optimistic means accepting two sides of any event. Thinking positively means to concentrate your attention on the positive side without completely forgetting your concerns. Overcoming negativity is a progressive task. The art of planning is not merely making a wish list, but knowing how to implement and execute deadline objectives. That is why you need abilities and accomplishments to confront the obstacles as you chart your organizational skills and revitalize your internal and external assets.

Organization is all about inventorying your resources, furnishing your ideas, and prioritizing your objectives. In any planning process, the implementation of a conscious SWOT (strengths, weaknesses, opportunities, and threats) analysis is important if you want to use the combined virtues and defects that any person or occurrence adds. Nevertheless, this should occur at the beginning of the planning process so when it comes time for implementation, the focus will be to maintain a positive attitude and commendable enthusiasm. After that, it would be easier to concentrate almost exclusively on the development of strengths and opportunities.

On the other hand, you should address difficulties in a timely and proactive manner. Remember, the worst enemy for implementing change and overcoming barriers is negativism. Correspondingly, positive energy and affirmative attitude must prevail when we convince ourselves of the value of our tasks and the rewards of reaching our goals. A plan alone does not guarantee success. It is just a strategy.

Finally, planning should not stand in the way of the power of imagination. On the contrary, it must emphasize and redirect the course of positive imagining. "Imagining does affect future events," wrote Norman Vincent Peale. "But the decision to do the imagining is yours" (Peale 1982, 159). Planning affects the setting of goals, but the time and strategy to reach them remains yours. Leadership ability and a commitment to achieve, whatever you imagine, rest almost exclusively in the planning process you establish.

The Importance of Leadership in Creating and Executing a Plan

To create and execute a plan, you need a project leader or commander. The importance of leadership stems from the acquisition of knowledge, expertise in solving problems, and sustainable leadership skills to communicate, connect, guide, and influence people by transforming private dreams into common goals. Leroy Eims defined a leader as, "One who sees more than others see, who sees farther than others see, and who sees before others do" (Maxwell 1998, 36). Leadership is granted by the power of influence and confirmed by the supremacy of intuition. Sustainable information, creative initiative, structured methodology, fearless approach, natural instinct, contagious passion, self-trust, and confidence are all characteristics of a leader.

THE CREATIVE ENERGY OF POSITIVE THINKING

A great leader has the ability to plan, the aptitude to organize, the capability to lead and delegate, and the management skills to follow processes. To lead is to transfer abstract intentions into concrete practices. It was not my objective to include an analysis of the qualities and advantages of leadership. However, since all of us have instinctively played leadership roles in our families, neighborhoods, schools, and social interactions, I thought I should acknowledge some principles of leadership.

Leadership is a transcendental responsibility. A leader helps others succeed. If you have not yet discovered your own leadership potential, this chapter may help you to recognize it and help others find theirs.

The following fable provides a good example of how your thoughts and attitude can affect the outcome of a situation. It's called "Two Wolves" and goes as follows:

An elder Apache was teaching his grandchildren about life. He said, "A fight is going on inside me. It is a terrible fight and it is between two wolves. One wolf represents fear, anger, envy, sorrow, regret, greed, arrogance, self-pity, guilt, resentment, inferiority, lies, false pride, competition, superiority, and ego. The other stands for joy, peace, love, hope, sharing, serenity, humility, kindness, friendship, empathy, generosity, truth, compassion, and faith. This same fight is going on inside you, and inside every other person, too." The children thought about it for a minute and then one child asked his grandfather, "Which wolf will win?" The old grandpa replied, "The one you feed."

With any decision you face and any challenge you confront, you always have at least two choices to make. This power of choices and decisions gives us the opportunity to utilize the gift of this transitory existence and make it valuable, significant, and laudable.

Leadership is an extraordinary talent that should be exercised in commanding any task, big or small, because any action affects our future. It is also an ongoing process of personal growth. Real leaders know that his/her role and influence come from his/her ability to inspire and relate to others. Therefore, leadership requires empathy and the use of affirmative statements, attentive listening skills, objective goals, and proactive actions. In his book, *The 21 Irrefutable Laws of Leadership*, John Maxwell points out that directly proportional relationship between people's dreams and their leadership abilities. One of the foundations of leadership is "The Law of Influence" (Maxwell 1998, 11). The ability to influence is necessary for any true leader because leadership is not a title that can be bought or transferred. It must be earned.

Personal efficiency, organizational effectiveness, and assessable productivity are measured by the intensity of your leadership skills, consolidated with what Maxwell calls "The Law of Process" (21). This law shows how leadership is a constant learning practice that requires discipline, perseverance, vision, respect, and emotional strengths that one develops through the qualities of experience, intuition, self-trust, and patience. In addition, a leader requires precision, agility, critical discerning, equanimity, and a balance between firm authority and sensitive social interaction. "Anyone can steer the ship, but it takes a leader to chart the course," says Maxwell (Maxwell 1998, 33).

I understand the importance of starting a project. However, the authentic test of leadership is measured by the leader's commitment to finish it, and that means a leader requires knowledge as well as intuition. In effect, Maxwell's law of intuition is based on an ability to balance facts and instincts, an ability that allows leaders to see the future in present facts. Accordingly, Maxwell tells us, "The leader finds the dream and then the people [...] People find the leader and then the dream" (Maxwell 1998, 145).

Since what we are is what we attract, we should lead by example. A leader should touch people's hearts before asking for support, contributions, or collaboration. People will take your leadership to heart when they understand not just how much you know, but how much you care. Great leaders are those who follow the experts, mentor those who are around them, and empower those who come behind them. "Great leaders gain authority by giving it away," advises Maxwell (Maxwell 1998, 128). Finally, the last of Maxwell's 21 Laws of Leadership involves legacy. "A leader's lasting value is measured by succession," he writes (Maxwell 1998, 215).

Succession is the most precious and enduring value of leadership. Any institutional leader should make his organization as strong as it can be, develop solid leaders, create teamwork and ownership, and prepare a successor. The lasting value of leadership is measured by a peaceful succession. Future leadership must be developed and nurtured. Remember that true leadership comes initially from a personal commitment but it is complemented and affirmed by the followers.

A position does not make a leader; it is the ability to lead that makes the position. Purely positional leadership can become a disadvantage. In fact it can harm an organization's image and the position's value. A true leader does not merely occupy a position. He/she leads and serves. A sensible approach, conciliatory tactics, and negotiation skills are abilities that differentiate great leaders from merely good ones. A true leader earns authority by his/her ability to lead and receives influence by his/her facility to relate to others. A great leader listens to and analyzes different viewpoints in order to make fair and informed decisions.

Leadership requires an attention to detail and respect for different opinions. When differences arise, a leader must maintain objectivity and not focus on subjective feelings or the personality traits of the people in disagreement. Leaders who object to the views of others in a constructive way are therefore not attacking the people who present their ideas, but only their ideas. When a leader disagrees, he/she should criticize in a constructive manner and do it in a diplomatic way by presenting alternatives.

Another fundamental characteristic for the development of leadership is credibility. In order to gain credibility, you must exercise integrity in everything you think, say, and do. "Integrity includes but goes beyond honesty," wrote Stephen Covey. "Honesty is telling the truth [...] Integrity is conforming reality to our words, keeping promises and fulfilling expectations" (Covey 1989, 196).

There cannot be credibility without trust, which is why it is important to recognize our mistakes and accept temporary errors as knowledgeable initiatives that will help you grow and increase your consciousness. During hard times a leader is not afraid to take responsibility for the failure of others. In good times, a true leader does not hesitate to credit results to his/her team.

One of the most ceaseless needs of our society is for true leaders, people who can demand respect and influence and demonstrate character, honesty, commitment, patience, and persistence. Leaders are commanders who make decisions based on plans and informed intuition and take into consideration the factors of time, environment, cause and effect, objectives, measurable outcomes, and predictable consequences. A typical leadership role requires the abilities to earn, execute, maintain, improve, and implant creative methods to achieve.

True leaders are usually familiar with planning skills and organizational strategies. Of course, too much analysis can result in doubt, procrastination, delays, concerns, and endless evaluations. Consequently, it is the leader's responsibility to address concerns or misconceptions in the planning process to avoid future problems and eliminate uncertainties. That is why leadership and managing are different. Once a decision has been made, there is not time to go back to the planning process. It is time to follow instincts and predict effects.

Sometimes a leader may make a course correction or even change a strategy without losing perspective of the team's ultimate goal. Leadership means taking the design and creating the pathway of a plan, while a manager has to be familiar with the plan and close to the process and procedures. Leadership is often focused on people; managing is more concerned with methods and practices. Warren Bennis made it even more clear by saying:

"Management is doing things right; leadership is doing the right things" (Covey 1989, 101).

A real leader accepts full responsibility for his/her title and dignifies it through challenges met and experiences gained during life's constant battles. Leadership is measured through the debate of ideas and reinforced by the call to action. It does not show itself in pompous ceremonies that so often characterize the appointments of situational or circumstantial leaders. A title does not make a leader, but the leader can make and dignify a title.

Planning requires objectivity while tactics look for priorities. Leadership seeks direction when designing and executing personal and institutional strategic plans. The leader's main role is to transmit a clear understanding of the vision and mission from the top to the base. That is why a leader should take charge in overcoming obstacles and facing challenges. Those times of adversity test true leaders and measure the loyalty of the followers. This is what gives leaders knowledge and experience. As Aldous Huxley pointed out, "Experience is not what happens to you; it is what you do with what happens to you" (Theibert 1997, 145).

Triumphs as well as adversities challenge character and assess talents. At such times it is okay to disagree and generate proactive discussions. However, we should be cautious lest an initial disagreement move beyond the consideration of different opinions to become a personal issue. Of course, that does not apply exclusively in the leadership role, but in any subject that involves cross-communication.

In summary, I am absolutely convinced that any person or organization can achieve their goals if they pay attention to the basic principles of leadership. The virtue of leadership is not in a title, but in the temperament, courage, and character of the leader. Great leaders are not evaluated only by their decisions, but also by his/her lasting influence. As Jose Ingenieros noted, "Those who deserve monuments do not really need them because his/her task and teachings transcend the fence of time and the circumstantial space of this temporary recognition."

Leadership can be learned. It's also an attitude that can help people discover their intrinsic potential. The greatest task of a leader is not necessarily to lead a multitude, but himself/herself. The greatest accomplishment does not come from challenging others, but by mastering his/her own thoughts. Finally, a genuine leader does not arise from self-nomination. In my view, authentic leadership comes from a collective consensus made by its followers. As Chris Widener says, "You can't decide if you are going to be a leader. You can only decide if you will become the type of person others want to follow" (Widener 2008, 28).

To be a leader, you can lead your thoughts, command your attitude, guide and control your feelings, and direct your destiny. In addition, it is always within your power to become aware of what is granted to you and use it wisely and assertively. Use your leadership to utilize your own time and resources—both those things that are seen and those that are unseen—and to plan, organize, and execute whatever you want to get from life.

Physical Organization: An Asset in Personal and Professional Growth

A classical definition of organization, from the business viewpoint, is "the structure of roles and responsibilities functioning to accomplish predetermined objectives." Organization is a virtue, an asset that must be learned and developed from a mixture of advantages and disadvantages, triumphs and defeats, and doubt and certainty. Organization is the foundation of planning, reaffirmed through knowledge and accumulated experience. Organization is fundamental for facilitating the execution, application, and achievement of a plan.

Physical order starts with yourself. You should exercise order in your home, office, room, and your personal possessions. One of the worst habits we often deal with in our house, family, organization, or institution is the lack of organization. Organization is fundamental for following plans, yet disorganization affects everyone without consideration of social status, economic class, or cultural background. Order is a matter of self-esteem and personal care. Taking real responsibility for yourself and being in charge of your own destiny requires that you make an inventory of your personal assets. Organization is a significant tool with which you can better utilize those assets and preserve structure in your projects, goals, and plans.

To maintain an up-to-date organization strategy, use techniques to prevent stress and better utilize your already busy time. Make a dedicated effort to sustain quality records of your files, belongings, actions, and commitments. Organization may not guarantee positive thinking, but you can be sure that disorganization will not help. Disorganization is a terrible habit that may start a slide to mental and physical desperation. On the other hand, a large amount of information can be a valuable resource if you keep it in order and accessible. Disorganized information will merely prevent you from finding data. I hope when you choose to improve your managerial skills you will make organization a key element of your strategy. The ability to organize is a skill that will help you avoid stress and depression. Organization will help you manage your resources, execute plans, and conquer objectives. An extraordinary ability to organize becomes an effective tool when you lead individuals and manage processes.

Organization is an asset for productivity and effectiveness. If you lack a solid plan and organizational structure, your project will suffer. Organization forms the foundation for executing action plans and choosing priorities. You will execute a plan by measuring the organized application of effort and talents, supported by the expectation you derive from your desired accomplishments. Organized priorities are mandatory if you want to decide what is important. Organization requires you to select and prioritize what you really need. It is why John Maxwell says, "A life in which anything goes will ultimately be a life in which nothing goes" (Maxwell 1993, 23).

The principle of organization is also a positive mental attitude that works with positive planning and affirmative action. Mental organizing devices are good exercises to clarify your emotions and promote a proactive approach to any new commitment. I encourage you to use such strategies to define your physical assets and material goods. Make periodic inventories of your clothing, papers, utensils, tools, files, and tangible resources. Maintain them in order and keep them classified, clean, and easily accessible.

Order and cleanliness are personal characteristics that expose your personality. In fact, order and cleanliness both arise mainly from self-appreciation. If organization is significantly important in utilizing planning strategies, then begin by assuring that your individual belongings are in place. I do not mean you should discard personal treasures or past memories, but order them systematically and accordingly to your immediate needs.

Once you have an orderly environment, facts, data, and memories become resources that you can use to enhance your talents and further your achievements. Organization and order is vital. To be effective, says Carlos Cuauhtémoc Sanchez, "A clean and ordered space is basically needed; however, cleanness should not be an obsession nor order an objective" (Sanchez 2003, 50). Organization is a tool to expand your talents and an instrument to bridge plans and bond accomplishment. Organization is important for maintaining a proactive environment as well as an attractive place where you can better enjoy your life and accomplish your objectives.

Organization requires both intellectual (attitude) and physical (aptitude) competencies. Attitude refers to the mental and rational organization of your thoughts, beliefs, and values. The main impetus for having organized thinking is to assure the predominance of intelligent judgment and controlled emotional interventions.

Aptitude or ability requires what Cuauhtémoc Sanchez called a "Strategy Cavern," an intimate space where you can meditate and approach decisions privately. Any space will do if it is organized and clean. Create a private space where you can have solitude and can talk peacefully to yourself. You may want to use it to think and make meaningful decisions as you approach your goals.

We should dedicate ourselves to make organization an unbreakable rule and discipline for our day-to-day activities. In order to think clearly, reduce pressure, and better analyze concerns, you must eliminate unwanted thoughts from your mind and unwanted clutter from your desk. Cleanliness and order are important for organizing your place and are a fundamental asset when executing your plans. I recommend using physically and mentally organized devices to pursue your objectives in sequence and harmony. Organization plays an important role in creating a purposeful, meaningful, and happy life. The choice is yours and so are the outcomes. The main premise here is that you should provide yourself with a clean space as well as quality time in which to organize your physical possessions and thoughts. An organized plan, adequate order, and effective management of your time are fundamental if you want to find happiness and success in life.

Time Managing: An Invaluable Source in Achieving Plans

Time management is an essential part of the planning and organizing process. Wasting your time on insignificant activities is just not fair to you or your loved ones. Time is a finite gift, so you must manage it astutely. Do not waste your time by looking for the perfect or ideal moment to do things. The ability to recognize opportunities will guide you on the right course and to the precise conditions you need to move toward opportunity and achievement.

Time is a mysterious treasure. Philosophically it exists only the present. Once it's gone, it becomes part of our memories. Of course, it is not my intention to philosophize in depth on this matter because the only thing that really counts is the present. On the other hand, the future remains unknown.

Nevertheless, you can plan for the future by considering the importance of time frame and deadlines.

As Albert Einstein expressed in his theory of relativity, time is tied to matter and space. All our actions or movements are linked with the space we inhabit and the time we use. Everything that we do happens in the context of time. Yet, is time a concrete reality or an abstract illusion? In the words of Eckhart Tolle, "Time is seen as the endless succession of moments [...] Even past or future only exists when you remember or anticipate them, and you do so by thinking about them in the only moment there is: this one" (Tolle 2005, 204). We live in a present that continuously makes a transition to the future. Time is volatile, a continual sequence of instants, but it exists only in the present.

I will spend no more time discussing the philosophy of time. I will leave the rest up to you. My sole intention here was to make you aware of a topic that relates to your entire life. It is my sincere intention that whatever you may understand about time, you can use the best of yours to pursue your dreams and spend its invaluable treasure in fulfilling your mission and purpose.

What does understanding the value of time have to do with positive thinking and the pursuit of happiness? That is a fair question. My answer lies in the fact that so often I hear extreme negativism, constant pessimism, and self-denial in mechanized responses that destroy the concept of happiness. In effect, when somebody asks, "How are you doing?" the most common responses I hear are, "Just existing" or "Living to survive." These phrases are pessimistic and negative. I realize that these feelings of conformism and hopelessness have sometimes affected me. My real intention here is to make you aware of the negativism that may surround you.

Negativism is contagious. It spreads like an epidemic and infects and contaminates even the strongest structures of positive thinking. You should be cautious when dealing with this destructive tendency and become persuasive when coaching your peers about the impact of negative statements. Lead by example and help people abandon the negative attitude of wasting their precious time on earth. If that does not work, you should escape before you become infected yourself and start to waste your precious time. As Alian Laken says, "Time is irreversible and irreplaceable."

Value the precious time you have, and invest it in the best and most meaningful way. Do not waste it. Use it! Appreciate, love, and enjoy it. Realize that time is fundamental for accomplishing your plans, organizing your strategies, and executing methods and tactics. If you want to learn effectively, you need a timeline so you can plan for future commitments. Keep a calendar, maintain an agenda, follow schedules, keep and uphold appointments. That will help you value your time and use it well.

Just as monetary budgeting is crucial for keeping your finances in control, the budget of your time is vital when planning and organizing your endeavors. The effective use of time is critical in any project or action plan. Doing something at the proper moment is "the art of doing the right thing at the right time in the right way" (Peale 1967, 98). One of the clearest definitions of time management comes from Charles Hobbs and his *Time Management Training Book* of the Pennsylvania Department of Public Welfare. For Hobbs, time management is "the act of controlling events to achieve an appropriate balance of priorities in order to focus on and accomplish our most important tasks."

Time management skills save valuable moments in execution, increase productivity, and create a better understanding of how to select priorities. Critical use of time is a very helpful administrative technique that allows people to gain a comprehensive understanding of analyzing priorities. Time management permits people to maximize this valuable resource and perceive the differences between urgent decisions and important ones. As you may know, "urgent" relates to time sensitivity while "important" means the matter has a direct relation to significant decisions that need to be made.

The important/urgent model represents a practical tool used by managerial and organizational disciplines and it is one that comes in handy in the personal field as well. Dedicate and invest your time and energy where you have strengths and delegate where you do not have much experience. That does not mean you should concentrate only on those things that you do best, but you should learn when to take charge and when to delegate. Empowering and supporting others are fundamental competencies that you should apply in a timely manner to avoid fatigue and keep from losing efficiency and effectiveness.

Delegating will help you avoid becoming overworked. At the same time it allows others to gain knowledge and experience by doing teamwork tasks. Having time to concentrate on your main responsibilities will help you select those priorities that will enhance your abilities. "Successful people don't find time, they make time" (Urban 2003, 131). In addition, another skill that you should be familiar with, in managing your time appropriately, is to learn to say yes or no and stick to it.

Saying "yes" or "no" reflexively, though, is one of the most common errors in time management and decision making. Saying "yes" before thinking is a clear sign of immaturity. You should deliberate about any new topic, activity, or responsibility if you want to appropriately plan, organize, and execute it. On the other hand, saying "no" in a respectful way is a normal choice and one you should exercise from time to time to avoid unexpected tasks that may alter your basic priorities, both in the workplace and in your personal life.

If you have set your priorities and designed your goals and plans in a predetermined period, then you will need self-discipline. Be prepared to say yes without pressure. Take your time and don't force yourself to make an immediate response. Analyze any new commitment very carefully and check your agenda and schedule before you overcommit yourself. There is nothing wrong with saying no. It is worse to say yes and not accomplish your responsibilities than to say no in a polite and respectful way.

Sometimes it even makes sense to put some important issues out of your mind, at least temporarily, to give yourself sufficient time to consider them later. This is why deadlines and the ability to focus your attention on priorities are necessary. It's important that you do not waste time in menial things or silly discussions. Time is precious, an invaluable resource that you should spend wisely and invest appropriately.

Therefore, keep track of details, analyze strategies, and design tactics that work in the context of your time. Remember John Maxwell's advice: "Reading a situation and knowing what to do are not enough to make you succeed in leadership. Only the right action at the right time will bring success" (Maxwell 1998, 203). Maintain priorities in everything you think, say, and do. That way you will give only the most important things in your life the care, emphasis, space, and time they need so you can become more effective and not just more efficient.

Several books on time management mention the concept of Pareto's principle, the equation I mentioned before that says 80 percent of our results flow from 20 percent of our activities (Covey 1989, 156). In other words, one-fifth of our time, energy, efforts, and mental or physical investment brings four-fifths of our benefits. That is why most of the time management strategies teach us to concentrate our time on important things and give special attention to the urgent ones.

Time management is vital for both business and our personal lives. Those in the management field apply it systematically, and people in leadership positions make practical use of it. As Goethe noted, "We always have time enough, if we will but use it right" (Urban 2003, 127). During our lives we all play different roles—as leaders or followers, manager or administrators, coaches or players, intellectual deciders or physical doers. In all of these roles, the wiser the use of our time, the more joy we bring to our lives.

That is why we should concentrate our efforts by applying the important/urgent principle. When you are acting in the managing field, you should redirect your energy in dealing with those things that are mainly important, but not necessarily urgent. A good plan will guide us to what is important so we can avoid the sense of urgency that arises from emotional perceptions. Of course, we must accept that urgent matters do require immediate attention. However, my intention is to deter the inclination to react emotionally to urgent issues. Instead, dedicate most of your time to what is important, but not urgent. This creates an environment where you can measure time and space, acquire balance, and control emotions. You want to apply the old adage of "thinking before acting" and avoid the common tendency to act immediately to confront concerns or pressing threats. The correct approach gives supremacy to rational thoughts instead of emotional impulses. Think before acting, but make sure you are aware of what you are thinking. As Eckhart Tolle says, "Thinking without awareness is the main dilemma of human existence" (Tolle 2005, 32).

The goal is not just to think deeply and listen carefully, but also to become conscious of your thinking process by creating awareness, which is the main factor in balancing perception and interpretation. Awareness arises when you analyze and explore what you perceive. Allow yourself some time to reaffirm your convictions and meditate on your intentions. Time is a precious resource, but our interpretation of time may differ because clock, biological, and psychological times can differ. Clock time is marked by the succession of hours, days, months, and years based mainly on astronomical movements. Biological time runs from the time of procreation until the end of life. A classic interpretation of psychological time comes from the famous book *Analects*, written by Confucius. He states, "At fifteen, I had my mind bent on learning. At thirty, I stood firm. At forty, I have no doubts. At fifty, I knew the decrees of heaven. At sixty, my ear was an obedient organ for the reception of truth. At seventy, I could follow what my heart desired, without transgressing what was right" (Renard 2002, 424).

Time is a very sensitive matter. It is a resource granted to us under the premise that we can adequately manage it. We cannot slow its course, but we can administer its influence. I would like to conclude this chapter with a reflection about time that a teenager with cancer wrote in a New York hospital. She wrote it after she was told that she had just six months of life left. This poem is called "Slow Dance."

Have you ever watched kids on a merry-go-round? Or listened to the rain slapping on the ground? Ever followed a butterfly's erratic flight? Or gazed at the sun into the fading night? You'd better slow down. Don't dance so fast. Time is short. The music won't last. Do you run through each day on the fly? When you ask; how are you? Do you hear the reply? When the day is done, do you lie in your bed with the next hundred chores running through your head? Have you ever told your child, we'll do it tomorrow? And in your haste, not see his sorrow?

Have you ever lost touch, let a good friendship die, because you never had time to call and say, "Hi"? You'd better slow down. Don't dance so fast. Time is short. The music won't last. When you run so fast to get somewhere, you miss half the fun of getting there. When you worry and hurry through your day, it is like an unopened gift....Thrown away. Life is not a race. Do take it slower. Hear the music before the song is over.

Life is beautiful, so you should treat it accordingly. Spend every second on those valuable things that bring goodwill and better friendships. Managing your time wisely and investing it proactively will help you enjoy the outcomes of life and share quality time with your loved ones, which is one of the approaches to true happiness. It is why Willa Cather says, "One cannot divine nor forecast the conditions that will make happiness; one only stumbles upon them by chance, in a lucky hour; at the world's end somewhere, and holds fast to the days, as to fortune or fame" (Breathnach 1998, 173).

Chapter 3

Positive Attitude

"There is nothing either good or bad, but thinking makes it so."
William Shakespeare

Chapter 3

Positive Attitude

———◆———

Attitude arises from an internal thinking process, one indirectly influenced by external forces we perceive through our senses. Our emotions, motivations, and instincts develop and stimulate our attitude, in environments each individual's personality constantly creates and recreates. Proactive attitude is an advantageous state that comes naturally from the combination of physical, spiritual, mental, and emotional resources, four basic elements that every person must grow and nurture. As mentioned earlier, planning and organizational skills play an important role in our lives. Nevertheless, they are usually invigorated by the confluence of two transcendent streams: aptitude and attitude.

Of course, people-planning skills and styles differ. However, efficient life skills exist mainly from a combination of rational, emotional, and spiritual dexterity. Attitude is a fundamental component for applying and implementing planning strategies. It is in the power of positive attitude and proactive perceptions that people find the best place and time to reach for their goals. This is not a common prescription or exclusive recipe for modeling our lives, but principles and guidelines you apply in correlation with your attitude. As

75

Daniel Goleman says, "One size does not fit all when it comes to formulating a useful agenda for your future" (Goleman et al 2002, 148).

Our attitude is the catalyst for connecting with and administrating our dreams and objectives. Attitude is the only thing that is truly and genuinely yours. People who take care of their attitudes bring something invaluable to their lives. "Attitude decides the size of our dreams and influences our determination when we are faced with new challenges," says Jim Rohn. Attitude is a personal asset that you must protect and control. Nobody can do that but you. Attitude is one of an individual's most valuable characteristics. It is a treasure of uncalculated value. In order to succeed in life, a person needs an affirmative attitude that includes big portions of confidence and passion. This does not mean just a great and contagious optimism, although that is a very good beginning. It means you need to incorporate passion into every single task you undertake. Consequently, a positive attitude is important, but to succeed and increase happiness you must love and believe in what you are thinking and doing.

A positive attitude is an advantage when you want to maintain an optimistic perspective, even when the circumstances appear awkward. Positive thinking engenders positive attitude, creates motivation, promotes proactive, reliable approaches, and sparks streams of enthusiasm. "Positive attitude causes a chain reaction of positive thoughts, events, and outcomes," according to an anonymous saying. "It is a catalyst; a spark that creates extraordinary results." Attitude results from people's inner choices, which give us the competencies that feed our self-esteem. Therefore, our thoughts are our most valuable asset. They form our character's values and the principles that shape the quality of our thinking.

When creative and optimistic thoughts prevail they generate a protective environment that helps deter negative thinking. I understand that we cannot always be filled with positive thoughts. However, we can generate positive thinking based on how we approach any issue we face. For example, a family loss, an unexpected accident, or terrible news can challenge our strongest predisposition to be positive as we experience pain, sorrow, and difficulties. In those times when we cannot change facts, we can learn from our experiences and use such episodes as opportunities to increase our maturity and strengthen our spirit.

If you don't control your attitude, it will inevitably control you. If we accept that we are in charge of our own lives, then it is reasonable to accept our responsibility for deciding the tone of our attitude. I encourage you to maximize your energy by bringing positive thoughts and implementing a proactive approach to any adverse circumstance. Any situation we experience is a new lesson to learn and another opportunity to succeed. When you foster productive thinking you will defeat negative thoughts.

Positive attitude is all about choices. Pleasure or suffering builds upon your inner self. We do not create it exclusively by what we think. We also influence it by what we do. Nevertheless, true happiness is an attitude that we find somewhere in between, in the middle of what we think and what we do. That is where the essence of happiness is so often hidden. When you hear something that appears to be bad news, you have choices to make. You can accept it as it is or delay its acknowledgment; analyze its causes or let it go; be a victim or learn from the experience. The choice you make depends on you.

This is why accepting responsibility for your actions, without blaming others, is one of the greatest virtues of self-growth and self-development. Life is all about choices. Only you can choose to be in a good or bad mood. Sometimes choices do not become immediately apparent. Many times your choices remain hidden and the positive side only appears after you do some critical thinking. As an old adage says, "There are no real problems to overcome, but opportunities to understand and options to learn."

Every single snag may look like an impediment to success. However, you can use your difficulties as opportunities to learn and a chance to understand better the unknown secrets of life. Success, respect, trust, truth, honesty, integrity, leadership, and happiness are some values that cannot be bought, but must be earned. You can achieve some of these aptitudes and attitudes through rigid discipline, spiritual empathy, and hard work. The process starts in our minds, no matter how big or small the project, dream, or idea may be. The important thing is to produce ongoing critical thinking so you can build a progressive positive attitude.

Positive attitude may not always bring your planned or desired results. However, a mind-set of positive thinking will show you clear, healthy alternatives as you dream and plan. Everything starts with the power of an idea. Nonetheless, every idea needs intention and objectivity to become reality. There is an old saying that goes, "A dream written down with a period becomes a goal; an aspiration broken down into steps becomes a plan; a plan followed by an action and filled out with beliefs, passion, and positive attitude makes a dream true."

Sometimes the future looks dismal. At such times you should not allow somebody else to control your positive thinking or even worse, allow any inanimate object or circumstance to ruin your efforts and attract negative thoughts. Why not think positively, intentionally, and productively? For instance, the phrase "I can't" is one thing that promotes negativity and limits proactive intervention. On the other hand, when we decide to change our habits and approach any situation with a positive attitude, ask instead, "How can I do it?" That becomes a great initial motivator to keep you thinking in a positive way instead of a preconceived negative one.

A positive mental attitude smoothes progress toward alternative solutions and allows us to express creativity and maintain enthusiasm as we overcome challenges. Another advantage of a proactive thinking approach is that it tends to embrace creativity and therefore gives us new ideas for generating success. Creativity comes from the art of collecting and connecting ideas. It ignites the power of imagination, which is the ability to visualize the objective in a future perspective. Therefore, my advice is to "keep going and doing" instead of merely trying. Opportunities often come unannounced or disguised in the form of misfortune and/or temporary barriers.

Positive thinking limits the presence of negative approaches by assuming controlled risks and meditated alternative solutions. As Napoleon Hill says, "Every successful person finds that great success lies just beyond the point when they're convinced their idea is not going to work" (Maxwell 2002, 147). Positive attitude is a key factor for elevating your spirit and recreating positive mental models. If you can't maintain it on a constant basis, then look for help and alternative ways to stay optimistic. For instance, reading is a great resource.

Attitude is your personal asset. It is a holistic resource, one you should feed and develop through an intimate relationship with your rational, emotional, and spiritual sources. You will find your attitude's essence in the deepest meditation of your inner being. If you can develop a positive attitude, then you can assume an affirmative environment instead of becoming absorbed by a negative one. In order to keep and promote positive thinking, revise your structural way of thinking, represented by the frame of reference where your thoughts are created and your responses generated. Positive attitude grants you greater options for fresh thoughts and bright ideas that will let you confront difficulties, defeat concerns, and accept challenges as a natural venue of life.

We encounter many pitfalls throughout our lives, and there are times when our positive attitude fails us. For instance, when my mother died I lost control and blamed others and even myself for such terrible news. Did I change the outcome of life's challenges? Did I help my siblings understand the situation? At first I didn't because I did not offer myself as part of the solution. Instead, I became another element of the problem. Since then I have learned that it is in such hard times that our leadership, strengths, and abilities are really tested.

THE CREATIVE ENERGY OF POSITIVE THINKING

Positive thinking does not mean that we must smile in times of sorrow or laugh in moments of suffering. Realistic positive thinking means to acknowledge and accept the conditions we face and apply wise, logical, and emotive alternatives to solve our difficulties. The fortitude of a positive attitude asserts itself when you take charge of your basic responsibilities, address your challenges with calmness, and confront any circumstance after appropriate study. In other words, positive thinking means to analyze the pros and cons of every situation. It also means you should act without allowing your impulses and emotions to overcome the rationality and spirituality that guarantee the harmony and balance of your initiatives and decisions.

You should always consult your rational side. On the other hand, emotions are important elements too, while spirituality provides purpose and meaning to our existence. It is the convergence of these strengths that feeds our moral and ethical norms and allows rationality and justice as well as love and goodwill to prevail. It is even better when your core values reinforce the prevalence of principles such as compassion, kindness, and solidarity. The fact is that we have the final option to make our own choices or select those things that make us feel confident to follow our dreams.

You are the only one who can decide what thoughts will prevail and what values will dictate your responses. Positive thinking can dominate your thoughts and influence your thinking. It depends on your attitude. Since attitude is exclusively a matter of decision making, the prevalence of a positive or negative approach relies exclusively on you, in the faculty of your thoughts and the harmony of your spirit.

Attitude and choice are very important elements for acquiring a positive thinking frame of reference. It is through freedom of choice that we assume the confidence to accept whatever occurs to us without losing ground as we move toward our life's purpose. Overcoming sadness is not easy and nobody is exempt from suffering. Accept that fact without allowing the claws of pessimism to sink into your positive mind-set.

Positivism comes primarily from your present attitude and the support of your mental, spiritual, and emotional connections. Optimism develops from learning experiences in the past and the desires we envision for the future. That is why we need unwanted events from time to time, so we can confront our insolence, vanity, and arrogance and develop an understanding and acceptance of the grace and beauty of life. It is by passing through uncomfortable scenarios that people find they can master life's challenges. Over human history, the wise application of fair judgments, the invaluable contribution of unrestricted moral initiatives, and the wise intuition of great thoughts have helped people transform their lives and form the benchmarks of civilization.

Remember that many marvelous inventions and creations were initially perceived as an absurd idea or an unusual way of thinking. If you are at peace with your values and feel confident with your principles, then you can pursue your dreams and follow your instincts before it is too late. "Regret is the only wound from which the soul never recovers" (Breathnach 1998, 57). Once you have the framework for understanding success you have the responsibility to move forward to take care of your projects, dreams, or ideas. It is up to you to convert them into plans and then realities.

Sometimes we experience fear, distress, procrastination, and doubt as we follow our dreams. Do not worry; these are all legitimate sensations. Remember that your mental attitude is influenced by past circumstances, present conditions, and future expectations. It is okay to feel these sensations. The problem arises when you let them persuade you to abandon or forget your mission. Sometimes you might have to postpone a dream. What you should not do is forget your dreams because of the difficulties you face or pessimistic advice you have received.

Self-restriction is one of the common things that traps people and forces them to fail their commitments. When following dreams, plans, and life's objectives, you will always need motivation, solid beliefs, and hard work. As Hal Urban says, "Any prize has a fee because nothing worthwhile ever comes easily or without a price [...] you have to give up something to get something" (Urban 2003, 118). Thomas Paine wrote something similar in his essay "The Crisis" when he said, "What we obtain too cheap, we esteem too lightly. It is dearness only that gives everything its value."

The main problem with our society is that negativism has become the predominant way of thinking. When we lack clear understanding of the power of our free choices or alternatives, pessimism can take over. Sometimes, this happens through an imbalance between rational and emotional perspectives that creates stress and leads to an underestimation of the power of possibility. In other words, the emotional side of your brain might conceive a brilliant idea, but your intellectual counterpart may not support it. This is why you need passion, imagination, and motivation in order to deter discouragement, hopelessness, and delusion.

Emotions arise in your mind, while commitment comes from your heart. Working together, emotion and commitment produce passion and create the positive mind-set you need to accomplish any goal, project, or dream. Napoleon Hill confirmed this principle in his book, *Think and Grow Rich*. "No one is ready for anything until he believes he can acquire it," he wrote. "The state of mind must be belief, not mere hope, or wish" (Hill 1983, 22). Positive attitude reminds us that we all have choices to make and decisions to take.

In order to attain success and happiness, you have to generate positive thoughts in your mind and passion in your heart. In order to keep your attitude positive, your enthusiasm must grow and your love and beliefs must become sustainable. More important, spread your positive thoughts beyond your circle of influence. That way you can maintain your devotion and bring positive thinking to all aspects of your life. Positive attitude provides the confidence to fuel the hard work necessary to pursue your dreams. It will not always guarantee positive results, but it will give you the energy and courage to continue.

On the other hand, past experiences, bad memories, and even failed intentions remain critical. Learn from them and use as them as strengths instead of setbacks. From time to time, we may feel temporarily defeated or experience the perception that we have lost a battle. Remember that you can lose a battle, but still win the war. As Charlie "Tremendous" Jones said, "Positive attitude will not get the desired result every time. However, a negative one surely will. [Therefore, you should always remember] Quitters never win and winners never quit" (Reid & Jones 2006, 72).

Passion provides the link between mind (hope and desires) and heart (commitment and devotion). To be passionate, you have to believe in yourself and imagine yourself living your desired future. This is what makes things happen. More importantly, this power of visualization allows people to live their dreams even before they happen. Love and commitment make it feasible; faith and devotion make it possible. In effect, one of the simplest ways to understand life is through the pursuit of dreams and the creation of great instants of happiness: "To love what you do and do what you love" (Reid & Jones 2006, 101).

Pleasure and sadness are two emotional sensations that relate to attitude. Both are normal human emotions that every human being experiences. They are also temporary conditions, and most of the time they are the outcomes of our own conscious and unconscious choices.

The decisions, compliments, triumphs, or incidents from the past affect our present actions and implications for the future. Therefore, it is important that we know and understand our past so we can face our future. Personal history is an essential part of your personality and identity. A person who does not know his/her past lacks the basic background to confront present problems and prepare a plan, goal, or future objective. Knowing your past can affect your rational and emotional responses in the present. Pleasant memories can provide ecstasy and excitement while physically painful or distressing experiences can alter your present responses.

Sometimes just remembering events can create a positive or negative attitude. When we revive an event from the past as part of a present condition, it can impact our choices. Positive feelings can play an important role in keeping alive a dream or an experience. Recalling a happy memory can help demonstrate that everything is possible and motivate you to succeed. On the other hand, reviving a negative experience from the past may regenerate negative situations that could affect your present behavior and influence the future.

One option is to keep your past events alive by balancing memories of worth and grief. You can advance or extinguish either sensation depending on your mood. A positive attitude should not ignore, but should address these feelings. A positive approach provides the substance to proactively deal with issues from the past as well as from the future. Proactive expectations and unlimited optimism may keep you psychologically equipped to address any scenario appropriately. As Kathleen Adams mentions in her book, *Journal to the Self,* "Acknowledging them [past events] and dealing with them constructively are the first steps in converting the energy to something healthy and positive" (Adams 1990, 39). To do that, you need the ability to establish the difference between remembering an event and reviving an episode. It does not matter if this concerns positive or negative feelings from the past. They have different effects on the present and future of the person who has experienced these conditions.

It depends on your attitude whether you use a remembering tool to overcome challenges or recall unhealed events. The second choice can become a heavy load that leads people to fall into a precipice of anxiety and distress. Remember that there is a clear difference between remembering an event and reviving a past episode. Remembering means to consider previous information, while reviving represents repeating, restating, or resuscitating former occurrences. These two terminologies may look similar but they have strong essential differences in their meanings. Remembering allows you to take into account your past so you can acknowledge the present and prepare the future. Remembering is one way people apply past positive episodes to confront similar present conditions in a creative and innovative way. You can use remembering to affirm your strengths and restate your attitudes, or to confront unexpected occurrences in a calmly and proactive manner. On the other hand, reliving an experience might keep you imprisoned in the past. If you constantly relive past episodes, that is a clear sign that you have issues and concerns that you need to address so you can find proper ways of healing.

Keep in mind that the burden of bygone actions, great or fearful, may deter your personal growth or even bring more difficulties to your present. Reliving a hostile or negative circumstance can discourage your best intentions of assertively controlling the future. It is why a friendly relationship with the past helps you determine the level of intervention you need to heal your soul and affirm your beliefs. Sometimes we carry out unresolved incidents from the past into our future relationships. At such times, unexpected responses tend to come from past pain or grief.

Such reactions can create unpredictable scenarios that can result in dangerous, risky, and irrational behaviors—behaviors that arise not from present condition but from past unresolved episodes. In these cases an emotional discharge can act as a healing agent and help us confront the issue. Since change begins in our inner self it becomes our duty to take action in consideration of our logical and emotional intelligence. We have to be aware of and actively involved in those things that occur inside us. As you know, internal and external circumstances can create stressful environments that may incite irrational and impulsive decisions. These negative tendencies interfere with what should be rational human interactions.

Since we control our thinking, one way to empower a positive attitude is through self-affection, love, and appreciation, characteristics so often needed to stimulate our selves. However, sometimes these exercises are not enough, due to the heavy burden of past experiences or negative influences that prevent you from treating yourself with harmony, generosity, and self-appreciation. In these cases, you need help to remove and discharge these past episodes. Counseling, therapies, healing exercises, and evaluation processes may be appropriate steps to take, depending on personal circumstances.

Nevertheless, therapy is not the only answer to our internal troubles. A self-help book, motivational speech, or counseling session can discharge the emotions. Self-talking procedures can facilitate the process of healing. In other cases, a deep commitment to spiritual healing can help you connect with your highest beliefs and discover the treasures hidden within yourself. This is why you should apply positive attitude by emphasizing that you can overcome any challenge if you explore optimistic venues and see problems as opportunities and any barrier as another step to growth.

Difficulties can be our best allies for uncovering our strengths and developing our maximum potential. As Nietzsche said, "What doesn't kill me makes me stronger." Once again it is by dealing with adversity that an individual tests his/her moral stature and uncovers his/her greatest abilities. When facing such concerns, use a proactive way of thinking and a positive attitude built on confidence and a sincere commitment to provide meaning and consistency to your life.

Depending on the dimension of the problem, the solution might be to break it down into a sequence of smaller challenges. This can help you take charge of the issue and assume the responsibility of your duties. Whatever the methodology you choose to confront barriers, it should be the full result of your choices. The fact is that so often a problem becomes worse when we ignore it or delay its solution. You should keep the whole picture in mind, but address problems on the basis of priority.

How you solve any problem depends primarily on your attitude. In addition, remember the words of Norman Vincent Peale, who said, "Every problem contains within itself the seeds of its own solution" (Peale 1967, 126). Focus your efforts in looking for alternative solutions instead of carrying the pain of negativism and procrastination. Positive emotions are the key to preventing persistent negative feelings. The only way to maintain confidence in what you are thinking, planning, and doing is by believing in yourself and appreciating your instincts. That will also motivate your intuition and exalt the worthiness of your values.

We all have unique talents that are both inside and outside our multisensorial perception. Seek those strengths that are necessary for your confidence and self-determination. I for one accept that the power of spirituality has played an important role in maintaining a positive attitude during my mature life. As Deepak Chopra says, our natural essence, the material wealth, is the energy while the character of our potentiality is found in the nature of our spirituality (Chopra 1995, 15). Therefore it becomes clear that the only person responsible for developing your vision and creating your mission is you. It is your responsibility to find your genuine meaning and spiritual purpose. You make your own choices to find ways to explore pleasure, satisfaction, and fulfillment and enjoy the exquisiteness of life.

You will achieve a positive attitude when you have a clear understanding of your purpose and mission in life. There is a difference between having a life mission and a living purpose. Nevertheless, there is also a strong connection that you can explore on an individual basis. Your life mission is supported by your outer goals, intentions, and lifelong objectives. Life purpose is an internal commitment that provides awareness of what is happening inside and around you. It is an emotional and spiritual devotion driven by everlasting convictions.

Your mission will become meaningful and your life enjoyable once you write down your action plan for your vision and mission of life. It is never too late to start but the earlier the better. Rejoice and relax your feelings by utilizing the power of your attitude to accomplish your main purposes and commitments of life. Our vision of life is an inspiration motivated from our core values and aspirations. It shows us where we are going while our mission states how our intentions can become realities. Our personal mission gives us meaning, importance, significance, and sense of destiny.

A mission acquires immeasurable value once you incorporate it into a strategic plan that you can update and reevaluate. Don't compromise your attitude to follow your personal legend. You nurture your life mission with intentions while you reinforce your life purpose by the way you pay attention to what takes place around you. Mission, purpose, and action plans are all interrelated. They become the foundation of living, an invaluable source of positive energy, and the origin of pleasure and happiness. "A mission statement gives me a meaningful purpose," says Jack Lannom. "A mission statement is a proclamation of what I am trying to accomplish [...] [On the other hand,] Vision speaks of the future. A vision statement identifies what you want to become" (Lannom 1998, 197).

A vision is what allows people to keep their dreams alive. It is not always easy. It requires self-awareness and self-confidence. To fight some self-imposed obstacles, we should utilize the power of our imagination to conceive the visionary pathway of possibility we will follow to achieve our dreams. Unfortunately, most of the time our self-imposed mental barriers keep the path hidden. Sometimes this negative tendency comes from skepticism and denial, an inability to believe in our own talents and abilities, as well as the lack of basic spiritual resources.

When the power of visualization is present, it becomes easier to transport dreams from your mind to your heart. Sometimes the opposite may occur, by which I mean that dreams can start in the bottom of your heart and later take analytical shape in your intellect. One way or another, visualization represents wider pathways of opportunities and possibilities. The power of having a vision gives people the ability to see what others cannot. It is in the foresight of the dreamers and in the execution of the doers where the subjectivity of the vision combines with the objectivity of the mission.

A mission is one of the greatest resources if you want to move forward and assume a forward-thinking attitude when facing concerns and addressing issues. A mission promotes objectivity, intention, and meaning. "Only meaning extricates man from mediocrity and propels him into magnificence," wrote Jack Lannom (Lannom 1998, 162). A personal mission creates challenges and recharges your initiatives. Your mission underscores the recognition of your self-identity and your internal values. You won't measure its success only through accomplishments; it may have diverse meaning and definitions. Nevertheless, you will find real success when you can balance both conquered achievements and the downfall of adversities. It requires humility in the triumphs and serenity in the difficulties. True success is not measured by what you have or what you have made, but who you are.

Being remembered for what you did is fine, but being remembered for what you were is what really counts. Before we are born we are no more than ash, residue, or spirit. When we die, we become ash, dust, and soul or essence, depending on your beliefs. Nevertheless, what really matters on earth is that we are in the middle of life. What we change, add, or create and what we leave for the incoming generations will have everlasting value at least for another person. Your vision gives you direction, intention, and meaning, which is why your mission gains so much value and worth.

Our self-identity represents who we are while our vision illustrates where we are going and our mission explains how we are doing. That's why a holistic strategic personal plan will help you with the directions, decisions, and strategies you need to find your purpose of life. A personal strategic plan includes, but it is not limited to, rationality, spirituality, emotions, values, beliefs, motivation, inspiration, and solidarity. The intention of a personal strategic plan is to discover your potential, develop your abilities, and define tactics and strategies you need to carry out your mission.

A personal strategic plan should include the four basic components of the classical SWOT analysis, an inventory of strengths, weaknesses, opportunities, and threats or challenges. Identifying your assets and needs is vital for developing your life's strategic plan without losing perspective of your own vision and mission on earth. Therefore, a personal strategic plan will help you focus on your mission and develop a purposeful life. Without purpose, we are not really living, but merely existing. Therefore, positive attitude is your best asset.

Positive attitude promotes positive thinking. If you do your best, it is certain you will get the best back. What you give is what you receive! Give the best of your talents sincerely and in a pleasant way. Do it without considering who the beneficiaries will be. Then follow Og Mandino's advice when he writes, "Work as though you would live forever, and live as though you would die today" (Mandino 199, 58). Positive thinking is based on the combination of rational aptitude and emotional attitude. It is supported by character and affirmed by strong commitment. Character is the best part of a person's qualities while commitment is the base for a person's actions.

Character and commitment provide the foundation for positive thinking. Without character, commitment is weak; without commitment, character is fractional. Positive thinking and positive attitude work with one another in a similar way. Without positive attitude, your choices become diminished and the initiatives of positive thinking merely co-exist. Without attitude, transformation becomes motionless. Life requires the best of us in order to enjoy the benefits of its sources. Attitude does not focus on great intentions, but proactive performances.

Without positive thinking, it is hard to get motivation and maintain creativity. Our attitude is the main component in life's equation while our actions signify the variable that determines our perception of gladness. Happiness is a condition that is intrinsically related to our attitude; therefore, attitude causes either prosperity or misfortune. Attitude is a fundamental part of our communication skills, so you should act cautiously when you express your opinions because you transmit your attitude through verbal and nonverbal messages. Attitude gives us reputation and trust. Attitude makes and defines us.

Natural Human Abilities

Creativity can be infinite, based on the ability of the mind and the unlimited power of imagination. Creativity requires decisions, courage, and commitment. It needs instincts, motivation, and continuity. One of the ways to approach happiness comes from your ability to take the present and imagine a future that harmonizes with it. You can use creativity to derive joy from former successes or even from the faulty situations of the past. With creativity you can gain from your accomplishments as well as your mistakes.

Creativity is an internal force that combines imagination and visualization to form mental pictures of your goals. These perceptions derive from your creative impulses. Enhanced by trustworthiness they allow you to experience the pleasure of achieving something without even knowing how the final result will appear. Creativity may come from your own ideas or somebody else's imagination. However, the essence of creativity is to convert a nebulous idea into a good one or a great thought into an even better one.

When we take the initiative to follow a path to a dream, we usually tend to focus attention on the desired ending rather than in the opportunities we find along the way. If we concentrate only on the results, we may overlook much of value that we could find during the journey. We can find happiness by understanding the greatest elements or by acknowledging the simple things, so pay attention to details too. There is joy in the discovery of the thousands of events that surround and make up life.

One way to feel spiritual fulfillment is during those times when a faithful commitment compels you to take full care of yourself. It would be even better if this ability led to a commitment to serve others. Our best practices are fulfilled when they serve us and become a bridge to serve others too. It is in the accomplishment of our duties that we exercise our elemental rights.

To enjoy life, admire those marvels that occur around us and pay attention to the hidden treasures in our everyday activities.

Both the objectivity of the task and the joyful approach of the journey measure the importance of achievement. Worries become barriers that prevent us from seeing the extraordinary events around us. This is why success is not merely the achievement of desired results, but the alignment of talent, interest, and intentional thinking. Two of the best natural human abilities, creativity and imagination, spring from the commitment to positive thinking. High achievers are those who accomplish their mental predictions while also enjoying their journey to the place where they achieve their dreams. You should not lose sight of the essence of the concept because you need that vision to make choices, keep promises, and hold principles. A typical environment that allows these practices occurs when we tend to minimize our victories or conform to initial or small achievements. Under this mentality, your lifelong dreams disappear as soon as you get a new position, career, or title that you may consider "good enough." Our own self-compelled limitations become the main obstacle to happiness.

Therefore, let us work to promote change, creativity, and imagination and be prepared to accept any challenges. As an anonymous philosopher wrote, "It is better to be prepared for an opportunity and never get one than get an opportunity and not be prepared for it at all." Being prepared will give you the opportunity for happiness, while being unprepared may push you along the pathway of misfortune. We all have the power of choice. By not choosing how you will act or behave, you have also made a choice. You must assume the consequences of your decisions.

Never allow your life to become expressionless and your dreams meaningless. Be aware of any situation that may convert your life into a mere routine of hopelessness, emptiness, and loneliness. The purpose of this book is to help you realize the potential of your choices and the virtue of positive thinking. As intelligent human beings we can develop our talents. That is a choice. So is contentment. Happiness is a temporary condition we can achieve with positive thinking because it is a reciprocal effect of the power of choice and attitude.

Life can be hard, but it is also full of beauty. Therefore, do not focus so much on the target and the ultimate goal, for in that way you may lose sight of the substance of life. It is not wrong to pursue a dream and work hard to accomplish it. However, any extreme creates a disproportion in the wholeness of life, so you must create the harmony needed to keep your decisions, primary purposes, and ultimate objectives in line. Do not let time slip through your fingers without having spent it with those who really matter to us.

Time is precious. Do not waste it in frivolities or in a stubborn intention of reaching artificial pleasure. Time is even more important than money, so measure your choices and question them if you are working all the time. Such choices make you what people call a "workaholic." Too often we tend to be "too busy" that we forget to pay attention to important details or to our loved ones. Balance your time and share it with your significant others. That is an ongoing commitment that can be very hard to meet. However, it is vital.

Investing time in our families does not mean disconnecting ourselves from our responsibilities to society. Delivering love, showing encouragement, and dedicating time to our loved ones should not take away from our citizenship duties. Maintain positive thinking and manage family and societal responsibilities by striking a balance. You define your priorities in life and the outcomes of your life's mission, so you must choose how to dedicate your time, efforts, and commitment to love and empower those who are around you.

The main principle of accomplishing your dreams, mission, and purpose is to follow a simple statement: "Work to live instead of living to work." Accordingly, find equilibrium and harmony on any decision that you may make. The flavor of a successful life comes from defeating obstacles. The spice of achieving is to make your best effort at success without leaving behind those who are around you. The opportunity to get pleasure and enjoy the beauty of life depends on your choices and the quality of your decisions in balancing time and responsibilities. Happiness comes from finding harmony in the time spent in those things that are important and necessary. Sometimes, we can find this trend in small achievements. Other times, we may get it solely in the greatest accomplishments.

However, so often we find happiness when overcoming barriers. Even in moments of pain and suffering, time remains an invaluable asset. The fact is that as you advance to maturity, you acquire increased knowledge and a sense of understanding, respecting and valuing the way you spend your time. To paraphrase William Shakespeare, time is too slow for those who just wait. It is too fast for those who are afraid. It is too long for those who weep for themselves and too short for those who celebrate. However, for those who love and are loved, time is eternity and love limitless.

Happiness is more than instant gratification. Happiness depends and relies on us. Happiness is inside, outside, above, and behind us because it is so often enclosed with the little events that we consciously and unconsciously may allow to pass by undetected. Both time and space play an important role in seeking happiness and in the pleasure of enjoying our journey of life. As John Maxwell says, citing Victor Hugo, "Our life is already short. However, we may make it ever shorter if we continuously waste the invaluable time that is gifted to us every day" (Maxwell 1998, 124-129).

Guidelines in Applying Emotional Intelligence

The power of your mind is immeasurable if you equip it with positive thinking and feed it with knowledge and understanding. It is an unlimited asset if you have a spirit filled with wisdom and a heart with persistency; if you combine patience with rationality and feelings with solidarity. Control your emotions, discharge negative influences, embrace enthusiasm, and keep yourself positive. Do it constantly by practicing and preaching on a daily basis. Positive thinking is all about attitude and making a convergence between rational ability and emotional intelligence. Apply these concepts and you will be free, blissful, and happy.

Experiencing this level of contentment requires that you sincerely engage in a deep peace of mind so you can attain the essence of happiness. Count your blessings, review the capacity of your instincts, utilize the positive power of your emotions, and continuously stimulate your spirit. This applies to both the smallest and the largest accomplishments as well as to tangible and intangible targets.

Use every second of your life to make proactive decisions and positive commitments to the opportunities that every day brings. Prepare and energize your activities with supplements of positive energy. Plan with intelligence and positive emotions each day you have the privilege to live. Prepare ahead of time how you want each day to be. You decide with your mind and in your attitude your predisposition to enjoyment. It is what I call commitment to life and faithfulness to pleasure. Stimulus and motivation play a significant role in maintaining positive thinking.

In order to fulfill your dreams and understand the purpose for your presence on earth, you should ask yourself what keeps you moving forward. As John Maxwell says, "Motivation comes not by activity alone, but by the [strong] desire to reach the end result [...] People are motivated when they know exactly what they are to do and have the confidence that they can do it successfully" (Maxwell 1993, 122). Motivation redirects inspiration and refreshes the conduit of creativity. It is in the ability to express your emotional intelligence where your power of determination influences your character.

Motivation, determination, and character create self-assurance and self-appreciation. These are the strengths that sustain commitment, another important element of emotional intelligence. Allegiance to our beliefs and devotion to our convictions fuel the power of commitment. Commitment without determination or determination without commitment are both worthless. They are interdependent principles and are both necessary to ensure accomplishment. "Commitment is the foundation on which determination and perseverance are laid," wrote Wally Amos (Amos & Amos 1988, 78).

To maintain proactive commitment, try making positive statements in the first five minutes after you awaken. Praise those gifts that are granted to you on a daily basis. Be grateful just for having the chance to live another day. One of the great deficiencies of humankind is lack of gratitude. We can change that by showing appreciation to those who share with us the privilege of life. Be grateful as well for the roof above your head, the food on your table, and the clothing in your wardrobe. It is even better if you can enjoy the companionship of your loved ones and friends and share your gifts and pleasure with them.

Our gratitude should not focus exclusively on material goods, but on all those assets that we earn rationally and emotionally. There are so many reasons to express our gratitude to God for His abundant blessings. I challenge you to read the obituaries that appear every day in your local newspapers and realize how many people die every second while you remain alive. Tell yourself, "I will live this day as though it were the last day of my life."

Even in difficult times, the hope that positive thinking brings, balanced by an optimistic emotional approach and confident spiritual trust, should persuade you that "everything that happens to you has spiritual significance" (Warren 2002, 195). Our life is not the result of random chance. There is a master plan for us individually and collectively. Therefore, practice gratitude at the beginning of each morning and at the end of each day. I have no doubt that the outcomes of this pledge will surprise you. More importantly, share the positive results with others and pass along your enthusiasm.

As you affirm positivism, deter pessimism, and overcome negativism, you will avoid wasting your time with menial activities and superfluous complaints and become more aware of yourself as an individual. It is as we exercise our consciousness that we find the main reason for articulating our thankfulness for our daily blessings. So be grateful for the things you already possess and seek to become more sensitive with the less fortunate. Remember that more than 900 million people live in social and economic survival mode, trapped in the struggle of poverty and lacking essential resources.

So why not praise the opportunities you receive every day? Would it not be appropriate to encourage yourself to live your life with intensity? That is the first rule I have personally applied while writing this book—become aware and thankful for the wonderful things that surround us. Remember that gratitude is a powerful tool for positive thinking, one that will fill your day with joy and your thoughts with proactive attitude. Thankfulness will also help you understand obstacles from different perspectives.

If you plant the seeds of positive thinking in your frame of reference, you will prepare yourself to confront all circumstances. Positive thinking is the essential element for dealing with unexpected conflicts. It is crucial for maintaining calm and assertively addressing any issue. Express sincere attention to those things that are important and bring a hearty intention to effect change whenever you can to implement your life purpose.

Paying attention means having a respectful approach to those around us, both people and things. On the other hand, intention is the ethical and moral target of any purpose or desire. Attention is a present attitude. Intention relates to both the present and the future. In effect, to paraphrase Deepak Chopra, intention is the spirit of the final target; it is the essence of content and the foundation of effort and action. A purposeful intention becomes stronger than the desire itself. The true power behind any aspiration is usually found in the final intention of the goals and objectives (Chopra 1995, 75-76).

Should you change the intentionality of your thoughts when uncontrolled events take place? You should pay attention to those issues that need your immediate consideration, but without losing perspective of your real intention.

A strong positive attitude will help you become amiable and enthusiastic as you defeat negativism. You can decide how any new day will look. You may not choose how it arrives, but you can elect how to respond.

It looks simple, but is it? It is not easy or so difficult. It is just a decision that you should make every morning. If you commit yourself to it as soon as you open your eyes, you will smile more frequently and express your kindness constantly as you praise and value others. Recognize the efforts of others and congratulate them even for small accomplishments. All human beings are delighted to be sincerely recognized for their virtues, talents, and commitments. It is another way to combine attention and intention, soul and feeling, thinking and action.

After connecting your spirit and emotions at the start of each day, strengthen your muscles and relax your body. Be sure your neck, back, and head are relaxed. Even a couple minutes of exercise adds great strength to your physical assets. It helps ensure that your mind (positive thoughts), emotions (enthusiasm), and body (physical relaxation) are connected. Exercising daily and maintaining a constant practice of deep breathing helps produce more oxygen circulation and strengthens the immune system. The combined exercise of body and mind will bring you greater opportunities to live better and enjoy more. Strengthen your muscles; release your bones, particularly your back and your feet. You could also take a hot shower in the morning to release body tension and again in the evening before getting into bed.

Some experts recommend deep mental exercises of spiritual meditation and mental relaxation to clarify your thoughts. Massages can also help your body and your mind. Of course, these are just a few alternatives that can help you prioritize your preferences so you can attain the power of your choices. Our thoughts are the elements that teach our brain to control our hormonal responses and nervous system. Our mind can manage stress and synchronize our actions, so we should practice healthy eating and frequent exercise to balance our physical, rational, and emotional resources. Follow the teaching of European psychiatrist Dr. Paul Tournier when he said, "Most illnesses do not, as is generally thought, come like a bolt out of the blue. The ground is prepared for years, through faulty diet, intemperance, overwork, and moral conflicts, slowly eroding the subject's vitality [...] Man does not die. He kills himself" (Peale 1967, 117).

Appropriate rest and periodic relaxation are fundamental. Rest is necessary to recharge and reenergize your physical and mental assets. Relaxation techniques influence the nervous system and improve the function of our organs. We need these resources to maintain vitality and prevent stress, depression, and impulsivity. Even a simple deep breath can help you biologically, physiologically, and psychologically. It can also remind you that you are in the present and alive.

Make this exercise into a habit. Practice it every day, even for just a couple minutes, and you will become more conscious of the beauty and precious moments that life constantly offers us. Furthermore, it will help enlighten your perspectives and perception and help you acknowledge the countless reasons you have for celebrating every brand-new day.

There is a great difference between knowing and acknowledging, even though these two terms can be interpreted as synonyms. However, I believe that to know a topic means to be aware of something, while acknowledging it is more related to a conscious understanding of the facts. For instance, when we read, we know about the topic; when we acknowledge, we understand and accept the facts as they are.

By acknowledging something, we reinforce our frame of reference and also validate our ways of thinking. The acknowledgment of credible information and a practical approach to living experiences will generate the confidence and wisdom you need to acclaim the virtue of positive thinking. Wisdom helps us differentiate between bad and negative, judgment and prejudice, real and artificial, and meaningful and worthless.

Physical activity and emotional discharge are important to refresh mind and body. When mind and spirit connect and you have avenues of emotional release, it becomes easier to maintain practical positive thinking. At such times the power of your mind can dominate your body and manage your physical resources. It is also important to include a healthy diet with your periodical exercise. But the most important thing is that in order to control your body, you should take care of your thoughts. As Rhonda Byrne says, "Stress begins with one negative thought. One thought that went unchecked [...] the effect is stress, but the cause was negative thinking, and it all began with one little negative thought" (Byrne 2006, 127).

If you harmoniously coordinate your thoughts, a balanced diet will help you control excesses and prevent extreme lifestyles. Changing lifestyles is a process, which is why I reaffirm the importance of seeding positive thinking in whatever we think, say, and do. If you can take care of your mind, you can control your nutritional lifestyles. Avoid junk foods and find a good balance of vegetables, fruits, whole grains, seeds, proteins, and carbohydrates.

However, depending on your age and eating traditions, you may need additional vitamins, minerals, digestive enzymes, or antioxidants. Furthermore, a balanced lifestyle should avoid toxins, trans fats, pollutants, free radicals, preservatives, and other nutritional deficiencies. Healthy mind plus vigorous body is an equation whose variables are determined by genetics, environment, nutrition techniques, eating methods, and lifestyles. Balancing them adequately is important because they will affect your way of thinking, acting, and living.

Of course, these practices require discipline, which is one of the most important factors for achieving great outcomes. It is also important for managing your body and your thoughts. "Discipline means doing the right things at the right time for the right reason," says John Maxwell (Maxwell 2002, 61). Positive thinking and discipline will help you to attain physical health, a good mental state, and spiritual satisfaction.

Another important aspect is digestion. When you dedicate time to eat, make sure you have time to assimilate it. Eat slowly and patiently. Give yourself at least 20 minutes. Feeding your body without distractions is a key element to preserving a great digestive system. I am sure that most of you realize that any substance abuse, alcohol or drugs, will interfere with good health.

It is your responsibility to address these issues. Positive thinking is not just a decision of the mind. It is also a resolution of the self. It is not a question of trying, but willing. Do not complain about what happens to you. Give thanks for what you have and for any opportunity you receive. Life offers us all opportunities to do something unique and great during our transitory existence. Is it not wise to justify our presence on earth? Shouldn't you create something or add something to what we find when we open our eyes? The great news is that we have that opportunity every single day. We can add value to any second of our lifetime if we are in charge and make the right decisions.

Sometimes we know what we get, but we rarely acknowledge what we already have. You must become aware that you can create positive thinking in yourself and in others. It is all in the power of your attitude. Make sure to focus your attention on the power of your assets and then use those gifts and concentrate your efforts on positive outcomes. Everything begins with individual commitment and the expectations of your inner self. Positive thoughts and spiritual convictions are unstoppable forces.

That is why we need a healthy body, strong mind, and robust spirit if we want to confront the challenges of life. Our entire organism works every second of our life. Some cells die and others grow; it is just a reflection, on a small scale, of the greatness of life's evolution. We must accept that body and mind become vulnerable to degenerative diseases as our immune system declines. Nonetheless, you should consider healthy choices and exercise as preventative measures to reduce painful and lethal diseases.

To enjoy your whole life and find physical and emotional stability, take appropriate care of yourself. In his *Discourse on Method*, René Descartes taught us, "To be possessed of a vigorous mind is not enough. The prime requisite is rightly to apply it." Whatever your choices, the most important thing is to make wise decisions and then follow and apply them consistently. That includes, but it is not limited to, giving love, sharing solidarity, procreating, and taking care of your own body and environment. If you add to these basic guidelines the important components of faith and emotional/spiritual confidence, then you can commit yourself to a trustful relationship with God.

Of course, that relies on the depth of your beliefs and convictions, but if you can keep these pieces together, nothing can change your positive attitude or interfere with your willingness to remain proactive and enjoy your life and opportunities. Positive and coordinated thinking is the best way to truly engage with life. Positive thinking provides the perfect environment for cultivating great habits and inspiring the visualization of great events.

However, positive thinking alone is not enough. Your beliefs play an important role in giving purpose and meaning to your life. This is why praying is a powerful tool for assessing both triumphs and difficulties. Worship can come from public inspiration or private reconciliation. Public praying brings energy from the whole to the individual while private practice creates a deep connection with your inner self. More important, praying is itself a call to act. As Dale Carnegie said, "Prayer puts into force an active principle for doing. It is a first step toward action" (Carnegie 1981, 437).

It is people with calm spirits who find the peace of mind needed to confront adversity and control impulsive emotional reactions. Start this process every day by desiring the best for you and others and remain thankful for all the gifts already granted to you. This is a proactive approach that will help you fill your life with pleasure and your journey on earth with accomplishments. At the end of the day, be sure to clean your mind from the influence of pessimistic forces. If you have to remove all impurities from your body and take a shower on a daily basis, then you also need a mental purification to release negative influences. Do this by using mental discharge conduits to clean your mind and release emotions, deter frustrations, reduce stress, and prevent depression. "You control your thoughts or they will inevitably control you."

You also need sleep to feel rested and energetic. Add quality to your sleep by quickly recounting the pleasant and unpleasant moments from your day. Focusing some attention on the unpleasant occurrences will help you release negative sentiment. More importantly, it will help you see the positive side of any issue, learn from the experience, and finally discharge it. You can do this by actively removing negative episodes from your mind. Feeling down from time to time is normal, but to remain in that state without addressing it will create problems that could affect your whole life.

Everything starts in your thinking process, so it's good to remove bad or unhappy sensations so you can avoid accumulating negative statements, pessimism, and self-denial. Intentional thoughts drive our behavior. They provide the conduit to our aspirations and they reflect our sadness and happiness. Our thoughts are the basic representation of who we are and they predict what we will become. Russ Harris said that thoughts are attachments that drive our ways of thinking and acting. "Thoughts tell us about our life and [they tell us] how to live it. They tell us how we are and how we should be, what to do and what to avoid. And yet they are nothing more than words[...] Our main interest in a thought is not whether it is true or false, but whether it is helpful" (Harris 2007, 38).

It is wise to eliminate anxieties from your thoughts through healing procedures. Conditioning yourself to make proactive responses is a process and therefore it can be a practice. In order to master it, heal your physical, mental, emotional, and spiritual assets by periodically expulsing all negative influences, past concerns, and old angst. That is what Dale Carnegie recommended when he said, "Act as if you were already happy, and that will tend to make you happy. Happiness does not depend on outward conditions. It depends on inner conditions" (Carnegie 1981, 67).

Use your enthusiasm and spiritual confidence to eliminate negativism that can thwart affirmative action and promote conformism. Remember, "We can't think intelligently while we are in distress" (Jackins 1994, 31). The ideal is to charge your mind, spirit, and emotions with enthusiasm and an array of positive thoughts. Usually the most difficult task is to convince yourself that enthusiasm is possible, self-motivation works, and positive thinking is achievable. To do that, visualize your talents, exercise your proactive skills, control your temper, and create appropriate responses to release your emotions.

To maintain eagerness and fervor, look at all circumstances as opportunities to learn and grow. Whatever the situation, maintain calm and remain patient. A single positive thought may not change all the problems or solve all the difficulties of the world, but it will feed your mental energy in a constructive way and make a difference in you and maybe in somebody else. Sometimes the root of a concern may not be an unexpected event, but a reminder of past feelings and emotions. Therefore, remain aware of previous circumstances that could interfere with your present commitments and weaken your future aspirations.

Stress and depression can arise from bad experiences that remain hidden in our subconscious. They may be unaddressed issues or the effects of dreadful episodes that have not healed. Be sure to clear your mind and determine to analyze such issues from the past. No matter how far back it occurred, you always have an opportunity to confront, accept, and forgive. Bitterness from past offenses can turn into a poison that can slowly kill your spirit, mind, and body.

Our future aspirations can also lead to stress or depression. As we deal with the present it can become burdensome to add the problems of the past or the worries of the future to our restrictive time constraints. It does not matter how many troubles we face, a positive attitude and a strong commitment to deal with one problem at a time is the best means for reducing stress. Take control of stress or it will take control of you. Stress can be a serious detriment to your attitude and it can infect your ways of thinking and acting. That is why Dr. Bernie Siegel says, "During stress, rational memory is impaired, and emotional memory predominates [...] Humans are at the mercy of fear impulses that override reason" (Siegel 2005, 27).

What is stress? How does it become part of us? The following story from an anonymous source helps illuminate the issue.

A professor was explaining the importance of stress management in people's lives. The speaker lifted a glass of water and asked, "How heavy is this?" Answers ranged from 20g to 500g. The teacher replied, "The absolute weight doesn't matter. It depends on how long you try to hold it. If I hold it for a minute, that is not a problem. If I hold it for an hour, my arm will ache. If I hold it for a day, I will have to call an ambulance. In each case, the weight is the same, but the longer I hold it, the heavier it becomes.

"That's the way it is with stress management," the professor continued. "If we carry our burdens all the time, those burdens become increasingly heavy until we can no longer carry on. As with the glass of water, you have to put your burden down for a while and rest before taking it up again. When we are refreshed, we can carry on with our burdens. So, before you return home tonight, put the burden of work down. Do not carry it home. You can pick it tomorrow."

Remain cautious of the tangible and intangible presence of stress. Take consideration of its influence so you can avoid matters that affect our communal affairs. At the same time, avoid public concerns that affect your individual private duties. We can all meditate about the essence of stress and how we can manage it through the power of our mind and a setting of straightforward positive thinking. Stress is a serious mental health challenge. But dealing with it does not mean to forget or delay. It means you must prioritize your needs and attend to one problem at a time. The first thing to do is relax and address your troubles after you have enough time to calm down, gain confidence, and act with restraint. Remember that life is short and you should enjoy it as much as you can. Apply positive thinking both in periods of fulfillment and in times of concern.

Social and emotional intelligence play an essential role in life's equation. To paraphrase Daniel Goleman, there are four basic elements of emotional intelligence, which is the ability to acquire what Goleman calls "personal and social competence." Personal competence requires self-awareness and self-management, while social competence represents social awareness and relationship management (Goleman et al 2002, 30). Emotional and social intelligence are crucial for positive thinking and the three basic inner skills you should acquire: self-awareness (understanding our emotions), self-management (the capability to balance our feelings), and self-development (which is nurtured by experiences and invigorated by challenges).

Our intentions do not necessarily reflect the facts of our realities; stressful situations do not necessarily arise from predictable conditions. That means we should act intelligently in the presence of either expected or unexpected events. By affirming our social and emotional boundaries we may find rational income streams of positivism and relationships of reciprocated respect. As Linda Andrews says, "Emotional intelligence is useful. It helps you get along with others and be more sensitive to their feelings. It gives you motivation to pursue your goals. And it puts you in touch with your own fascinating feelings" (Andrews 2004, 69).

The power of emotional intelligence works even though it can be difficult to maintain the same mood all the time. How you react to life's circumstances becomes the main challenge that confronts a positive thinking mind-set. A simple discussion or social occasion can turn into a mental bullet that impregnates your subconscious in a way that may affect you forever. The best course is to prevent such reactions or illogical impulses. Make a meditated reply that comes from a deep analysis. If you do not appropriately address such an offense, it could displace your enthusiasm and bury the magic of life. It will be even worse if you carry that heavy weight in your heart and become a source of negative energy, a conduit of lethargy, or a spreader of apathy.

It is always better to express your feelings and points of view clearly. Maintain respect and understanding for other viewpoints. Sometimes it may be difficult to properly consider offenses, transgressions, or frustrations. It may require specific attention and selective intervention. At all times try to maintain reconciliation with your inner self and learn to forgive with your mind and with your soul. Forgiveness is the first step in finding equanimity within your inner self and approaching reconciliation and peace of mind.

Past episodes can have a long-lasting effect whether the offense was made by you or against you. Remember that bad thoughts, negative feelings, or malicious approaches affect the giver more than the receiver. Reconciliation with your spirit and self-controlled emotions will help your mind and body balance your attitude, release fatigue, and discharge sentiments that block proactive ways of thinking. Consequently, you must develop confidence in your abilities to control and release feelings, which is part of basic emotional and social skills.

Both past and future episodes can give you satisfaction or distress and affect your ability to develop your mind's emotional intelligence. Self-confidence becomes an essential element for the creation and the development of emotional intelligence. When you have confidence, you trust yourself and your own capabilities. Do not harbor rancor in your soul because it will also affect your mind and body. Instead, release negative emotions and pardon any offenses. "He who is slow to wrath has great understanding, but he who is impulsive exalts folly" (Proverbs 14:29).

Jesus Christ provides us another example by demonstrating love and compassion for others. More importantly, in His last minute on earth He asked for forgiveness for those who mistreated Him even though they knew He was innocent. In fact, Christ said, "Forgive us our trespasses as we forgive those who trespass against us." So it is with us. Let us forget bad episodes from the past. More importantly, let us use any affront, offense, or misfortune as a learning experience. Let the purity of your heart, the comforts of your emotions, and the faith of your spirit heal your mind and feed your soul with love and peace.

In order to love others you must love yourself, without egocentrism or narcissism. That is a supreme principle taken from the divine advice of "Loving one to another." This thesis replicates Jesus' teaching about avoiding judgments and promoting love and compassion. It does not mean deterring your natural right to become productive and self-sufficient. It merely calls for the amazing grace of loving one another.

Do this by considering the welfare of the whole instead of the particular interest of the few. This is your commitment to share and exercise solidarity. Distributing your wealth does not necessarily mean taking away or splitting your assets. It means to share the abundance of your resources— intangible and tangible—with those less fortunate. That includes resources such as kindness, appreciation, a sincere smile, or a real hug. Those are things we can freely share on a continuous basis. Keep in mind Norman Vincent Peale's saying, "You never have continuing flow of abundance if your thought is only for yourself" (Peale 1967, 196).

The art of giving comes from a spontaneous desire to help those who are less fortunate. Giving is never mandatory. We can all give something away, but most of us also need something from others. We need one another. So why not give out what we may have in abundance? As Saint Francis of Assisi said, "All getting separates you from others. All giving unites to others" (Maxwell 2002, 129). It is in the power of giving and sharing that we promote and attract positive energy. Periodic giving is another way to enjoy the beauty of life.

The first step in changing your frame of reference is to consider all situations as learning experiences. Change the things that you can and accept those that pass beyond your control. As Epictetus said, "There is only one way to happiness and that is to cease worrying about things which are beyond the power of our will" (Carnegie 1981, 328). Be generous in giving those things that do not have monetary value but provide emotional gain. Do not match up your spirit to so few. Ignite your intuition, embrace your originality, and think bigger.

To summarize, it is indispensable to rest your body, mind, heart and spirit. Refreshing and relaxing your mind and body will recharge your attitude and improve performance. On the other hand, be sure to practice the art of giving and exercise the greatness of solidarity. Affirm your actions to the utmost and conquer your projects. Eliminate denial and put the word impossible out of your mind. Positive thinking will help you find the connection between giving and receiving, loving and caring, praising and affirming. As the Dalai Lama said, "The more we care for the happiness of others, the greater our own sense of well-being becomes."

Positive Thoughts Are All About Controlling Your Emotions

The purpose of this book is to utilize the power of positive thinking so you can enjoy the best of life. However, as Dale Carnegie advises, "Circumstances alone do not make us happy or unhappy. It is the way we react to circumstances that determines our feelings" (Carnegie 1981, 324). Rationality is just one part of your brain. The second part is the emotional component shared by your mind and feelings.

In our interaction with different personalities, cultures, and traditions in the world, we often find disagreement. This is why we need an open mind, positive attitude, and proactive emotional approach so we can adjust our frame of mind and better understand differences. This is where our emotional side plays a significant role in maintaining positive thinking. It affects both the way you treat yourself and the way you deal with others. Consequently, try to keep all disagreements in the field of ideas instead of the sensibility of emotions. It is normal to disagree but unproductive to argue. When confronted by a difference of opinion, speak out about anything related to the subject but try to avoid involving personal or cultural differences.

The only exception to mentioning the personal characteristics of an individual would be when you are making positive comments. Otherwise it is best to keep your mouth closed. Sometimes that is not easy, but you can do it. It will help your relationships endure and improve. It is a valuable attribute to remain humble during triumphs and acquiescent in failure. It is a matter of wisdom to show real interest, compassion, and solidarity for others instead of merely criticizing or censuring.

Do not judge. Analyze issues instead of personalities. Do not dwell on things that did not occur or might never happen. It is unproductive and usually results in broken relationships. Often when you judge and criticize others it comes from a lack of sensitivity and poor management skills. Fear of our own limitations is also a factor, especially when we are facing risk. Still, it is better to make mistakes than to fail to take the initiative and confront your own fears. It is worse to react to the failure of others with sarcasm or accept the accomplishments of dreamers with envy.

Take the lead! Make your best effort, and learn to do even better the next time you receive an opportunity. When you are positive and act in a proactive way, you reduce the need to criticize others, who may be doing their best to improve or become independent. It is selfish to focus your attention on the public failure of others instead of on their private virtues. Avoid criticizing. If your opinion is requested, be generous in your comments and diplomatic in your censures. It is one of the wisest rules for gaining friends and avoiding enemies, seeking happiness and lowering suffering.

We should rarely criticize people in private and never in public. Not only do you risk losing the person's confidence, you will also probably win antagonism instead. Even when you are right, develop the ability to listen to others' views and the humility to express your own. When you are wrong, learn the virtue of recognizing and accepting it calmly. Sometimes, having the right information does not mean that we possess the truth. Even Socrates with all his wisdom remained humble enough to say, "One thing only I know, and that is that I know nothing." So why should we jump to conclusions and scold those who may be wrong in their approach but unaware of it?

Is it fair to embarrass people instead of giving them an opportunity to demonstrate their abilities? Why offend them instead? Why be rude even when we have reason to support our views? Remember, "Humility places us in the state where learning becomes possible" (Ferrucci 2006, 201). Be sincere when praising people and be slow in criticizing or condemning others. Address mistakes calmly and proactively. Use prudence, tact, and diplomacy.

You will face conflict. When you do, remain aware and carefully measure the consequences of whatever course you pursue. It will also help if you challenge the normal human tendency to condemn others. "Even if we are right and the other person is definitely wrong we only destroy people's ego by causing someone to lose face," wrote Dale Carnegie (Carnegie 1981, 212). Criticism promotes resentment while denigration seriously hurts people's pride. Concentrate your energy in recognizing virtues rather than hunting defects.

The art of building relationships with reciprocated respect demands that we concentrate our attention on the qualities and capabilities of others. Sometimes this isn't totally realistic for those in supervisory positions. However, in general you should concentrate on the virtues while minimizing errors. For instance, if an action leads to a mandatory disciplinary action, handle it in private and be respectful by first emphasizing the person's qualities and ending by citing required improvements. As John Maxwell said, "If we take people as they are, we make them worse. If we take them as they should be, we help them become what they can be" (Maxwell 1993, 118).

Negativism can be habitual or situational. Habitual negativism operates on the conscious and unconscious levels through a reflexive pessimistic outlook. It arises from conditions in the present and involves a refusal to change or innovate and/or unshared expectations of future outcomes. Situational negativism is a negative response that usually arises from unexpected circumstances.

I certainly believe that we should avoid persistent and customary negativism in order to protect our decisions from pessimistic effects. Since our reactions drive negativism, my first recommendation is that you take time to explore your options so you can reduce or eliminate any tendency for auto-imposed negative responses. Keep in mind that such negative responses influence your decisions, hide opportunities, and create additional concerns. Most of the time, negativism arises from the sense that bad moments will last forever or the assumption that there are no manageable solutions. That is why a minimum requirement for assuming a positive attitude is to focus your attention on options and solutions instead of complaints and self-deprecation.

Avoid negativism by concentrating your efforts on evidence-based initiatives balanced with solution-focused approaches. Reactions do not measure consequences. They do not provide options, only random emotional responses. We should subordinate reactions to rationality. "Reactive people are driven by feelings, by circumstances, by conditions, by their environment," writes Stephen Covey. "Proactive people are driven by values carefully thought about, selected and internalized values" (Covey 1989, 72). Negativism usually tends to escalate from disagreement to hostility and from verbal disagreements to physical conflict. Pessimism, lack of sensitivity, and miscommunication can transform a passive disagreement into an active altercation.

According to Lani Arredondo, negativity expresses itself in three basic modes: defensiveness (which comes from a reaction originated to protect oneself), hostility or resentment (the tendency to blame somebody for bad events), and chronic complaining (seeing any event or circumstance in a pessimistic way) (Arredondo 2005, 17). A negative approach can originate from different reasons and circumstances. However, it is at the most critical moments when you must manage any disruptive manner calmly but firmly and slowly but consistently.

Habitual negativism is a psychological contagion that poisons our rational and emotional ways of thinking. It corrodes and destroys trust and confidence. Avoid it. I realize that changing people's minds is a difficult task, which is why it has been said, "It is always better to avoid a conflict than win one." In conflict you always lose in one way or another. Therefore, eliminate personal and destructive criticism in order to maintain healthy relationships.

Pay special attention to the judgment and comments you make while remembering how different your life would look if you focus on the good things. Determine today to become more sensible about praising people's qualities. I find it hard to understand why people bring flowers, send cards, and provide limitless good comments after someone has died. Positive thinking should take place when people are still alive because the practice will bring comfort and peace to mind and feelings, calmness to hearts, and harmony to souls. As the great philosopher Zoroaster said, "To do the right thing is not just a duty, but also a pleasant sensation that lasts forever."

Offer love instead of odium and acceptance instead of intolerance. Remember that to denigrate and punish others, physically or mentally, is a terrible disgrace, a practice that people around the world should condemn. "The wounds of psychic abuse are far easier to camouflage than the bruises of the physical batterer," said Sarah Breathnach. "This makes them even more dangerous. What is hidden cannot be healed" (Breathnach 1998, 295).

No doubt you have heard that you should act towards people as though they were going to die tomorrow. That is another tactic to help you focus your attention on the positive capabilities of others. Even a small misunderstanding or lack of attentive listening skills may distort the actual intention of a discussion, and that is why effective communication is so important if you want to maintain respect and interact well with others. Make it a permanent practice to make good comments about people. Do not allow irrationality or emotional reactions to hurt others or even yourself. In order to think positively, eliminate these tendencies by applying positivism. Collect facts calmly and analyze all the consequences to avoid losing your temper or hurting others. Emphasize your efforts to bring out the positive side of people's behavior. Positive attitude is a combination of proactive analytical thinking and positive feelings, while positivism is the firm conviction that any event is circumstantial. All things must pass. Anger management is one of the most difficult things to master. As I've mentioned, when you hit with an object, you damage a person's body. When you hit psychologically, you damage a soul.

Anger is a powerful weapon that usually arises from assumptions, reactions, and mixed impulses. A bad word spoken is like an arrow or a bullet. Once it's released it cannot be called back. You have to live with the damage you cause to those you injure with your words. To win friends and influence our peers, we must smile and give them a sincere appreciation. It is as Dale Carnegie said. You should be "hearty in your approbation and lavish in your praise" (Carnegie 1981, 29).

I have also seen that when people face hard situations, they tend to deny the power of their internal spiritual resources. This tendency can even limit your opportunity to view concerns from different perspectives. It's a reaction that typically appears during moments of pain and sorrow or in the wake of some unexpected circumstance. Such sensations can limit your capacity to address an issue in a positive and proactive manner. Just remember that responsibility and accountability means accepting conditions as they are. Use your capacity to manage opportunities and learn from them. The next time you experience something similar, you will be prepared to offer kind words and sympathy to invigorate your inner self with enthusiasm and understanding. Be affable, be thankful, and show appreciation. By giving love, you get love. By promoting peace, you find peace.

Confronting difficulties is part of the maturation process. You have the power of choice and the ability to decide how to respond. It is up to you to apply positive thinking. Keep in mind that you have the power of decision when confronting challenges. You can act proactively without assigning blame. The power of acquiring success and resolving problems comes from the infinite supremacy of your mind and your belief that anything is possible. In addition, it is complemented when you apply pragmatic instincts, informed intuition, and knowledgeable decisions. Even when sad news comes unexpectedly, your first approach should be to acknowledge and accept grief as a natural fact. Grief, as Russ Harris says, is "a normal emotional reaction to any significant loss. [Consequently] It is in the period of acknowledgement and acceptance that the grieving transaction is assimilated and over-passed by applying both rational and emotional intelligence" (Harris 2007, 24).

The power of your mind is unlimited. When you add the fortitude of your spirit, you have an invincible force that you can use to construct your desired future while healing the effect of past painful actions. Keep away from distressful experiences because they can clog your enthusiasm and interfere with positive thinking. Use prayer and spiritual commitment to prevent resentment and maintain peace with yourself as well as others.

You can discover the power of your mind by balancing it with your heart. It is not a matter of wishing, but of practicing. Norman Vincent Peale said that enthusiasm is a powerful force. Controlled enthusiasm can create, invent, and produce, although if left uncontrolled, enthusiasm can break, split, and destroy (Peale 1967, 6). Remember that financial resources and material comfort are important assets, but you should develop other resources that have more worth than money. Things such as faith, enthusiasm, and health will bring you closer to happiness.

To summarize, praying can help you connect mind, heart, and soul. However, do not squander your time by asking for material goods, titles, or physical possessions. Seek wisdom, understanding, patience, and perseverance. Wisdom is one of the most valuable things you can find through faith. Use it by praying and acting at the same time. Prayer without action is like planting without water. "The Serenity Prayer" is one of the best and simplest ways to ask for orientation and directions. It says, "God, grant me the serenity to accept the things I cannot change, the courage to change the things I can, and the wisdom to know the difference."

Ask for guidance, and live each day by enjoying and utilizing the power of enthusiasm and the greatness of motivation so you can intelligently carry out your plans and attain your desires. Do this by constantly utilizing creativity and imagination. Remember Dale Carnegie's advice: "Act as if it were impossible to fail [...] The best is always yet to come." Then, seek things that make you feel special and underscore your uniqueness. Leave the ordinary behind and become an extraordinary human being by discovering those qualities that highlight your authenticity.

Positive thinking is the mental commitment to accept any circumstance as an opportunity to create and recreate your authenticity. It is part of the journey to discover your talents and accomplish your higher goals until you reach the point where you find consciousness and awareness. You will find a satisfactory life in the pieces of happiness that lie all around us. You can also find pleasure in the ignition of an idea and the execution of your final aspirations. Learn to be authentic and accept who you really are in order to enjoy your gifts and recognize the multitude of your blessings. As Pope John Paul II said, "The value of a man isn't measured by what he has, but by what he is."

Your self-identity is a conscious acknowledgment of the real you and a rational analysis of yourself. It is a reflection of the knowledge, skills, and abilities that lead to your social competences. Avoid trying to imitate somebody else. Just try to be yourself! Discover your own self and attract positive ideas and motivations that are connected to your self-identity. Since positive thinking, proactive attitude, and affirmative emotional intelligence arise from our inner self, self-appreciation becomes important in the process of maintaining a positive attitude. Your self concept helps you find your emotional intelligence. Be generous with yourself and praise your talents by recognizing your virtues.

Positive thinking is invaluable. It cannot be purchased or given, although you can learn personal virtue and transform it into a habit when you have trust, commitment, and spiritual comfort. When you have an environment where intellect can act freely and in a proactive manner, you can control your emotions and discharge them in a comfortable way. Strong beliefs allow the growth of wisdom, develop self-confidence, and affirm trust. When you have all that in place, nothing can impede a joyful life and a proactive approach to solving concerns and finding a supporting affirmative attitude.

Positive Emotions

Positive thinking and awareness are fundamental factors for feeding positive emotions and connecting to the broad spectrum of possibilities. It incites creativity and provides the confidence you need to acknowledge things as they are so you can prepare a pathway to the future. Positive controlled emotions emphasize the need to combine rational thoughts and emotive feelings in a realistic yet visionary way. You can apply it to create dreams or overcome unexpected difficulties. In all cases do not judge events by making assumptions. Accept them as they come. That is the only way to determine factual reality.

Seed and nurture positive emotions. Most of the time we can do that by aiming to "do what we love and love what we do." That is a key to maintaining positive emotions. Create an environment where creativity, inventiveness, and critical and positive thinking can thrive. Assume the responsibility of accepting what you really are. Challenge your self-imposed limits.

Positive emotions mean more than displaying humor or being entertaining. A positive emotion is a quality. It is an opportunity to discharge stress and a resource for escaping life's tension so you can create or explore your imagination. In fact, in her book, *Understanding Poverty*, Ruby Payne says, "Sense of humor and entertainment are a key element in generational poverty." What she's saying is that people who live on the margins find that emotions represent a way of healing or a way to survive. Just keep in mind that we must learn to not take life too seriously or too lightly.

Smiles and laughter are positive emotional assets that help you relax, revive your spirit, and renovate your attitude. That is why everyone needs a sense of humor, no matter your education, culture, or status. Smiling is free and precious, a gift that people can give without cost. It helps both the giver and the receiver. So enjoy your journey, smile as much as possible, and laugh whenever you can. "Live well, love much, and love often," says an anonymous piece of wisdom. That is a daily prescription for your soul that will provide wonderful strength for your heart. Living, loving, smiling, and laughing combine to create a great recipe to enjoy life and increase your physical, mental, and spiritual welfare. "One can live magnificently in this world, if one knows how to work and how to live," said Leo Tolstoy. "To work for the person one loves and to love one's work" (Haidt 2006, 220).

Laughter is a healthy means to well being. In fact, Hal Urban's medical research showed him, "Laughter can enhance respiration, produce morphine-like molecules called endorphins, increase the number of disease –fighting immune cells, reduce stress, stimulate the internal organs, and improve the circulation of the blood" (Urban 2003, 24). Are you aware that children laugh an average of almost 200 times a day while adults manage an average of only 20 laughs? Adults should take a lesson from children. Avoid complaints and embrace laughter.

Children, too, have their own problems and concerns. However, poor ways of thinking have not yet contaminated their lives. In general children receive what we give them. They model their behavior on what they see and repeat what they hear. It's when they are still young that children can freely release their emotions and enjoy life. Adults, however, are more resistant to change, learn, and try new adventures. Because adults are so often concerned with the future they often lose perspective about the present.

Laughing and smiling are natural abilities that help both mind and body. A lack of laughter and smiling will make a significant impact on the regeneration of positive emotions and affirmative ways of thinking. Doesn't it make sense to enjoy whatever you are doing at this instant? Shouldn't you find reasons to rejoice instead of being angry, worried, tense, and depressed? I challenge you to look at your peers and pay attention to their faces. Notice their expressions and consider the fears they have about the outcome of their decisions. You don't need to ask them anything. You can see it in their expressions. Do they look positive? Proactive? Are their expressions charged with enthusiasm? Why do so many people look sadder and more stressed than ever?

The magic of positive thinking allows us not just to see opportunities, but also to create them. Negative thinking, on the other hand, may not just obscure opportunities but also create failure. Avoid this trap by being aware of what goes on in your life. What we do is what we transmit. What we touch is what we connect. What we feel is what we receive. What we perceive is what we internalize. This is why the impact that you have on people can influence them positively or negatively. The energy that you generate becomes part of your environment. As Rhonda Byrne states, "The greater the love [and peace] you feel and emit, the greater the power you are harnessing" (Byrne 2006, 20).

I will demonstrate the genuineness of this thinking with a practical example. Recently I observed more than 100 people who were just passing by. I wanted to study their attitudes, see their faces and expressions, and observe how they behaved on a typical day. I was surprised to see so much anger, sadness, anxiety, and distress on their faces. At one point I had been just like that, until I became truly aware of the issues I outline in this book. The ideas and examples I present in these chapters have helped me understand and become truly involved with my daily tasks and enjoy their outcomes.

In a meeting I attended that day, I found a similar situation. I became concerned about the behaviors I saw and reflected on the poor attitudes people brought with them. I also recognized that situations I observed on the street were a little different in the meeting, where people interacted and participated in discussion. When people make direct contact and communicate in face-to-face discussion, they release emotions that impact the interaction. That indicates the importance of social interaction.

Companionship is important. We need other people, not just to love and appreciate, but to complement each other. Men and women cannot live in isolation. Our triumphs or failures require the presence of others. That is why we must connect with our coworkers, neighbors, classmates, and friends, actively and constantly. It helps us communicate our perceptions, discharge our emotions, and release our tensions but also transmit love, appreciation, and friendship. Loneliness is a terrible thing. "No matter how powerful a single person may be, without other human companions, that individual person cannot survive," says Howard Cutler. "We all are interdependent, we all depend on one another for our livelihood" (Cutler 2003, 38-43). Therefore, it is not only the spiritual law of loving one another that prevails, but also the necessity to become involved and connected. That is what we need to truly live.

Positive emotions help us relate to one another as well as ourselves. They provide substance to our visions. They help us connect with others and they link the elements of body, mind, emotions, and spirit within ourselves.

Life is fun. It is a blessing. It is a privilege. You do not have any right to lessen it by taking it either too seriously or not seriously enough. It is enough to end any self-compulsory suffering. Release all bitterness from your soul and pay attention to the amusing things that nature constantly offers us. "Joy always overcomes fear," says Dr. Bernie Siegel. "Love creates [enhancement], but laughter is the cement that holds our lives together" (Siegel 1998, 155). Another link is the supremacy of love. "The power of love overcomes the love of power," according to an anonymous saying. We need to create avenues that will give us joy and opportunities to interact, transmit, and share love and kindness.

Unfortunately, too often people focus solely on financial concerns to fulfill their aspirations. In fact, one of the greatest problems of society is the love of money and material possessions. Comedian George Carlin addressed this tendency when he said, "The paradox of our time is that we have taller buildings but shorter tempers; wider freeways, but narrower viewpoints. We spend more, but have less, we buy more, but enjoy less. We have bigger houses, but smaller families; more conveniences, but less time. We have more degrees, but less sense; more knowledge, but less judgment; more experts, yet more problems; more medicine, but less wellness."

That still applies. We have become so misguided that we have replaced adventures with status quo, innovation with tradition, affection with hatred, and true laughter with artificial smiles. As Carlin stated, we may have multiplied our possessions, but we have reduced our values. We talk too much, love too seldom, and hate too often. We write more, but learn less; speak more, but listen less; text more, but talk less. We plan more, but accomplish less. We have learned to rush, but not to wait.

So let us use our best assets and promote our admiration and appreciation for others. Do not postpone any gratification, pleasure, and/or satisfaction that you could enjoy today. Articulate positive statements sincerely and frequently. The best time to express gratitude is now. Do it in the presence of those who serve, contribute, and collaborate with you. Be sure you express sincere intentions. Praise people profusely. Smile often and laugh regularly. Humor is not just a supportive way to release emotions; it is also a natural medicine for your soul and body.

Scientists and health professionals have concluded that laughter performs an important function for human life. It releases positive energy that helps to circulate the blood, stimulate the hormones, and increase stamina. Unfortunately, so few of us use this tool well. Try it out! Smile to yourself. Look in the mirror. See yourself and observe the power and energy that you create just by laughing. You may be surprised by the changes you can create with the powerful energy you transmit.

Living well, loving a lot, smiling frequently, and laughing often are great ways to relieve stress and avoid depression. The sense of joyfulness is a mental and physical commitment that comes from your inner self and flows out to others. To tap into it I recommend starting your day by dedicating a few minutes to watching a favorite cartoon before you tune to any other program. Something as simple as that can help you energize your day. Life is a serious commitment, but it is also something you should enjoy. Discover the pleasure of accomplishing simple or difficult tasks. Learn to smile at your mistakes. Positive emotions are not just a way of thinking, but also of acting.

It is necessary to find fun even in the most difficult times. It helps you separate your emotional feelings from specific circumstances so you can find better solutions. You will discover the balance of positive mental emotions when you assume responsibility of your acts and grant yourself the right to pleasure. Remember that rational intelligence, what Linda Andrews called "ordinary intelligence," is mainly the intellectual approach of using ideas, facts, words, numbers, logic, and analytic inductions and deductions when thinking and acting. On the other hand, emotional intelligence is the intuitive knowledge and assertive management of feeling and emotions (Andrews 2004, 8).

The balance between analytical and emotional intelligence is necessary to sustain our decision-making process. Analytical sagacity means logical rationality. The emotional approach represents creative and imaginative intelligence. If we can utilize these two elements in a positive and emotionally controlled manner, we will gain what Harvard professor Howard Gardner called "practical intelligence," which is mainly "the ability to understand and solve real-life problems" (Andrews 2004, 11).

Wally Amos says that nothing can change the facts. Therefore, "You can only deal with your problem once you separate your emotions from the fact. Gain control of your situation and make the moves to resolve it" (Amos 2006, 32). Sometimes we have to detach ourselves so we can concentrate on the denotative meanings, the factual ones, without losing sight of the subjective, connotative ones. Thinking before acting becomes essential if we want to avoid reactions and impulses that lead to long-lasting mistakes. When impulse or immoderate reactions lead to poor decisions, you might lose the chance to learn from the experience.

Unpredictable circumstances can end your life or ensure that you spend the rest of it imprisoned. Avoid this by acting in a positive, balanced manner or you will surely be corroded by negativity. Jealous reactions, poor anger management, or a predisposition to violence can spur aggressive reactions that dictate your behavior and even drive you to commit horrendous crimes or make terrible mistakes that will mark you forever. That is why it is indispensable that you think before acting and measure causes and consequences before performing. Weigh your present decisions with their future implications. Learn to control your emotions—sometimes even detach from them—to allow critical thinking. Assume a conscious approach to dealing with life issues. Acquire problem-solving skills. The development of emotional intelligence becomes a fundamental component of a positive thinking strategy. To paraphrase Linda Andrews, emotional intelligence is an asset that helps people to control their tempers, increase motivation, cope with bullies and negativism, and improve intuition and sensitive perceptions (Andrews 2004, 11).

Make sure your instinct and intuition remain connected. Remember that every incident has a reason and every event a purpose. Be patient, revise your options, and find possible solutions. Once you do, apply those solutions without fear. Use your instincts and apply informed intuition to address your emotions. As Sarah Ban Breathnach says, "My intuition [is] my capacity to know something without rational evidence that proves it to be so. Intuition has been called our sixth sense, and like our imagination, it is a spiritual gift" (Breathnach 1998, 277). Be aware that all setbacks are temporary. Even more important, every obstacle brings with it the opportunity to excel.

For any situation, determine the greatest thing you can get from it. Seek alternative solutions. These options can come from your mind, but confidence and commitment come from your heart. Open your mind to inspiration and discover your inner values and assets. Understand that anything is possible if you use your resources correctly. "The only thing that stands between a man and what he wants from life is often merely the will to try it and the faith to believe that it is possible," says Richard Devos (Maxwell 2003, 29). Positive emotions will help you endure setbacks and exercise your talents to fulfill your expectations.

You have an emotional balance in place when, in addition to rational analysis and pragmatic emotional conviction, you dedicate yourself to getting fun as you reach your objectives. In order to use your emotions intelligently, you should always keep a big smile on your face and a strong commitment in your heart. If you do, you will find the fortitude necessary to confront adversities and accept any situation that comes along. "The expression of your feelings will reflect the transparency of your soul, while the manifestation of your emotions reveals the pleasure in your heart."

So let us laugh and smile as often as we can. As I've said, a smile makes a strong impact on those who give it and in those who receive it. It is a win-win scenario, so why not use it? As Wally Amos says, "Age may wrinkle the face, but lack of enthusiasm wrinkles the soul" (Amos & Amos 1988, 159). So smile. You can do it without much effort. If it is sincere, it has long-lasting benefits. A smile is a free gift. Take it; use it; spread it. "It costs nothing, but creates much," says Dale Carnegie. "None is so rich that they can get along without it and none so poor but are richer for its benefits. [...] It is rest to the weary, daylight to the discouraged, sunshine to the sad, and Nature's best antidote to trouble" (Carnegie 1981, 69).

In closing, positive attitude is tied to positive thinking. Positive attitude gives you the ability to measure your perceptions and accommodate them to realities without limiting your goals, mission, or purpose in life. Positive emotions combine the rationality of your judgments and the emotionality of your sentiments. It is your choice whether you accept an event as an opportunity and a learning experience. Pragmatic thinking will become the core of your accomplishments and the essence of life's challenges. You can select what you think and do and what you achieve. The best part is that you have a choice.

Motivation and Intuition, the Greatest Assets in Maintaining Positive Attitude

One way to stimulate motivation and inspiration and develop your intuition is to maintain an open mind and think outside the boundaries of your senses. You can bring fresh thoughts and alternative views to your mind when you are open to accepting new ideas and different perspectives. You create what Og Mandino called a "receptive frame of mind." That means you are prepared to learn from experiences and accept that differences exist in relationships that contain diverse personalities, cultures, and spiritual orientations.

Motivation provides the generation of purpose, motives, stimuli, or incentives that enter our mind and influence our emotional structure. Motivation is one of those internal assets that you should stimulate and nurture with positive thoughts in order to ensure a proactive and consistent approach of positive thinking. Inspiration is another internal asset. It derives exclusively from an individual's choices and decisions. However, when you have an open and sensible mind-set, that does not mean all thoughts are equal or that you should accept any opinion as truth. Truth is relative, so a proactive way of thinking means to explore ideas and opinions with sensitivity but without compromising your own beliefs and values.

Sometimes people must temporarily change a dream's course. That is just part of life's game, a stratagem that tests the will and illuminates the complexities we face. Often people must accept different options to accomplish a goal. It is part of the learning process. Any event might generate a state of mind that misdirects your intentions or tests your willpower. At those times motivation becomes a strong pillar of support for your decision making. Motivation is a powerful tool that helps us overcome resistance to change. At the same time, intuition can help you find ways to stimulate your senses and discover incentives to pursue your ultimate goal.

One strategy to motivate yourself is to visualize your desires and accomplishments in advance. Once you live those desired moments in your imagination you may develop a different mind-set that will reshape your thoughts so you can emotionally confront any barriers or obstacles in your way. Imagination is a priceless tool for creating motivation and intuitiveness. Just remember that imagination differs from fantasy. Imagination derives from the power of visualization, where fantasy originates in illusion.

One advantage you get from positive thinking is the chance to apply affirmative autosuggestion, which is like a covenant between your conscious and subconscious minds. We are all masters of our own minds and architects of our self-created environment. That means we have the power to influence and tune our awareness. If a higher purpose leads your mind and spirit, if you are filled with love and solidarity, then you certainly can succeed in whatever action to which you commit. Motivation is the essence of inspiration. When people are truly motivated, they find the ladders that reach success.

When you can choose freely, you should be satisfied with whatever result you obtain. It comes from your free will, so you must accept the result of your own choices. Never attach the blame from mistakes to others.

Let us claim ownership of our own decisions and live with the result of our choices, whatever the outcome may be. That is both the risk and the advantage of taking charge of your own decisions and destiny. "When they exercise their personal power of choice and opt to take the bolder path, we celebrate them!" says Jack Lannom. "Even if they do not quite get the right results" (Lannom 1998, 228). The essence of positive thinking arrives along different avenues. You can approach it from different perspectives. One way is to visualize accomplishments ahead of time. Positive thinking with clear faith and spiritual commitment is unstoppable. Moved to action and hard work, supported by constancy, it is invaluable. When you ignite your positive attitude with passion it becomes an unconquerable strength. Positive thinking makes anything possible even if the whole world conspires against it.

Passion is an important element of positive thinking. It keeps you connected to the realization of your goals. Passion is a sparkplug for creativity and a powerful force when you must address concerns. Passion is directly related to your feelings. It is a priceless component of emotional intelligence and an advantage for enhancing a person's quality. Motivation without passion is like a river without water, a book without pages, or a garden without flowers. Positive thinkers understand that passion generates creativity and transforms impulses. They know that it multiplies their options for exploring more and better ways to execute their dreams.

One way to acquire passion and inspire motivation is to utilize the mental model of visualizing future accomplishments. Try to see in advance the final product of your imagination. Project an image of the future in your mind's eye and start moving back to the present. In effect you are planning backward. When people use this technique, they create a mirror of themselves conquering their dreams. It is a description that your conscious mind processes to create a practical and concrete approach that will convert a dream into a goal. If you have motivation then you will be more willing to identify the right steps along the pathway to your goal.

We tend to find the best of our rational responses when we can tune our thoughts by acquiring what psychologists Peter Salovey and John Mayer call "emotional perception" (Andrews 2004, 13). By that, they mean the process I described of imagining the future and using that image to explore the power of possibilities. Then, move back mentally from your visualized future to your current situation and determine the steps you must take to accomplish what you have conceived.

Doing this exercise gives you the wonderful opportunity to live a result ahead of time. It also makes any dream accessible and achievable. Of course, you can't just think. You have to act too. You will need to become account-able to your projects. Positive attitude and motivation will be fundamental factors when you embrace the art of possibility. These two pillars of posi-tive thinking stimulate people to generate positive ideas and transform imag-ination into plans and initial fantasies into progressive realities.

In the field of emotional intelligence, the power of decision is the mas-ter key you need to recharge your mind and take command of your actions. If you want to achieve, you need the ability to plan, the motivation to change, and a concrete approach to measure consequences. Being able to predict fu-ture perspectives in a tangible and proactive manner will help you attain clar-ity and objectivity in your commitments. Even better, it will give you effective means of understanding future conditions and the affordable choices you need to make to get there. A concrete understanding of the mental model of positive imagination can lead you to a better understanding of the abstract concept of change and the best approach to flavor accomplishments and re-alizations.

I have to accept that this process may not work identically for everyone. Emotions have different implications for different people when they set out to manage personal and public interactions. There is no single pattern of emotional reaction, because it depends on your unique personality, charac-ter, confidence, and style in facing life's challenges. No matter how you take this option, you have the free discretion to use it. The bottom line is that it works and it will change your life. One of the main purposes for developing emotional intelligence is to become aware of the factors that affect your choices and use them as an asset instead of letting them boomerang against you.

Self-awareness and confidence in managing your assets and addressing both expected and unexpected tasks is one of those gifts that positive thinking will bring you. In the view of Linda Andrews, self-awareness is "the act of paying attention to both your emotions and your thoughts about those emotions" (Andrews 2004, 34). Keep in mind that you have everything you need to succeed in life. So start today to invigorate your intuition and ignite your motivations to accomplish your main goals and projects. I admit it will not be easy, but you can do it. When you analyze your options calmly and figure out alternative solutions to any problem, you will become accustomed to rely on your instinct, the extra sense that comes from the development of your inner intuition.

Instinct, common sense, and unprejudiced perception become extra assets when you make meditated decisions. Intuition is part of the subconscious. It becomes present in the light of motivation. In addition, the power of intuition becomes self-evident to the beholder. That means that intuition does not mean the same thing to everyone. What one person observes so clearly, others cannot even see. According to the Webster's dictionary definition, intuition is a "direct apprehension of a truth without reasoning."

Positive thinking is a mind-set; it is the foundation of optimism. Even so, the continuous process of maintaining positive settings derives from the capacity to increase your motivation and the ability to expand your informed intuition. One result is wisdom, which arises from the interaction of instinct, motivation, and intuition.

Success comes from your inner self, which is where you find motivation and intuition. Creativity's best friend is motivation, while the best way to encourage your senses is by conceiving a desired result in your imagination.

Nevertheless, a wrong mind-set, such as extreme criticism or the unconscious influence of negative thinking, can hurt creativity and stimulation. In other words, an environment or a circle of influence can manipulate your way of thinking. Sometimes, the enemy is not necessarily outside, but inside. One example is when we fail to release attached emotions or traumatic experiences from the past. Such unresolved fears feed negativism, reactive behaviors, and lack of confidence.

If you do not address these issues they can create a gap between present conditions and desired realities. It is what James Garbarino calls "emotional disassociation," which means performing almost without emotions or by giving a false impression of your feelings. That can become a behavioral health issue, one that tends to hide the real intention of your emotions. Emotional intelligence starts by acknowledging your impulses, reactions, and past behaviors. It releases creativity and motivation. In fact, creative thinking and motivational thoughts arise from an environment where imagination and inventiveness spread.

The whole process of thinking lies in the power of your decisions and the free exercise of your choices. It is in the mind-set of positive thinking that incentives and motivations can provide access to creativity and originality. You express the most extraordinary capacity of your mind in images and mental models created by the power of visualization. If you combine imaginative thoughts with passion and enthusiasm, the images you visualize will become an irrefutable reality.

Imagination is another of abilities that people do not use often enough, despite its importance for creativity. "Imagination is even more important than knowledge," said Albert Einstein (Canfield & Hansen, 174). In my opinion, that is a relative truth. However, I complement Einstein's thought with a point of view from Arnold Bennet, who says, "There can be no knowledge without emotion. We may be aware of a truth, but until we have felt its force, it is not ours" (Andrews 2004, 21). Consequently, intuition, motivation, and imagination are wonderful assets for creating, retaining, and developing positive thinking.

Proactive Decision-making
Is Not Just Inherited, but Learned

I am sure that most of the time people narrate their chronicles not from narcissism or egocentrism but as a way to share their experiences and thoughts with others. Consequently, when we study the great legacy of positive thinkers who have published their thoughts, we find their writings offer many ways we can accept life's concerns and uncertainties. Most of us, in one way or another, have struggled with the avalanche of life's issues and obstacles. Even those who consider themselves without gifts can use the writings of great thinkers to learn, practice, and master enthusiasm and positive thinking.

Successful people use different approaches to find wonderful opportunities and deterrents to lethargy. Many authors share their experiences with their readers because they know that it is not what you get, but what you add to life that really matters. That is why I am grateful for the privilege I have had writing this book and sharing passages from my life to use as examples of how to apply positive thinking. By doing that I am following a principle that Aldous Huxley expressed when he said, "Experience is not what happens to you. It is what you do with what happens to you" (Warren 2002, 248).

Experiences become fundamental tools for modeling accomplishments and lifestyles. It is why I emphasize in this book the transcendental role that homes, neighborhoods, or schools play in our lives. These environments form us as citizens, parents, bosses, and leaders, thus adding to the wealth and strength the nation finds in its families and the strong relationships among its communities. If you as parent lack the skills or abilities to influence or at least express the importance of choices to your children, then ask for assistance. The most important legacy that we leave to our kids is the combination of quality education and a family environment filled with love that teaches by example and preaches with practice.

Our primary social responsibility is to take care of our family and ourselves. In order to accomplish this role, one that is essential for the future of humankind, you should offer your children a positive role model. What you do is what you exhibit; what you exhibit is what you model; and what you model is what you reproduce. Therefore, your children will be influenced by whatever they see and/or whoever makes the best impression to them.

To make wise and rational decisions about raising your children, it's not necessary to know the entire process of childhood development or be present for the whole pathway of your child's journey. To be a good parent or to create a responsible child and civic-minded citizen, you need to embrace commitment and supply support for building values and teaching principles for success in life. Accept your parenthood with responsibility, acknowledge your commitments, and take full accountability for your acts. Remember that the fortitude of a man or woman is not measured in glorious triumphs, but in how he or she deals with difficulties.

An exceptional human being is a person who remains faithful at all times. The stature of men and women only increases when they show they can get up as many times as they fall down. More importantly, parents are judged by their ability to fulfill their family duties and their commitment to nurture productive citizens for the community. Remember that knowledge is not exclusively learned, but inherited; attitude is not solely built, but developed.

I feel fortunate that you allow me to share some experiences that have helped me to remain positive and embrace optimism in my life. Let me start by describing some experiences that really transformed my life. When I was four, I was involved in a car accident that almost killed me. I cannot explain how I survived. It seemed to me like divine intervention. The incident reaffirmed for me that we all have a mission and a purpose to achieve on earth.

It reminded me of the greatness of the Creator to make me aware of the value of life and its wonder. I knew that I had a mission to accomplish and a life to enjoy during my walk on earth. Everything happens for a reason. Every action has a reaction and every life a purpose.

A couple years later, when I was six, I started wondering how I could find productive ways to get resources to become self-sufficient. Although my parents had come from backgrounds of poverty, they still provided us with love and comprehension. We grew up in a very strict and disciplined environment. A lack of monetary resources was always a concern, but we always had love, compassion, and understanding.

Later I learned about the struggles my parents faced when they were young. They had experienced real poverty as they immigrated to big cities and fought to overcome social stagnation. Fortunately, we did not lack food or shelter, as do millions of families that experience severe poverty all around the world. More importantly, my parents always stressed the importance of education and advised me to become "somebody" in life. Their voices still resound in my ears and remind me of the necessity for gradual improvement. These wise teachings came from my parents, even though they had never advanced beyond elementary school. However, they made sure their children understood that education and hard work would always be necessary if we wanted to succeed.

They did a great job. They gave us the tools for growth and the skills to move ahead. This demonstrates the importance of exposing our children to positive and proactive living experiences. What you get in your childhood, especially at a very early age, will always live in your memories. Consequently, parents should always provide their children with an environment of positive thinking. If you come from a negative or dysfunctional home, then you should make a conscious analysis of your early years and maintain what positive things you can and expunge any negative memories from your mind and your heart. Life should be a paradise of love. However, some behaviors do not necessarily result from current circumstances, but rise from unhealed episodes of the past. That is one reason why there is so much hate and odium in this world.

When I was seven I took it upon myself to go out and sell bread in the theaters. A couple days later, my parents heard about it and they punished me. At the time I did not understand why. Later, I discovered that my parents were angry because of the poor image I made for them and the embarrassment I had caused. This temporary job experience really touched me. It does not matter that it lasted just a couple days. It helped teach me how to become later independent and self-sufficient. Later, when I was in the highest grades of my elementary school, I conceived different ways to get some extra allowance for what I considered natural children's necessities. From that experience I learned my own definition of autonomy and the importance of creating and pursuing dreams.

As I grew I started seeing the social and economic interactions between those who had plenty of material possessions and those who struggled to meet their basic needs. A couple years later, my father hired me to clean his taxicab so he would not have to pay somebody else to do it. Of course, that gave me some extra revenue. In addition, when my mother started a small business that involved neighborhood deliveries, I volunteered to visit people's homes and distribute products. That provided more income for me.

Why I am sharing these stories with you? How are they related to the idea of positive thinking? The fact is these stories include several lessons, including the need for hard work, the conviction that everything has a price, the value of nourishing your thoughts about your early years, and the importance of healthy relationships.

I am not necessarily advising young people to do something similar. What I want to explain is that it worked with me in my circumstances. These experiences helped me understand that real meaning comes from the intentions, motivations, and imaginary awards we gain and not merely from the actions or monetary rewards we receive from others. I should mention that

I never forgot my duties in school or at home. It was my own decision to become self-sufficient and productive during my early years.

Later I started a short but successful sales career during my first years in college. The experience helped add to my character, increase my confidence, and enhance my ability to believe in the power of choice. Additionally, I gained enough confidence to become independent. I learned to trust myself in pursuing post-secondary education and I made a commitment to take care of myself. In all this the privilege of having parents who taught me fundamental values, high ethical and moral standards, and a deep trust in God and His spiritual connections, which helped me persevere.

My parents' house offered me some assets as I grew up that helped me make right choices later. When you grow up in poverty you find that the few resources you have become even more valuable. I learned to value the gifts I had and the hidden treasures we all possess. The best gifts I received were the concepts of caring and loving, taking care of our responsibilities, and learning to love ourselves as well as those who are around us. The promise of love and compassion was a powerful message I received from my mother's spiritual convictions. When you can build strength like this in your soul, your spirit acquires vigor and you become proactive in whatever you think and do. You feed your self-esteem and outfit your thoughts with optimistic and confident thinking.

Self-esteem is a powerful tool for influencing positive attitude and the wonderful initiatives that come from positive thinking. High self-esteem is a fundamental asset when you deal with life challenges. A high level of self-esteem becomes a crucial factor for maintaining coherence and equilibrium as you attempt to master self-awareness and self-acceptance. It is always easier if you are encircled by an affirmative environment of positive thinking instead of pessimism. Your self-esteem needs reinforcement if you want to confront challenges effectively and face adversities assertively.

The higher your self-esteem, the better your responses will be in the face of unexpected occurrences. To paraphrase Russ Harris, we have a portion of our intellect that thinks and acts and another part of our brain that just observes and contemplates (Harris 2007, 150). In effect, the two parts of the brain participate in the thousands of events, images, and ideas that permanently cross our mind and senses. Additionally, there are other elements, such as emotionality and spirituality, whose interventions play important roles in steering the direction of our thoughts and ultimately the course of our lives.

The priority of your choices and decisions may differ. However, you should understand that you are not alone or affected exclusively by accidental or random circumstances. Your ideas, actions, and choices come largely from intentional, creative, and reflective thinking. Self-esteem plays an influential factor in the self-decision process and the achievement of goals and objectives. This is why I stress the importance of developing self-esteem. It helps us prepare ourselves to accept whatever circumstance we confront.

Getting back to my story, when I accepted a position selling books, I found it difficult because I had to sell them through catalogues. I did not have the opportunity to show a customer the actual book, only a brochure. In addition, I lacked knowledge about the diverse personalities I would find when I dealt with different clients. I lacked experience in the ways of persuading or influencing people from dissimilar environments. I learned it by doing it, and I earned respect by acting instead of merely thinking about it.

The sales job was a wonderful experience and an introduction to the power of relationships. Of course, it also gave me income and social exposure. I was proud of what I did. More importantly, I felt satisfied with the services I provided. Keep in mind that I was just 17, maybe a little immature and with too little experience. Nevertheless, I really appreciated the self-esteem I had received from my parents and several positive role models around me. All these episodes helped me build the courage and strength to see life from a proactive and feasible perspective. As a result, I earned an income that was good enough for my age. I also made new acquaintances and some very good friends.

One of the lessons I earned was the importance of relationships. At that time I had no clue about networking, effective communication, or the power of influence. I had some intuition about knowing people, but very little information about bridging social and economic divides. Consequently, I knew little about the necessity of investing in interpersonal activities and social cross-system connections. Today I realize that networking is a powerful tool for strengthening personal and professional relationships.

In any situation where you have the opportunity to interact with people, you always have the possibility of enhancing your network and building or extending your relationships. Whether you are just talking or making a business transaction, you always have the potential to build strong connections. Networking is a way to cross social boundaries and create business interactions and interpersonal relationships with the primary intention of knowing people and becoming known by them.

I have another anecdote that relates to the appointment I received from the government of Ecuador as Regional Director of Alcohol Control. It happened when I was 21. Due to my age, the appointment surprised me but it did not scare me. On the contrary, it became a challenge that I could accept, thanks to the things I had learned from past experiences. In fact, I had the opportunity to manage a group where the newest employee had at least five years of experience while the oldest veteran had been there for 35 years. Yet, I earned respect, commitment, and collaboration from my coworkers because I was able to influence rather than merely persuade.

Of course, I also intended to be fair and firm in any decision that I made. Yes, I probably made many mistakes; however, I learned that tough times help you grow just as errors help you mature. You have to accept your problems instead of letting them make you angry or provoke you into an immediate reaction. Problems worsen when you react without measuring the consequences of your decisions. Something similar occurs when you express reactive feelings focused on the symptoms instead of concentrating your efforts on the causes of the problem.

The essence of people's experiences reveals itself in the values they carry in their minds and the virtues they utilize in their practices. That is what really counts. I am not saying that whatever you have is enough or that what you have learned is sufficient. What we know is just a start in the wide constellation of the universe. You may know a lot, but it is still very little compared to what you can learn and acknowledge during your lifetime. Welcome circumstances as they come and accept challenges as opportunities. Keep your sight on the final objectives instead of becoming troubled by the presence of temporary misfortunes.

You lose confidence when the visualization of future commitments and dreams become hidden in the shadows of auto-imposed reservations. In my case, the maturity I gained in acquiring positive ways of thinking came partially from the experience I accumulated over the years. I also benefited from the advantage of healthy relationships and from being around some informal tutors and coaches. These people helped me to redirect the potential granted from my divine creator to serve and help others and the conviction that confidence, enthusiasm, and positive thinking are ongoing mental processes that lead to self-achievement. Making clear decisions and assuming any risks involved with them is one method for getting positive results.

Dreamers can form ideas in their minds, picture things from the perspective of an imagined future, and transform fantasies into realities. To do that, they need to make careful planned decisions about the steps that allow them to pass from a dream to a pragmatic objective. At times that requires meditation and times of solitude to conciliate values, principles, and feelings.

When I reached the age of 25, I received the opportunity to embark on a career in civil engineering, one that let me maintain my passion for interacting with all kinds of people. Later, I studied international relations and diplomacy, an opportunity that enhanced my fervor for supporting peace, conflict resolution, human rights, and community advocacy. I had a great future back in my country of origin. However, my destiny lay elsewhere. I didn't know it at the time, but greater avenues for opportunity would become visible as the course of my life changed. It was as Daniel Goleman described when he said, "People's dreams and aspirations change as their careers unfold, reshaping what they consider important in life and work" (Goleman et al 2002, 124).

My family and I talked things over and we decided we would emigrate to seek other horizons and find new opportunities that were unavailable where we were. It is not my purpose with this book to talk about the subject of immigration and its causes and effects. Nor is it my intention to focus on my personal life, except when it's necessary to outline my perspective as the author. For instance, I've stated that sometimes you must deal with doubts and uncertainties, and that was the state of my family at the beginning of our journey to this country. Nevertheless, my wife and I discovered that it was our destiny to be here. We received confirmation of that when we received the greatest news of our lives in the birth of our daughter, Bonnie, who was born in Pennsylvania.

As you can bet, right then we received the answer to many questions about the sudden change in the course of our lives. And we made sure that Bonnie Zenobia grew up in an environment of love, faith, hope, and multicultural opportunities. Remember, your thoughts determine how your day and life will unfold. Your thinking is the indicator that assesses your feelings. It can also allow you to feel a sense of belonging, which some people lack because they become so concerned about noting differences and errors that they lose perspective of the things that really matter in life. We detach ourselves from one another as we listen less and judge more. We lose insight into our own lives as we defend our privileges at the cost of the rights of others.

Many times such reactions arise from a lack of a clear purpose and a sense of conformity when we make our choices. If you want to gain peace of mind and commitment to love, do not let yourself become devoured by routine and tedious patterns of living a self-imposed boring life. Our time on earth is so short that we must not waste our time pursuing the monotonous. Seek for those things that bring you pleasure. Change the status quo, take the lead, take action, and stay in touch. Leave behind the lethargy of self-isolation, which is just a way to refuse involvement with human need. Sometimes, of course, solitude is necessary, but do not confuse solitude with loneliness.

If you need privacy, use it to meditate and self-evaluate your own actions. When you reflect on your performance on earth, consider it analytically, emotionally, and spiritually in order to gain your precious desires. I do recognize the fundamental role that spirituality plays in reaching holistic confidence. It brings self-reliance and trust to the things that have outstanding value in our lives. It is fundamental for understanding that the essence of happiness is not necessarily found in material goods, but in those little things that money cannot buy nor power deliver.

Meditation and solitude can help you discover who you are instead of just what you do. Nevertheless, do not confuse these practices with lethargy or a disinterest in chasing your dreams. Beware also of exhausting yourself by always working. That will make you lose perspective about the real meaning of life. You need to find equilibrium through a balance that allows you to enjoy calm and peace. Character determines your potentiality; your challenges reinforce your strengths; your thoughts determine your feelings; and the equilibrium of them all reveals the quality of your life and the extent of your happiness. Seek what Deepak Chopra called "the perfect equilibrium of the coexistence."

Any serious decision you make should come after a conscious analysis of your options and the diverse alternatives that are sometimes hidden along the pathway of possibilities. If you have confidence and trust in who you are and what you can do, any place and event provides an opportunity to succeed. These options are intrinsically linked to an investment in the acquisition of knowledge, the worth of your relationships, and the power of your decisions as you achieve your purpose.

When you create a relationship with a sincere intention for mutual benefit, you can use your interpersonal abilities to transform a simple business connection into the superior category of friendship. By maintaining positive thinking you can create enough energy to transform passivism into activism. Do this by creating a foundation of hope, the greatest link to motivation and a wonderful igniter of enthusiasm. Keep in mind that love creates passion; passion helps to develop your potential; and your potential helps you to discover your talent and gifts.

To summarize, positive emotions, motivation, intuition, and choices are necessary if you want to keep your dreams active. The spiritual and intellectual connection you make with your inner self will allow your subconscious to fuel a passion to journey toward your goals and objectives. It does not matter how difficult the goal may be. It is always present if you have the knowledge, love, passion, and confidence to keep trying even when you feel like you have lost direction or a sense of accomplishment.

Predisposition to Change

"There is nothing permanent except change."

Heraclitus

Chapter 4

Predisposition to Change

———◆—◆———

Change can be natural or artificial. Change can arrive from different avenues and perspectives. Any change involves mental, physical, spiritual, and emotional movement based on a transformation from one condition to another. Change comes from many factors and causes. It can happen gradually or suddenly. It can be temporary or permanent, forced or unforced, intentional or accidental. Change can also be a movement from one behavior to another. It can be a modification, an alteration of status, a behavior adjustment, a motivational transformation, a religious conversion, or a simple natural variation in the fields of temperature, time, weather, sea breeze, and so forth.

Change happens all the time with or without our consent. Change makes us different. Change transforms people, systems, thinking, and actions. As John Thompson defines it, change is a shift to something (the desired destination) from something else (the status or condition). A practical definition of change, from a positive-thinking perspective, involves a mental or physical shift or alteration, which occurs when a main objective has been defined and a movement in visualizing the desired destination inspires its transformation. The status or condition is the place where we come from or currently inhabit, while the final objective or destination is what initiates the real essence of change.

Take into account that it's easy to confuse the concept of mental change with the sense of extricating yourself from a current condition without specifying a reason or destination. When you look for change you are appealing for transformation, so you should certainly know where you want to go. If you just seek to alter, move, or modify a situation, then you want an adjustment or amendment, but not true change. To initiate real change, you must have a clear destination or final objective.

Change is a shift *to* something *from* something. Consequently, a logical approach to change means first and foremost finding the place where you would like to go. By this I mean you should employ visualization or make a mental picture of your dream. Later you will also need to relate that visualized future to your current status. Change starts with a mental attitude, a motivation, and a specific course or direction. It comes from your thoughts. You conceive it in a mental model you design through your intellectual and emotional capability.

Without a clear destination and sustainable motivation, the process of change may not happen because it lacks meaning and therefore incentive. "Most people change only when one of three things happen," says John Maxwell. "They hurt enough, they learn enough that they want to, or they receive enough that they are able to" (Maxwell 2002, 122). The essence of change becomes apparent when you recognize that life is not a static condition, but a constant motion. There are no limits to embracing change. It comes mainly through the development of your analytical approach and positive sensorial perceptions.

Change may become apparent as soon as you can clarify your beliefs, intensify your curiosity, and amplify your choices for reaching your objectives. Change occurs when people realize that the emotional side of their dreams can fit together with the intellectual part of their aspirations and the spiritual segment of their convictions. People who want to achieve must keep an open mind so they can acknowledge alterations and learn new ways of thinking and acting. In addition, we should link our instinct to apply change with the acknowledgment that we have limitless opportunities every day to discover the wonders and beauties of the world.

If you want to predict future perspectives in a tangible and proactive way, make it a habit to accept and reinforce your predisposition to change and accept the consequences of your choices. This conviction will open doors to a wider range of possibilities and will help you find a more effective method of understanding future conditions and the implication of your choices. The presence of positive expectations, motivated by the visualization of future transformation, is crucial. It will enhance your feelings and motivate your intellect so you can lead the way to better understanding of the common barriers to change.

One of the benefits of change is that it can help you discover your own self and highlight your authenticity and therefore help you polish your uniqueness. The authenticity of any human being does not depend on things like titles, positions, or labels. These are artificial distinctions that serve to accommodate the perceptions of others. In fact, Hanoch McCarty says that the essence of authenticity is a person without titles, status, culture, traditions, customs, experience, inclination, affiliation, or spiritual orientation. According to McCarty, these are just shields that protect the appearance of your inner self (Canfield & Hansen 1995, 54).

Authenticity is a fundamental requirement if you want to open your heart to love and your mind to peace. Authenticity is closely related to your spirituality and intrinsically connected with the essence of your self. The true purpose for change should take into consideration authenticity and the substance of identity.

Change can occur in you or around you and from controlled or uncontrolled forces. Consequently, positive change happens in relation to your attitude and the balance of your aptitude. As John Burgh says, "Most mental processes happen automatically, without the need of consciousness, attention or control [...] [On the other hand, controlled processes are] the kind of thinking that takes some effort, that proceeds in steps and that always plays out on the center stage of consciousness" (Haidt 2006, 14). Change will happen, so why not make use of it for good reasons instead of bad?

Positive change comes from a practical commitment to move physically, intellectually, psychologically, and spiritually from a current condition to a desired place. It starts when we become aware of the facts and conditions that are already present. Proactive change is complemented by your predisposition to modify and become prepared for a better future. As an old Bosnian proverb says, "If better is an option, good is not enough." Even greatness would never be enough because there is always an opportunity to improve and a possibility to excel.

Components of Change

There are two basic components of change, "To" and "From." "From" is the place, situation, or condition where a person or object is currently positioned. "To" is the location or destination where people or objects are moved or transported. In order to process change, it is necessary to make a movement that involves a direction or trend that will help transform or modify a present condition. That is a very important part of change. In this chapter, I partially credit some of these thoughts to John Thompson and his booklet, *The Truth About Change*.

Components of Change

FROM ⟶ PRESENT (SITUATION OR LOCATION)

MOVEMENT ⟶ DIRECTION (COURSE OF ACTION)

TO ⟶ DESTINATION (INTENTION OR ULTIMATE GOAL)

Taken from *The Truth About Change* and adapted by Hector Ortiz

Destination is the place, status, or future condition that will be achieved through the movement or direction made by change. The intention and direction to reach the final destination depends on the commitment, confidence, and informed decisions involved in the essence of change. Dreams are important components of destination. In fact, dreams, goals, and objectives provide the motivation to change and therefore alter the current course of action. Change makes it possible to alter a way of thinking. In other words, personal change takes place when a decision has been made to modify, transform, or revolutionize a way of acting or thinking.

A final destination may incite the components of change and the subsequent steps taken to modify a situation. Change alters a present condition based on choices; it occurs by adjusting direction or course of action. The direction taken is the real stimulation of change. Change is different from mere changes. Making changes involves little more than just making a movement. Change is an attitude. Changes are actions based on facts and measured by performances. Change is a cause. Changes are the effect of these actions. Change is the analytical process of transformation. Changes are the outcomes that come from alterations. Change affects us physically, mentally, and spiritually. Changes include situations, circumstances, strategies, and processes. Change is in the context of intention. Changes are in the framework of actions.

Change starts and finishes in the deepest attitude of your mind and in the sincerity and commitment of your heart. This is why a true scrutiny of your actions should not been seen exclusively with the eyes, but in the deepest reflection of your heart. It was Antoine de Saint-Exupery who said that the most essential of humans' virtues are usually invisible to our eyes (Canfield & Hansen 1995, 81).

In summarizing my thesis of the components of change, I want to stress that it is essentially intellectual decision making. It is an emotional determination to move to one place from another. Attitude and aptitude form significant aspects of change and become fundamental assets to transform an existing step to a different one. A receptive and open mind allows for positive change and provides a strong inclination to convert ideas into actions and commitments into realizations. Predisposition to change is a powerful force that influences your character, attitude, views, and life commitments.

Steps of Change

There are four steps of change: desires, destination, location, and direction. The foundation for change comes from our dreams or desires. Once we have desires it becomes possible to find goals and objectives that can bring us to the destination with purpose. Then we need a plan to transform our dreams into goals and our wishes into objectives. In order to form a plan, we must select a destination with at least two basic properties: intention and purpose. Once you have established the destination or final desire, the next step is to understand your present condition. That means identifying where you are so you can acknowledge your starting point and feed yourself with personal motivation to pursue your goals. The last step is the direction or design. This is the stage when real change occurs and therefore it requires attitude, passion, and commitment.

Steps of Change

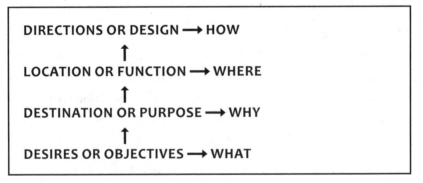

Adapted by Hector Ortiz from *The Truth About Change*, John Thompson, 2004

Destination or intention is the beginning. It comes from different processes such as brainstorming, inspiration, dialogues, or ideas that you can convert into future requests or expectations. In the first step of changing, you may see your dreams as magic sensations or imaginary assumptions. You can have a firm resolution or merely an initial sense that an idea can become true. Desires may be just wishes or requirements to address present or future expectations. Nonetheless, they can become goals and objectives once you explore resources and include a timeline. This represents the "What," or definition of what you want to accomplish. This is an initial approach to behave based on what you expect to accomplish.

The second step is destination or purpose. In short, it is the "Why" part of the equation. It requires the conception of clear and perceptible outcomes that you would achieve when realizing these dreams. Destination implies a motivation to embrace a different attitude and a mind-set to learn skills and acquire the ability to make informed decisions in order to accomplish an objective. It is the phase where time investment becomes welcome because the final result, such as the pleasure of achievement or the rewards of accomplishment, are clearly in your mind.

The third step is the location or site where you currently exist in the present. Awareness of your physical and mental positions allows you to identify your real situation. Knowing "Where" you are and where you come from is basic for helping you recognize your personality and reaffirm your identity. Combining and measuring fact and reality with intention and idealistic perspectives will help you prepare a scenario for achieving your expectations. Your physical site is your geographical location in the world or your place in a social or economic structure or a mental position.

There is an intrinsic correlation between your ways of acting and thinking. Actions and thoughts spring from coherent decisions brought forth by the rational approaches your intellect develops. In order to promote deep change, your emotions must play a significant role in supporting your way of thinking. Perceptions and feelings are also important in decision-making. Furthermore, factors such as personality type, attitude, mission, purpose, and spiritual beliefs will affect a person's decision to change.

The last step of change is direction. It implies a design or course of action that will take place as you achieve change and pursue your final dreams. It is the "How" part of the process and involves the strategies and schemes you will use to achieve your desired results. Design or direction is the step where you decide how to act or track anything that you would like to pursue. You must have preconceived plans and goal-setting objectives in place. True, sometimes you may decide to act without waiting for the specific match of your individual assets. That is preferable to always waiting for the perfect moment and the ideal place to act. This is why a road map or design often helps people remain alert and take the lead in creating change and seizing the opportunities that life offers all of us on a regular basis.

You might have to deal with fear and uncertainty on the road to change. You might have to confront adversity and unexpected setbacks. Nevertheless, we can still promote positive change and realign our actions with our original intentions. As Eckhart Tolle says, "Some changes may look negative on the surface but you will soon realize that space is being created in your life for something new to emerge" (Tolle 2005, 272). That just reaffirms that nothing is absolute; all is relative.

Do not wait too long for the right design, the correct moment, and the appropriate resources. A Nicaraguan's proverb tells us, "You make the road by walking on it." If you stop because you worry about making mistakes, you will remain trapped by the fears of past failures. Of course, planning is important. In fact, it is what design is all about. Nevertheless, you need to strike a balance to avoid extremes. You must be prepared to act despite the unexpected circumstances that so often occur. This is why any design should contemplate alternatives and basic expectations.

Remember, your direction or design is a matter of choice, although the combination of the three fundamental forces—body, soul, and spirit—is not. Making that combination is a mandatory, natural, lifelong task. They came together; they are together; they will be together. However, the questions of when, where, and how to use these combined resources is our exclusive option. No human action is complete without a physical disposition to go ahead, a mental predisposition to get your objectives done, and a conscious guide of spiritual comfort.

Consequently, an openness to change is the attitude that creates opportunities for you to carry out your mission and purpose in life. Keep in mind that true change is a difficult commitment. It requires time, effort, motivation, and sensitivity. In order to lead proactive change, you should liberate your mind to new ideas, release your feelings to different sensations, and open your heart to love and kindness.

In addition, to make dreams come true and wishes turn into factual reality, a predisposition to change is mandatory for creating mobility and adaptability to the variables of change. In other words, in order to escalate the steps of change you must nurture a tendency to transform and accept diverse ideas. Predisposition to change will help you find purpose in your life, objectives in your earthy mission, and spiritual comfort in your human interactions. The use of your physical, mental, and spiritual resources will help you measure your strengths, pursue change, and achieve your desired lifelong commitments.

Dimensions or Aspects of Change

Change involves the insertion of other elements that may affect your ability to alter a current circumstance. As I explained, the foundation of change starts with a dream—a desired destination—and knowledge of your current position. Once you add direction or design you have clearly identified the steps for the structure of change, which represents what I call the dimension of space. In summation, the aspects of change involve destination, location, and direction.

The first dimension of space represents the application of our physical, rational, emotional, and/or spiritual resources, which allows us to move to a different place or situation from a determined circumstance or condition. The location of your starting point and your aspiration to reach your ultimate desire or destination is the fundamental part of any project, objective, goal, or plan. The direction, design, or course that you establish in the dimension of space will affect, recreate, and define your future accomplishments.

As I mentioned before, the emotional and spiritual resources you need to affect change include purpose, stimulus, and motivation. Consequently, the aspects of change create the perfect environment to utilize the steps of change and transform those initial ideas, which are just dreams at the beginning, into existing realities. The dimension of space (steps of change) is intrinsically related to the dimension of time, which implies that past, present, and future all have an influence on change. It is the past and future events that really count in our lives.

That may sound paradoxical, since I have also mentioned that the current moment is the most important time of our lives. However, the present is just a tiny fraction of time. As soon as you move or breathe it is transformed to the future. In other words, the only aspects of change that really count are past and future, even if you make your decisions in the ongoing now. The present is a situational circumstance where you are consciously and unconsciously deciding your future and every single second becomes an opportunity to move from existing to living. As Piero Ferrucci says, "The time is intangible [...] the past is already past. The future, however promising, is still a fairy tale. Only the present is—and we cannot grasp it. Yet we are always in the present" (Ferrucci 2006, 72).

In other words, aspects of change include characteristics that occur in the dimension of space and which you analyze with other factors related to past, present, and future. Additionally, the dimension of the aspects of change takes into consideration the input of rational and emotional intelligence. It certainly implies the next dimension of the aspects of change, which is the dimension of action. To paraphrase John Thompson, this aspect of change takes into accounts the thoughts and things that you can control as well as those that you cannot control, at least temporarily (Thompson 2004).

The thoughts and things that we can control include physical and emotional responses. Those that we cannot control include unpredictable circumstances that you cannot predict. The first component of the dimension of actions depends on both aptitude and attitude. The second element relates to the environment and its natural laws. That is why, in addition to rationality and emotional intelligence, you need a positive attitude to redirect your thoughts and pass from mere wishes to realistic dreams.

Furthermore, positive thinking will allow you to explore those things that you can control and accept those that you cannot. The things we usually can control are those facts that can be touched, perceived, or observed. These are pragmatic events, sensible acts, or clear facts, even though they may rely on things that remain invisible or undetected. For instance, faith and spiritual confidence allow you to create instinct, intuition, motivation, and emotions to adjust those feelings and sensations that you can control.

On the other hand, there are some things and thoughts that you cannot control, but you can manage them. You cannot change the facts but you can handle a situation or condition in a way that allows you to create opportunities for achieving purposes, goals, or objectives. Uncontrolled circumstances can arise from a natural disaster or a living experience that abruptly stimulates or diminishes your predisposition to change. I accept that you cannot prevent or predict some occurrences. Nonetheless, as things happen you can expect, plan, or even predict some things.

That brings up the last element of the aspect of change, the dimension of occurrence. This aspect describes those things, controlled or uncontrolled and seen and unseen, that take place suddenly or gradually. Remain cautious, because such facts and sensations can affect your way of thinking and your disposition to change. In this case, the dimensions of time and space play an important role in redirecting your attitude so you can deal with such things. In order to acknowledge the aspects and dimensions of change, you must visualize time, space, actions, and occurrences in a holistic and sensitive manner.

Remember, time is a frame of reference that passes from one place or circumstance to another. Therefore, past and future become factors that mark the bypass of change. However, as I mentioned, any step you take to create change happens exclusively in the present, however small or fleeting that fraction of a second may be. Change is an attitude. Change is a state of mind, a situational or permanent circumstance that occurs naturally and artificially. It is up to you to confront the past as you advance to meet the challenges of the future. By acting in the present, you decide what you become in the future.

Dimensions or Aspects of Change

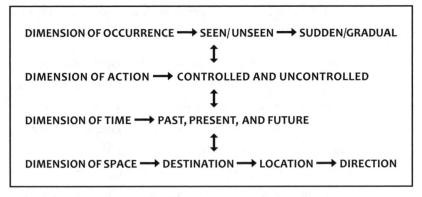

Aspects of Change; taken from *The Truth About Change*
(Thompson 2004) and adapted by Hector Ortiz

The viability of utilizing the dimension or aspects of change effectively come from the proactive expectations you set primarily in your own frame of reference. Since positive thinking comes from an elemental predisposition to change, everything relies in the power of your decisions. Remember that all life is movement and, as an old axiom advises, "If you are not moving ahead, you are falling behind." The real endorsement of positive thinking occurs when you empower your thoughts to change so you can pass from the theoretical plan to a concrete application.

According to the law of energy, nothing remains static; all is moving. The earth turns, while nonliving systems are always being altered. As Napoleon Hill says, elementary physics teaches us that "neither matter nor energy (the only two realities known to man) can be created nor destroyed. Both matter and energy can be transformed, but neither can be destroyed" (Hill 1983, 101). No condition is ever permanent, but nothing is lost, only altered. Therefore, change allows for the transformation or regeneration of matter and thoughts from one status to another. Remember the words of Heraclitus: "There is nothing permanent except change."

Stages of Change

The stages of change refer to the emotional mind-set of the individual. Stages of change are the basic principles we use to accept that a situation exists. It means we must assume responsibility for our own behavior, generate positive attitude, and reduce or eliminate the barriers to change. Those barriers include fear of new and unknown situations in the present or of risky scenarios of the future. That is why we need a psychological setting to apply the aspects of change.

This part of the study comes from the Transtheoretical Model of Change prepared by Dr. James O. Prochaska and Dr. Carlo C. DiClemente as adjusted by the author to link the stages of change with the positive thinking mind-set. In fact, it considers five stages of change: precontemplation, which I will call awareness; contemplation, which I describe as reflection; preparation, which I call stimulation; action or business plan; and maintenance/relapse, which I call assessment, evaluation, or feedback (Aha! Process, Bridges out of Poverty Train the Trainer, 193).

Stages of Change

→ AWARENESS ↔ PRECONTEMPLATION

→ REFLECTION ↔ CONTEMPLATION

→ STIMULATION ↔ PREPARATION

→ ACTION ↔ BUSINESS PLAN

→ ASSESSMENT ↔ MAINTENANCE

Taken from The Transtheoretical Model prepared by Dr. James O. Prochaska and Dr. Carlo C. DiClemente and adapted by H. Ortiz

The first stage of change is the awareness of the issue, problem, concern, or situation. Before this stage takes place, events that happen to an individual remain unknown conditions. People may not even be aware of the behavior or circumstance at this point. It can present itself as two opposite conditions. In the first case, as Dr. Prochaska and Dr. DiClemente mention, people ignore a problem or do not know that a dilemma exists. The second case is called indifference. There is a lack of concern or interest in resolving the issue.

Awareness of a problem becomes an important asset when you want to analyze the behavior and social interaction of people. If you ignore the individual's behavior, it becomes hard to ensure consistency and persistency during the process of change. It becomes an easy way to waste time and dilutes resources before a planned action takes place. It is important that family members, relatives, friends, neighbors, coworkers, or church members ensure that the person is aware of the current circumstances. Awareness prevents the creation of assumptions about the behavior and social and/or economic condition of any individual whom you want to help by introducing a perspective of change.

In the first period of the stages of change, awareness, we must know of an issue's existence. More importantly, the stage of awareness helps us acknowledge the causes and effects of circumstances or behavior so we can determine consequences and predict the outcomes of predetermined behavior or attitudes. It also implies, from the object of change, our acknowledgment of previous and potential future conditions that we need in order to stimulate and motivate the activation of change.

The second stage is called reflection. This is where people become aware of the current situation but lack the resources necessary to get out of it. This is an important piece of the ladder of change. It is here that we need to conduct a mental auto-analysis to address the issue actively. Depending on your attitude, this reflection can be simple contemplation or a more intensive, critical thinking process. The idea is to closely study whatever factors affect your life or project.

The next stage is stimulation. Once you have identified the problem and reflected about it, stimulation becomes necessary. It is fundamental if you want to ensure commitment and a sense of obligation to the serious responsibility of promoting change. Stimulation is the buy-in of change and it requires motivation, self-encouragement, impetus, self-value, or worthiness. It requires continuous care for your emotions and a permanent feeding of your self-esteem. You can enhance it by making mental commitments and visualizing your eventual satisfaction.

Stimulation is the incentive that fills your life with alternative ways of thinking. In this stage, accessibility to immediate mental and physical gratifications will help you think in different ways and recharge your environment with positivism. More importantly, stimulation can offer you clear flashes of opportunity and lucid sparkles of possibility. It is the part of the process of change that lets you see problems from different perspectives and become proactive and confident as you find new ways to confront issues and deal with challenges.

The fourth stage of change is action or action plan. This is where you find the real meaning of change. As you know already, in the steps of change, desire identifies your dream; destination recognizes where you want to go; and location describes where you are currently. Now the steps of change and the stages of change meet to form the action plan—the design or directions that impact the virtue of change. In order to pursue action steps you need awareness, receptiveness, and a critical thinking approach. In addition to physical and mental abilities you require incentives, stimulation, and inspiration to implement the spirit of change.

Any dream or desire to move forward, change behavior, or achieve a goal requires a plan and the development of action steps. It demands diverse resources, programmatic research, realistic time, procedural steps, and prediction of unexpected circumstances. To attract positive change, you should periodically revise your values and principles. Something similar should occur with your feelings, sensations, and emotions. Your body changes internally and externally and so do your thoughts. "Change involves risk," says Russ Harris. "It requires facing your fears and stepping out of your comfort zone—both of which point to one thing: change will usually give rise to uncomfortable feelings" (Harris 2007, 204). Finally, if you want to acquire and maintain a positive attitude about change you must ask yourself for feedback. Make continuous assessments so you can make improvements and implement change. Change is an endless practice that you should reevaluate persistently. Often one person can change without even knowing if it is for good or ill. So remember that change is not a static condition, but an ongoing process.

Phases of Change

There are six basic phases of change. They are related in various ways to the components, steps, aspects (or dimension), and stages of change that we explored in the previous pages. The phases of change are as follows: incident or occurrence; personal awareness; decision-making; commitment or passion to buy in; process or conception of a plan; and finally the outcomes or results of change.

The phases of change begin with an event, incident, or circumstance. It can happen at any point in your life. This is the phase where your emotions become exposed and memories manifest themselves in a relationship with the essence of that experience or occurrence. You pass to the next phase by creating awareness. It may come consciously or unconsciously through a workshop, book, sermon, movie, story, difficulty, or accomplishment. Awareness is the factor that allows you to compare the outcomes of past circumstances with your current situation. A book or lecture can help you with this, but the decision to change comes only from you. A story or example just provides a point of reference that can promote change, but it is the awareness of the condition and the stimulus you grasp from it that create an environment to engender change. Reading a book may not change you at all because "information [alone] does not transform people," says Dr. Bernie Siegel. "Change requires energy, and you must supply the energy [...] I cannot change you. Only you can change yourself" (Siegel 1998, xxii). You have two options. You can take an occasion to explore opportunities for change or you can maintain the current status quo. Awareness is the factor that makes you conscious of your options and choices. Awareness occurs when you trigger your feelings and utilize your thoughts to transform an idea into desire.

The third phase of change, choices, explores the decision-making process. This phase goes into effect once a circumstance has created awareness and moves us to reflect (the third stage of change) and consciously take the initiative to find solutions. This is where you may launch an intellectual approach to find alternative conclusions about how to transform an existing situation. In this phase, you must think critically to keep your mind moving and your initiatives alive. Only then can you spark intuition and conceive alternative solutions.

The fourth phase of change is commitment. It is similar to the third stage of change, which we called stimulation. Commitment is the bridge between mind and heart. In this phase, your passion acquires the power it needs to spur decision into action. Commitment is fed by stimulus and incentives that transform promises into realities. Commitment is the force that brings fortitude and reinforces your determination to change.

Similar to the aspects of change (direction), the steps of change (design) or stages of changes (action), the fifth element of the phases of change is process, the phase where direction, design, or an action plan takes place. It is the most important and fundamental part for building the ladder of change. The action plan is a key element, which processes or produces change. Action without a plan is like rowing against the current; a plan without action is like assuming you'll win the lottery without buying a ticket.

A process or plan allows transformation; it creates the procedures you need to assess and analyze strengths and weakness. A process is a plan's execution. It involves a fair examination of the available resources, expected inquiries, enforced time, and the efforts necessary to achieve your goals. A plan should have purpose, intention, destination, direction, and an awareness of predictable events and even unseen circumstances as well as any alternative solutions you might need to accomplish the desired change.

The last segment of the phases of change is called feedback or self-assessment. It completes the cycle of the processes of change and the accomplishment of your desired outcome. I realize that some occurrences may force you to act so quickly that you skip some action steps of the plan. Since change may alter your thoughts, attitude, and behavior, the real process of change takes place once you analyze its phases and become conscious of the impact that it has on your life. This is the stage where true change occurs and you can apply your decision making and reach a real commitment to succeed.

The objectivity and subjectivity of your acts are relatively important. Objectivity represents wisdom, analytical judgment, and intelligence applied to promote logical changes in your life. Subjectivity encompasses the feelings and emotions that ensure commitment and urge you to pursue change. It does not matter if you seek a better life or to find peace and love. Subjectivity will also enhance family connections, increase understanding, and upgrade the mission or purpose of your life.

All prospective conditions arrive initially in the form of an idea or mental visualization of the future. An ability to plan becomes a key element for developing goal-setting strategies, action plans, diagrams, steps, stages, phases, and procedures to achieve a mental model of change. The ability to plan is one of the skills you need if you want to succeed in life. I reinforce this concept to remind you of the importance of goal setting and planning in relationship to your predisposition to change.

You create the bridge between present moments and future conditions through your ability to plan and a clear commitment to organize your thoughts and actions. An action plan is designed to accomplish change so you can follow the course of your self-imposed destiny to succeed in life. The ability to plan is also related to your attitude and your predisposition to change. Positive thinking allows you to create the vision necessary for setting goals. It will help you balance present conditions and future aspirations with realistic tactics of measuring the results you make as you execute a plan.

Planned change is an important step to acquiring purpose and fulfillment in all your activities. Make sure that any specific goals you set are measurable, challenging, achievable, and time specific. Other important factors as you move forward include creativity, an open mind, and a fair commitment to improve your lifestyle and generate ongoing and progressive positive thinking. In addition, methodic and systematic change should include planning and organizational skills. In fact, good organization is like an art. It is wonderful when you want to assess your abilities and categorize assets. Gary Kreps defines organization as the process of developing the coherence, coordination, order, and direction necessary to succeed in any activity (Kreps 1995, 14).

Organization is a coordinated course of action taken to enhance talents and resources as you accomplish tasks, activities, projects, or missions. It does not matter if you carry it out at the personal or social level—any goal or objective has a better chance of realization if it is systematized and categorized for creating organized change. Organizational change is necessary to make the connection between plan and order. As I've mentioned before, a plan requires organization and organization demands a plan. A plan without organization will result in chaos while organization without a plan will not help you approach your dreams. To put it another way, a predisposition to change is not necessarily an intellectual issue, but an attitudinal one. Change relies on fact even if it is based on a future orientation. The important thing is to see and understand change as an opportunity to learn and improve your life and as an essential element of self-motivation and innovation for acquiring the desired outcomes and expected results.

In conclusion, the phases of change are tools you can use to implement creative and strategic change. Positive change starts when you analyze a situation objectively to create true awareness of the factual conditions in the present. After that, conduct a deep survey of the circumstances and research the opportunities. Then, any resolution should come from informed decisions, strong confidence, and a solid commitment to convert ideas into realities. Finally, if these ideas arrive in an organized and sequential way, then an organized plan supported by achievable action steps will be the best way to reach your planned outcomes and desires.

Phases of Change

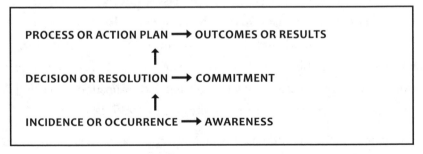

Phases of Change. Adapted by Hector Ortiz

The Cycle of Change

The key to any change is developing a clear understanding of the advantages that the change offers. A successful application of change means defeating initial resistance and keeping the original dream unaltered. More importantly, the change should belong to both its executers and beneficiaries. This is why I insist in stressing that change is a continuous process. It is a transition from a current physical or mental site or condition to another place, location, position, or state.

People resist less when they understand the future compensations and benefits of change. A person who promotes change should be driven by example. As John Maxwell says, "He [or she] must first understand the two important requisites to bring about change, knowing the technological requirements, and understanding the attitude and motivational demands for bringing it about" (Maxwell 1993, 52).

A typical cycle of change starts with an initial approach, defined as the intention to move from past condition to future expectations. This is when the processes of creation and imagination take place. The next stage is identified as defensive or resistance. This is when the protection of customs and traditions stand in opposition to alteration. To paraphrase John Maxwell, as change moves from the initial creation process to subsequent resistance, it faces criticism and negativism. This is an environment where doubts can flourish. Following clarification, measurement of expectations and consolidation of gains, change moves into the phase of acceptance, an invitation to enjoy the tangible benefits brought by the implementation of change (Maxwell 1993, 60).

The Cycle of Change

CREATION ⟶ CONSERVATION ⟶ CRITICISM ⟶ CHANGE

True change involves mobility and involvement. A task requires both personal and collective efforts. Individuals can better achieve personal goals when they are also engaged in common initiatives. We find our strongest commitment when it comes from a common goal instead of an exclusive or individual one. Nevertheless, change starts in yourself. The predisposition to create organized change takes place in the harmony, serenity, and wisdom of your thoughts, decisions, and actions.

Transformation is great experience, especially when it comes from organizational change. However, the process of change is not always easy. It may even be uncomfortable. It is difficult to remain open to new ideas. You need more than just the willingness to practice change. You need preparation and work. Change will often force you to leave your comfort zone and face unknown or unexpected challenges. Change is an option, but it offers you a way to improve your life. The decision is yours.

The Sequence of Change

The succession of true change requires the alteration of status, beliefs, comfort, and practices, usually driven by an intention to solve a present need. The pressure of immediate needs creates awareness and acknowledgment of the issues at hand. It is during the sequence of change that desires and aspirations tend to impact the development of knowledge, abilities and intentions as you find solutions to current problems. In order to effect change, you must develop a plan and include the processes needed to implement it.

The Sequence of Change

```
CHANGE ⟶ NEEDS ⟶ AWARENESS ⟶DESIRES ⟶ PLAN
OR PROCESS ⟶ IMPLEMENTATION OF CHANGE
```

Consequently, it is during the sequence of change that we experience the essence of the organizational culture of change. Any measure of what we assess, judge, perceive, and feel is what really counts in the essential context of human accountability. According to an anonymous saying, "Whatever we think, say, and do about any person is usually a reflex of what we have inside of us." The predisposition to change may be more easily supported by a balance of internal and external factors as well as rational and emotional insights. As Daniel Goleman says, "Structural change comes mainly from rational goals, clear mandates, and biological processes" (Goleman 2002, 196).

In conclusion, change requires creativity, innovation, and transformation. You cannot pretend to create change or innovate by always doing the same old thing because "to repeatedly do the same thing and expect different results is considered a strong sign of insanity." Instead, be proactive and open yourself to change. Action plans, dedication, and sacrifices are required. Hard work and a commitment to finish are necessary, as is the faith to believe that anything is possible. Therefore, creation, resistance, and criticism play different roles in acquiring the predisposition to change and a commitment to open your mind to the art of possibility and the implementation of positive thinking.

Finally, let us encourage ourselves to pursue true change in our lives and in our world by pushing the boundaries of what we think and do. Let us ignite the fire of curiosity and commit ourselves to improve and advance so we can see what we have not seen yet. Challenge yourself to create, invent, and innovate. That is what the great thinkers did in the past to leave us those things we have inherited today.

Why don't we promise ourselves a periodical commitment to analyze our thoughts and reflect upon the impact that they have on our actions? The significance of people's accomplishments is measured by the service that they provide to others and the opportunities they generate in helping someone else succeed. It is the prime value of success and a priceless attribute of extraordinary human beings. As George Bernard Shaw said, "Some men see things as they are and say 'Why?' I dream of things that never were and say, 'Why not?'" (Maxwell 2003, 170).

THE CREATIVE ENERGY OF POSITIVE THINKING

Predisposition to change is the main force behind creating, rediscovering, and inventing avenues of happiness, pathways of opportunities, and a wider spectrum of possibilities. We cannot resist change. That goes against nature. It is opposed to evolution, hostile to growth, and adverse to development. We should not refuse the advantages and rewards of promoting and enhancing positive change. So let us implant in our minds the seeds of positive thinking and the commitment to accept, deal, and promote change. It is our personal and social responsibility for all of us and for future generations. As Howard Cutler says, "All things lack the ability to endure, lack the ability to remain the same. And since all things are subject to change, nothing exists in a permanent condition; nothing is able to remain the same under its own independent power. Thus, all things are under the power or influence of other factors" (Cutler 1998, 163).

Chapter 5

Faith to Believe

"Some men see things as they are and say 'Why?' I dream of things that never were and say, 'Why not?'"

George Bernard Shaw

Chapter 5

Faith to Believe

⸻ ◆ ⸻

Faith is a fundamental spiritual resource. It represents those internal qualities that people may carry, feel, express, or transmit to enhance and support their life purpose. Spiritual capital is an invaluable asset. By sharing it, people give affection, devotion, and respect to others. Commitment to faith is one of the most powerful avenues of positive emotions. It is an infinite strength that you should support with spiritual conviction and the power of praying. When you do, make sure that you ask for guidance instead of material goods, and peace instead of superficial satisfaction.

Faith generates spiritual and positive emotions that transform regular thinking into the extraordinary confidence of its spiritual counterpart. When your thoughts become interconnected and aligned with emotional and spiritual vibrations you receive a continuous injection of confidence for organizing plans and supporting your intentions. Getting in touch with your spiritual resources provides an elemental spark for directing, controlling, and reinforcing positive ways of thinking. The power of faith and the conviction of your beliefs is one of the strongest forces for reshaping attitudes and building confidence.

Faith is a state of mind that comes from a personal decision to believe in something higher than the mind itself. Faith can be induced or created because what you generate in your conscious intellect influences the permanent responses of your subconscious. The spiritual approaches we generate from our subconscious are continuing sources of stimulation, motivation, and inspiration for our intellect. Faith and spirituality help us accept problems as normal occurrences but temporary conditions of life.

The faith to believe is an exceptional resource. It helps you eliminate negative feelings. It reaffirms your genuineness and legitimizes the roots of your beliefs and your connection with your commitments. Faith helps you find the authenticity of your inner self by invoking a religious creed or spiritual belief. Keep in mind that spirituality doesn't necessarily have religious implications, although some religions intrinsically incorporate spirituality.

Spiritual beliefs involve perceptions, stimulations, and convictions. Spiritual conviction is a supreme force whose presence, usually unseen, guides our life, beliefs, values, and/or religious orientation. As Ana Adams says, "Spiritual experience is often beyond words and beyond cognition" (Tisdell 2003, 58). Faith and spiritual confidence are influential sources that come from a fervent conviction of the existence of a higher and omnipotent power. It is through faith that people can accept that the universe's marvels derive from a supreme force. Faith and belief are personal spiritual assets that vary depending on cultural and ethnic background and social or economic class, education, age, gender, religion, heritage, or personal research. Faith means you trust in those things that you can't see. Faith means devoting yourself to something you consider reliable. Faith involves fidelity, knowledge, experience, and values that we accept intrinsically as true.

Faith is not just a blind trust or an emotional approach that springs from despair or hopelessness. Faith is an informed decision, which may be or may not be based on solid corroborative evidence. Nevertheless, when it is supported by fact, it may come with tools that help enrich our spirituality. It is, as Libby says, "One of the ways people construct knowledge and meaning" (Tisdell 2003, 20). Faith is an incommensurable resource that represents a steady expression of hope and a coherent reaffirmation of values. In *The Case for Faith*, a book written by Lee Strobel, Bill Craig says, "Faith is trust or commitment to what you think is true [...] When you understand faith in these categories, you can see it's entirely compatible with reason" (Strobel 2000, 74).

To cite more from Lee Strobel, I would like to highlight six basic arguments defending the existence of God, and consequently faith. The first argument is what Strobel calls "random chance" (Strobel 2000, 100). Some say the universe originated "by accident" and that our world came from nothing and by nothing. These theorists cannot sustain this hypothesis. Whatever exists in nature has cause and effect, so the idea of accidental creation makes so sense at all. Nor does it explain the way all the living creatures on earth are precisely correlated with the environment. Observe a living system and its reproduction of life and you will understand that an intelligent connection occurs between our bodies and the complex work all our organs do. More importantly, energy, gravity, and all the elements of nature are perfectly arranged for all human functioning. All this indicates there is only one explanation for existence, and that is the presence of a supernatural and intelligent creator.

The next theory is related to the universe's complexity. Strobel calls it "self-ordering tendencies" (Strobel 2000, 102). He explains that the cosmos is so complex, precise, balanced, and perfectly articulated that it could not have come from accidental or random circumstances. The birth of a universe that organized stars, planets, water, and life cannot be explained through biology, chemistry, or all the learning of modern science. It requires the existence of an intelligent designer.

Subsequent arguments involve the origin of life. According to Charles Darwin's theory of evolution, "Life began millions of years ago with simple single-cell creatures and developed through mutation and natural selection" (Strobel 2000, 91). In addition, Carlos Ayala says, "All life is the result of timeless evolutionary forces [...] the result of a natural process, natural selection, without any need to resort to a creator" (Strobel 2000, 89). But one essential thing that Darwin could not explain was how life initially began.

Darwin based his theory on the premise that our world changes through a process of natural species selection where the stronger ones prevail. In effect, his theory states, "Those species that possess characteristics most useful for physical survival will remain, while those species with traits that leave them vulnerable will not survive" (Lannom 1998, 140). This hypothesis demeans the unique intelligence of the human being, created in the image of the deity, by denigrating the marvel of the original conception so it becomes a mere evolutionist survival of the fittest.

Strobel calls his next argument "chemical affinity." It says any hypothesis that supports the assumptions that life could have emerged from non-living chemicals or automatic biochemical development lacks relevant and scientific proof (Strobel 2000, 101). Similar objections apply to the theory of assembling cells and the protein molecule theory of chemical evolution (Strobel 2000, 107). Living and even nonliving systems are so complex that they require many conditions in the right sequences and connections. There is no logical explanation to replace the presence of an intelligent creator in creating life and the universe. Thus, as Professor Walter Bradley of the University of Texas says, "If there is no natural explanation [of the origin of life...] it is appropriate to look at a supernatural explanation" (Strobel 2000, 108).

How could be life arise as a result of a random explosion or coincidental gathering of all the necessary elements? That question has challenged atheists and agnostics forever. Jack Lannom denies the coherence of the evolution theory by saying, "If we are, as the theory of evolution proclaims, merely a cosmic accident, how can you possibly ascribe any value or worth to anyone we meet or anything we do? We have no identity. We have no foundation to build upon. We are working for an identity, rather than from one" (Lannom 1998, 10).

It is not my intention to make a deep analysis of the controversial theories of creation or natural selection. My main purpose is to highlight the importance of faith for the construction of positive thinking. Faith can also provide an incentive for the development of our own spiritual journey. It adds extra sources we can use to explore and analyze our world and find answers to our questions and concerns. As Hamilton and Jackson noted, spirituality is fundamentally about three main themes: further development of self-awareness, a sense of interconnectedness of all things, and a relationship to a higher power or higher purpose (Tisdell 2003, 30).

I respect everyone who may offer different viewpoints, although it is hard to believe in the theories that cite the non-existence of an intelligent designer. We have plenty of evidence of the existence of a supreme force. The marvels and astonishing events of our cosmos are enough to show that a universe without the divine presence of God is inconceivable.

To continue our discussion of Strobel's writings, his next argument is based on "the objectivity of moral values" (Strobel 2000, 79). The existence of God is mandatory if we want to understand the objectivity of ethical and moral values. If God did not exist then human beings would be mere accidents of nature. Then we would have to accept the atheistic version of the influences of morality.

Strobel's last argument is the evidence of Jesus Christ's resurrection. Four pieces of evidence demonstrate this event. Jesus was crucified and buried; it was confirmed that His tomb was later found empty; several individuals testified to His resurrection and appearance after His crucifixion; and Christ's disciples believed in Jesus' power even more after His death and resurrection. Is there a more logical explanation for why they were willing to die for their belief? (Strobel 2000, 267-269)

As you know, some people believe that life arose from a cosmic accident and that human beings are the result of an evolutionary process. Others believe in the undeniable presence of a supreme maker. To support their beliefs, people have used cosmology, geology, anthropology, and evolutionary and theological perspectives. Lately the debate has concentrated on evolutionist and creationist theories. However, it's best not to take any of these approaches as an absolute lest they block your view of life's purpose.

Evolution leaves us with an empty sense about our values and life's purpose. On the other hand, believing that God creates everything that happens is also a fallacy. We cannot blame God for our laziness and bad choices. However, if you choose to become an agnostic or an atheist you may be unaware of the priceless resources that come from our spiritual richness. If you accept the presence of God, you can pray and rely on a spiritual foundation that will help you accomplish your life's mission.

The reaffirmation of our faith and the growth of our spirituality is an internalized task as well as an essential one. As Libby Tisdell says, "Understanding more about spiritual development is part of our search for wholeness" (Tisdell 2003, 182). It remains your option as well as your personal responsibility to analyze and clarify your spiritual and religious views and match your thoughts and actions with them to understand life's purpose.

Whatever your beliefs make sure your viewpoint does not turn into a paradigm where freedom does not exist, moral values do not make sense, and life has no purpose. I believe that concepts of evolution and divine design are fundamentally different. Debate them internally and find your own truth. Keep in mind that scientific theories alone have not been able to explain the origin and mission of life. Faith remains the element that will help us identify our spiritual convictions so we can understand the complexity of the universe and its link to all living things.

So should we accept that moral values are just a result of socio-biological evolution and exist merely to assist survival and procreation? Keep in mind that moral and ethical behaviors form the foundation of any civilized society. The Ten Commandments that Moses brought have served as the basis for governments and set the standards for human behavior. The ideas of honoring our parents, not seeking vengeance, preserving life, respecting the lawful possessions of others, and maintaining ethical and moral principles come from this unique set of values.

Life without purpose makes no sense at all. Living without mission is like climbing aboard a train without a destination. People who are not sure where they came from or where they're going have trapped themselves, consciously or unconsciously, in an illogical life of merely existing. Knowing your mission and purpose in life is the first step to rediscovering your faith and spiritual values. I've offered reasons for believing in the miracle of creation, but the final testimony you should depend on should be your own rational, emotional, and spiritual experiences. Use them to find meaning that gives significance and purpose.

You may still have reservations and uncertainties. According to Lynn Anderson, who graduated from Abilene Christian University, intellectual doubts often arise around the boundaries of what he calls "seasons of life." We all need time to reflect. Sometimes personal or family struggles lead to feelings of anguish, melancholy, or suspicion. This is not from a lack of faith, but from the presence of doubt. I firmly believe we need faith to understand our purpose in life.

We also need spiritual commitment to better understand differences, tolerate adversity, and accept that pleasure and melancholy are mind-sets that arise independently from our positive or negative moods. The moods themselves are alternatives that we can choose. They are connected to the ways we think and to our spiritual perception of happiness and sadness. But they are choices.

We are the architects of our own destiny. Our thoughts or the negative influences we get from others will affect our rational approaches to positive thinking. They might enhance our appreciation of life and our religious orientation. Or they may have an adverse effect. To avoid that we must identify and eliminate all negative statements from our vocabulary. Positive thinking should be present in all aspects of our life. However, as Lynn Anderson pointed out, "Faith is not always about having positive emotional feelings toward God. [...] A faith that's challenged by adversity or tough questions or contemplation is often a stronger faith in the end" (Strobel 2000, 233-234). Keep that in mind as you confront doubt. It is one healthy way to solidify your faith. I encourage you to discover your strengths in the solitude of your soul and the expressive manifestation of your feelings. As Sarah Ban Breathnach says, "Our senses speak the secret language of the soul [...] [While our] spirit attempts to restore the Divine Connection through our sensory perceptions. When we lose touch with our true natures, we become unable to create boundaries that protect, nurture, and sustain our self-worth" (Breathnach 1998, 276-311).

There is a difference between spirituality and religion, but I remain convinced that faith is an internal manifestation of a spiritual self-confidence. I also accept that faith may not exclusively be interpreted as religious although rational faith and spiritual beliefs often overlap. As you explore your power of faith you will find that its real conviction arrives once you have discovered your life purpose and your own definition of truth. As the Apostle John said about Jesus, "Those who follow Him will know the truth and the truth will set them free" (John 8:31-32). In order to accept that our beliefs are truths, we must learn it by ourselves.

You may base your faith on facts, reasoning, and commitment, but trust and self-confidence reaffirm it. As the Lord says, "Blessed are they who have not seen Me, but still believe!" (John 20:19-31). The value of faith and the sincerity of our beliefs come from a strong spiritual commitment to believe in a purpose in our life.

Some beliefs are initially shaped by our family environment and fed by our culture, traditions, and communities. We learn some beliefs in our childhood and develop them over our lives. We can acquire beliefs and explore and evaluate them. As we do, we find that they shape our personality, build our character, and affirm our confidence in life and purpose. Just as we cannot find happiness without looking inside ourselves, faith and belief also must be discovered inside us. That is what Agnes Replier means when she says, "It is not easy to find happiness in ourselves, but it is not possible to find it elsewhere" (Breathnach 1998, 189).

Life without faith is like a life without a mission or purpose. If your life does not make sense, then clearly you lack a spiritual or religious component. Life without faith creates doubt and uncertainty. Life may be a mystery, but it is our personal task to analyze different theories about its meaning and live according to our faith and spiritual commitments.

What about the afterlife? There are many doctrines about the afterlife, and they differ according to religion or spiritual conviction. Although I will not discuss the question of the hereafter in depth, I do want to mention two comments that involve the questions of how to live. "Death is not the end of life, but the beginning of a different mode of existence," says John Renard. "Death is the doorway to a world beyond this. But since each person is responsible for his or her choices in life, there will be an accounting called Judgment" (Renard 2002, 141). Other religions offer different interpretations of the afterlife. The Muslim religion believes an afterlife is an inherent part of their values. In the Christian faith, the resurrection of Christ gives people hope for a final judgment where people are held accountable for their acts. "Death is not the end of life," says Renard, "but a transition to another level of existence" (Renard 2002, 130).

The conception of life after our death depends on the spiritual conviction of each individual, so I will not discuss it any longer. I will say, though, that the soul cannot die. It can, however, be hurt. You can live a successful life if you design it with your inner self. You can find the authenticity of your faith, the conviction of your spirituality, and the arguments for your own truth in your heart and soul. The prospect of an afterlife provides another incentive to reorder your thoughts even if it challenges your relationships with culture and religion, faith and spirituality, and creed and superstition.

You will find the perfect harmony when you create a balance between a legacy in the present and the rewards of the future while maintaining the conviction to enjoy the gifts you have. Exercise your talents and share what you have been granted. That is how you can enjoy the privilege of life. All of us have our own definitions of faith, success, and happiness. There is no one formula. Each approach has its own unique and personal quality.

People can learn from past experiences, receive motivation from multiple resources, become energized by prayer, or become spiritually connected to a supernatural power. There is no exclusive success story that works for everyone. Create your own method for enjoying your present and for embracing an existence in the afterlife. "There is no one-size-fits-all perfect formula for living a significant life," says Pastor Jim Graff. "The key is faith that God honors his word and delights in empowering [us] [...] to be all that we can be" (Graff 2006, 224).

Faith is an invaluable asset. It converts ordinary thoughts into extraordinary spiritual ones. When we act according to our faith and principles and willfully dedicate our best effort to accomplish our life's mission, we should follow our spiritual guide, instincts, and religious motivations. It is important that we maintain a balance between our spiritual, physical, intelligent, and emotional commitments to pursue our dreams and find our purpose of life. "Faith and work are not at odds with each other—they go hand-in-glove together [...] Faith without work is dead" (Shelton & Quinn 2005, 71).

Spirituality is a holistic element of our core values. Its influence helps us discover the essence of our inner self and connect it with our main purpose of life. Religion, on the other hand, is a creed or doctrine whose principles guide us as we reach our sense of wholeness. It helps us understand the beginning and end of life. It is why John Renard says, "Religion means adherence to a set of beliefs or teaching about the deepest and most elusive of life's mysteries" (Renard 2002, 3).

We should all try to understand different religious approaches and recognize spiritual differences. "Pluralism is an obvious fact of life," says John Renard. "Mutual understanding is no longer a luxury but an absolute prerequisite for peace in the world" (Renard 2002, 33).

Finally, faith is a choice that we can support with evidence, testimonies, and experience. Happiness is an attitude that you can feed with positive thoughts and proactive energy, and faith can connect you with these resources. "Faith is the centerpiece of a connected life," says Terry Tempest Williams. "It allows us to live by the grace of invisible strands. It is a belief in a wisdom superior to our own. Faith [is an internal force that] becomes teacher in the absence of fact" (Breathnach 1998, 213).

Faith is a personal determination we need to make the link between positive thinking, success, and the pursuit of happiness. Consequently, it is through the strength of our faith and the harmony of our beliefs that we can use our positive thinking to move from primary desires to progressive actions. Our accomplishments rely on the confidence of our faith, which helps us intensify the power of visualization. Faith makes it easier; faith makes it simple to pass from an imagined aspiration into a concrete and reachable reality.

Religious Diversity and the Analysis of Doubts in Dealing With Spiritual Resources

There are many diverse religious movements around the world. The largest classic world religions are those that scholars call the "Big Five." These five religions are Christianity, Hinduism, Islamism, Buddhism, and Judaism. In addition there are movements and non-religious groups such as agnostics and atheists.

As I discuss the concept of religion and its connection to faith and spirituality, I am using the classical definition of religion by Emil Durkheim. He defined it as "a unified system of beliefs, and practices relative to sacred things, that is to say, things set apart and forbidden—beliefs and practices which unite into one single moral community [...]." It is not the target of this book to discuss the similarities or differences of religious groups. My main purpose is to assure you that these resources are available and they can help people understand their purpose in living on this planet.

For instance, I believe that a commitment to pursue moral and ethical standards is an important motivation for choosing a religious direction. However, this is a personal choice that belongs to you. The essence of positive thinking is to ensure that you analyze all alternatives so you can find what you consider to be inalterable truth. My humble advice is that any religious and/or spiritual path you choose should include the existence of the law of cause and effect (related to choices) and the expected understanding of life's purpose (linked to consequences).

Our religious conviction and the depth of our spiritual faith are key elements in our determination to accept that a divine power is behind the creation of all living things. The idea of a purposeful life brings sense to moral and ethical standards. Consequently, the liberty behind our actions makes us accountable for our choices and responsible for our blessings.

After you have made your own internal analysis and have arrived at an informed decision, you should pursue your instincts and live according to your principles while respecting the values of others—provided their values include preserving life and the dignity of the individual.

The real purpose of faith is to ensure that people do not just follow traditions, but beliefs. In other words, spiritual resources become stronger when accompanied by faith, which transforms the blind following of tradition into a strong and informed conviction of belief. "If a man will begin with certainties, he shall end in doubts," said Francis Bacon; "but if he will be content to begin with doubts, he shall end in certainties."

As John Renard says,

Belief, understood either generally or as a reference to a particular tenet, refers to the content of a tradition's central teaching [...]

Faith is the act or process of relying on or assenting to realities that one might not be able to prove as easily as one might like. But what finally distinguished religious belief and faith from their more mundane counterparts is that religious believers are willing to live without conclusive proof indefinitely (Renard 2002, 11).

A strong belief becomes faith once we accept those things that we internally know exist, but cannot prove. Informed faith requires both the internal force of your spirit and the pragmatic approach of your intellect before you can follow any religious track. Since doubt is a normal step on the path to discovering truth, I would like to include a text written about the existence of God. It replicates a conversation between a college teacher and students that took place many years ago.

"Did God create everything that exists on earth?" asked the teacher. "Yes, He did," one of his students said with conviction. "If God created everything, then God created evil," the teacher replied. He was pleased with himself because he felt he had demonstrated that faith was a myth.

Another student asked, "Professor, does the cold exist?" "Of course it exists," the teacher replied. "Have you not ever felt cold?" "No," said the student. "It does not exist. According to physical laws, what we consider cold is simply lack of heat. All bodies or objects possess energy in the form of heat. Without heat a body is inert or cold. As a consequence, cold does not exist; we create it to describe our feelings when heat is absent."

The student asked another question. "Do you think that darkness exists?" "Of course darkness exists," the teacher replied. "No, darkness does not exist," said the student. "What really exists is light. It can be studied, while darkness can't. In fact, the prism allows us to learn that white light is composed of diverse colors. You cannot conduct such an experiment with darkness. How can we determine how much darkness exists in any given space? Darkness is a definition created by people to explain what they see if there is no light."

Finally, the student asked, "Does evil exist?" The teacher answered, "Yes, it does. Notice how many crimes, robberies, and rapes occur all around the world to sustain it." "Evil does not exist, or at least it does not exist by itself," the student responded. "Evil is just the lack of good. Evil is just an invention to describe the lack of God. As an analogy, the same thing occurs with the body when there is no heat or the darkness when there is no light. Evil is an invention of human beings due to the lack of God."

Life on earth is finite. We have only a short period of time to exercise our free will and choose how to live. We all have the free determination to follow our instincts and select our faith, beliefs, and religion. Believing in the existence of God is a personal decision. It may give you the strength to assume responsibility for your acts and the confidence to ask for help and guidance where you may need it. If it is your situation, do not forget to give thanks to Him for everything He has granted you. The problem is that we tend to act only when we are in desperate need of divine intervention.

I have known people on both sides of the spectrum. I have seen those who were at the height of their careers but fell due to their lack of spiritual beliefs. I have seen those who rose from the shadows because their beliefs helped them find their purpose of life. The first case can happen to those who have been blessed but forget their mission and life purpose. As a result, they lose the love and peace of mind they need to explore happiness. Financial resources are important, but they alone are not enough to grant us the real meaning of life. "He [God] does for us what we cannot do for ourselves, causing us to be all that He has called us to be!" (Shelton & Quinn 2005, 57)

On the other hand, those who struggle every day against financial difficulties can still enjoy the pleasure of life by living in accordance with their moral and spiritual values. There are many cases where people who were abandoned by society or even by themselves learned to raise their self-esteem and correct their characters. They left bad habits and attitudes behind, thanks to an encounter with that supreme voice called the spirit of life.

This is what Libby Tisdell had in mind when she said, "Spirituality is about making sense of our chaotic lives [...] what all these experiences have in common is that they offer hope, healing, or affirmation" (Tisdell 2003, 67-68).

Positive thinking and the pursuit of happiness are possible when peace and alternative tools for conflict resolution become accepted as the best ways to resolve human differences. We will better understand how to achieve peace and broker human relationships when we gain a clear understanding of poverty, explain religious diversity, and share on the national and international level. A serious understanding of these issues requires not just tolerance, but acceptance and understanding. We must encourage religious freedom and implement inter-religious dialogues if we want to accept the contributions of our diverse community.

Remember that acceptance does not mean you must agree with all practices or opinions. As I mentioned, some people take extreme positions or assume ways of thinking that are life threatening or run contrary to our moral and ethical standards. In encounters with them, I recommend that you maintain a prudent distance, but still avoid being judgmental or intolerant.

On the other hand, there are some governments that encourage a fundamentalism that is radically opposed to our conception of religion. Keep in mind that culture and spirituality are often connected, and therefore spirituality may be influenced by cultural traditions. "Culture is not just about symbols," says Dr. Libby Tisdell. "It includes mannerisms, nonverbal interaction, speech patterns, music [predominant religion and ancestral traditions]" (Tisdell 2003, 12). This is why both individual and collective identity plays an important role in defining people's authenticity and their free will to express opinions, faith, and spiritual conviction.

Spiritual resources are supported and sustained by faith. God and His presence are a reminder that we are blessed and gifted. However, sometimes our stubbornness tells us that all our assets come exclusively from our efforts. That attitude may make us blind to our own possessions and cause us to lose perspective of our real purpose in life. The world suffers from an absence of spiritual resources, a lack of love, and the egocentrism of those who never are satisfied with what they already have. There are too many people for whom enough is never enough. What should be unlimited are positive ambitions and long-term dreams, but we must guard against the insatiable desire for power or excessive material accumulation. To paraphrase Alan Cohen, the truth of our authentic welfare is directly related to what we provide. As soon as we sincerely give, we receive (Canfield & Hansen, 65).

Never think that the power of your influence, resources, or status makes you superior to others or allows you treat them differently. In the First book of Samuel the Lord said to Samuel, who was seeking the new king of Israel, "Do not look at his appearance or at his physical stature, because I have refused him. For the Lord does not see; for man looks at the outward appearance, but the Lord looks at the heart" (I Samuel 16:7). That is why servant leadership is an asset that benefits society as a whole. However, I have to emphasize that ultimately such leadership is more helpful to the provider than to the receiver because the power of service pays us not just at the end of our lives, but also in the spiritual and emotional gain of life itself.

We must accept differences if we want to understand and to be understood, to love and to be loved, to bring light and become enlightened. If we open our minds, eyes, and hearts we will recognize our richness and blessings. Nevertheless, as St. Augustine said, "We must love in order to see." The lover sees with the heart, not just the eyes or the head. We must start doing the process by being thankful for all the gifts we receive and we should demonstrate it by expressing our sincere gratitude to our creator. A perfect example of this was provided by Dr. Martin Luther King, Jr., when he said, "I decided early to give my life to something eternal and absolute. Not to these little goods that are here today and gone tomorrow, but to God who is the same yesterday, today, and forever."

That is another approach to understanding the importance of finding a purposeful and meaningful life. Of course, everything has a price. The correlation between giving and receiving is based on the premise that any work deserves gratification and any effort should receive a proportional reward. As John D. Rockefeller, Jr., said, "I believe that every right implies a responsibility; every opportunity, an obligation; every possession a duty" (Maxwell 1993, 41). I accept that some elemental rights are an essential part of human dignity and so they should prevail. However, even those basic rights exist in a reciprocal relationship of elemental responsibilities.

Jesus of Nazareth confirmed this connection between rights and responsibilities when He said, "Everyone to whom much is given, from him much will be required" (Luke 12:48). Of course, this balance between rights and duties should not be used to discriminate against one another. True religious freedom and human rights means you can express beliefs without being forced to do so by dictatorships or other government forces. It was Pope Benedict XVI who said, "It is essential that people and governments recognize they are not the creators of human rights and they cannot limit them [...] The rights recognized and expounded in the [universal] declaration [of human rights] apply to everyone by virtue of the common origin of the person [...]" (The Catholic Witness, April 25, 2008).

Most religions tend to embrace the virtues of recognizing our gifts and encourage us to accomplish our basic responsibilities. For instance, in the Jewish view, as John Renard pointed out, "Since life's gifts don't always simply fall into one's lap and take care of themselves, believers need to work toward worthy goals and care for gifts attained" (Renard 2002, 83). Life is a gift, a great and invaluable gift that comes from God. That is why we must offer up the season and the turnings of our lives to serve others and ask God's help to learn and grow.

Our methods of prayer can change but the essence of our basic guiding principles should prevail. For example, Hinduism requires that the cardinal virtues are based in personal justice and righteousness (Renard

2002, 263). On the other hand, the Confucianism notion of life, purpose, and common pledge is based on The Five Basic Dues of any human being: reverence always, joyful service, solicitude for ailing parents, sincere grief at a parent's death, and proper ritual veneration thereafter. Additionally, The Five Constant Virtues of person's superiority are "self-respect, generosity, sincerity, responsibility and openness to others" (Renard 2002, 435-436).

The Egyptians had something similar in the Ten Virtues of Ancient Kemet, which refers to thoughts, actions, purposes, and life mission. Patricia Gadsden cites the Seven Principles of the "Nguzo Saba," which includes Umoja (unity as a person and as a community), Kujichagulia (self-determination), Ujima (the importance of collective work and accountability), Ujamaa (cooperation and sharing profits), Nia (the necessity of having a purposeful life), Kuumba (creativity), and Imani (people faith and beliefs) (Gadsden 2002, 15).

To summarize: faith is not just a subjective belief. It is an active commitment and a personal responsibility that helps us control our anger and unconscious predisposition to hatred and selfishness. The lack of respect for different cultures, religions, and ways of thinking has created insensitivity in our communities. In this situation prayer and faith are not enough. We must maintain our pledges while moving our spiritual forces, intelligence assets, and strong feelings to action.

One of the fundamental pieces of faith is prayer. It is a great way to recognize our gifts and become aware of the abundance granted to us. However, praying should not come just in response to events. Prayer should be a daily pledge, not a last resort. Praying is fundamental for faith; nevertheless, as Lee Strobel says, "Faith is an action; it's never just mental assent. It is a direction of life" (Strobel 2002, 241).

The Spiritual Transcendence of Praying

Praying is a spiritual experience you can do in solitude or with companions. It is a deep communication with your inner self and your spiritual guide. The action of pledging is one of the most comfortable ways of healing and gaining confidence. A sincere prayer is not merely asking, but pledging. Praying is a faithful trust in God's decision. It is a request for wisdom for your mind and keenness for your heart. The power of prayer comes in a renewed way of thinking that you should match with a commitment to action.

Whatever the reason for prayer, it is always recommended to implore with faith and move to action. It is a wonderful resource when seeking guidance and life directives. You should make it a habit. Do it in times of health as well as in periods of sickness. Pray when you are happy and sad and not only in times of need. Prayer will connect your soul with supreme spirituality in times of pleasure as well as those moments when you need alternative means to joy and greatness. To paraphrase Anthony Campolo, what we really need is not necessarily being cured, but healed (Campolo 2002, 36).

We find peace and happiness in the healthy environment of our souls and the vigorous temperament of our spirits. Saint Francis of Assisi provided us with a great example about how to make requests of God in one of his famous prayers. In this pledge, he asked for directions to replace love for hatred, pardon for injury, faith instead doubt, hope for despair, and light for darkness. This beautiful expression of love is complemented when he said: "Lord, may I not so much seek to be consoled as to console; to be understood as to understand; to be loved as to love. Because it is giving that we receive, in pardoning that we pardoned."

If we are absolutely committed to the divine presence of our creator, then it is absolutely right to pray for direction as you seek solutions to your daily problems. The most valuable asset that any human being can be granted is the capability to identify the wisdom needed to deal with human matters.

THE CREATIVE ENERGY OF POSITIVE THINKING

Some difficult situations can brings us to desperation, especially in scenarios of sicknesses, loss, or death. At those times we need calm, patience, and trust to prevent angry reactions and complaints when we don't receive an immediate response to our prayers.

I understand the initial frustration that occurs when we don't get the solutions we seek through prayer. There might even be times when we blame God for our own mistakes. The real liberation occurs when our feelings exit our senses and we're granted intellectual, spiritual, and emotional expansion in our mind, soul, and heart. We achieve our highest spiritual elevation when we contact the presence of a divinity, a release we find in the deepest exercise of praying. It is what Abraham Marlow calls "peak experience" and Jonathan Haidt describes as "Awe, agape or Moral elevation" (Haidt 2006, 193).

The mystery of spiritual affection and the confidentiality of our reflected faith allow us to feel and experience internal peace. It doesn't matter how we pray—in a group or alone, with psalm or poems, or by singing or dancing. Sometimes we need a moment of silence to promote deep self-discerning. A very important rule in praying is persistence, which teaches us patience and helps us develop the ability to accept whatever decision our intelligent designer makes. If we place God in our hearts, He may refresh our memory by helping us reaffirm our trust in Him.

Prayer should comfort your soul and improve your wisdom. Your social elevation, economic status, or educational level does not matter. It is always necessary to worship and thank God for everything you have. It is best to balance your emotions so you can find a thankful attitude for recognizing your blessings and asking for the compensation of your needs. As Norman Vincent Peale said, "Don't ask for it as something to be granted later, but give thanks for it as a current fact" (Peale 1967, 110). Understanding this truth is a virtue that you will acquire through faith and a trusting relationship with your spiritual beliefs.

Remember that enthusiasm has a positive effect on your decision making, and that is because a deeply enthusiastic attitude is directly involved with your spiritual elements. The point is to ask God to guide your path and decisions and then you will be prepared to follow your intuition and instincts. Faith is a personal conviction that will help give purpose and light to your life but it is an internal decision that must come from your rational, emotional, and spiritual intelligence. It is up to you to acknowledge faith, religion, spirituality, and divinity. Then you can begin the investigation to find your own truth.

If you are a non-believer, I cannot pretend I will convince you to follow a particular spiritual path. It is your life and your decision. I consider myself a believer. Yes, I have seen both the terrible injustice of the world as well as the immeasurable kindness of the creator. Millions of testimonies affirm the presence of the superior force that fills my thoughts and gives purpose and motives to my presence on earth. Consequently, I have to share the conviction of William James, who once said, "Faith is one of the forces by which men live [...] and the total absence of it means collapse" (Carnegie 1981, 428).

I respect your views even if they differ from mine. However, I challenge you to reconsider your ways of thinking and see if it brings you confidence, self-reliance, and trust. In the end, what really counts is that you connect the elements within yourself and invigorate your soul. Since the essence of faith grows not in the mind but in the heart, I do not expect that everyone sees this world and their purpose of life through the same lenses. However, it is through the guiding principle of faith that the soul becomes the only immaterial part of our self. It is what Dr. Andrew Weil calls "the immutable essence" whose foundation lies on the value of our beliefs.

Faith and prayer are irreplaceable assets that reaffirm our hope, values, character, attitude, dreams, knowledge, and relationships. As Lee Strobel says, "If God does not exist, then [it just means that] life is futile. If the God of the Bible does exist, then life is meaningful" (Strobel 2002, 256). Remember that nothing comes with us nor belongs to us. Yes, we get a life that is truly ours. Nevertheless, life lasts just an instant, so enjoy it intensely by discovering and following your main purpose in life. More importantly, remain thankful for all the gifts that have been granted to you. Share them with those in need because sharing is one of the beauties of life.

In summary, praying is a virtue and it is best when it comes from a real intention to request guidance and wisdom. Praying is the best way to reach the highest conception of faith. It is on this level that people find a connection with spirituality and the sublime feelings where believers can find wholeness and peace. If you want to live in faith and remain connected with your divine values, you must align your spirituality with your transcendental purposeful life and the intrinsic power of love. Faith without love is like a car without battery; a pool without water; or a dream without a plan.

Faith exists, but it is difficult to utilize if we don't have love. The presence of love results in the creation of a significant, altruistic, and meaningful life. Our thoughts and spiritual convictions positively influence our values and principles so we can succeed and transform our lives. Remember, though, that we are always one decision away from paradise or torment. It all resides in the power of our thoughts.

When seeking happiness you need a predisposition to enjoy life as it is, with all its pleasures and difficulties. Always give your best in any situation. What we think is what we get; what we attract is what we reflect.

The purpose of this book is to show you different ways to see things from a positive perspective. You are the only one who can decide how to think and how to construct your values, faith, and beliefs. You can decide to pursue whatever gives meaning and sense to your life. That is the way to find joy and contentment. First you must balance your thinking, logically, emotionally, and spiritually. Your definition of God remains a personal issue, although I think that the following definition fits the essence of most theological perspectives. As Rhonda Byrne says, God is a force that "always was and always has been, never can be created or destroyed, all that ever was, always will be, always moving into form, through form and out of form" (Byrne 2006, 159).

Everything relies on your ability to connect your inner self with the reality of giving meaning and purpose to your life. Everything starts with your commitment to your own views and your willingness to be aware that others may disagree with your convictions. That is why I have continuously emphasized the importance of respecting differences. "Acceptance does not mean putting up with or resigning yourself to anything. Acceptance is about embracing life [...] it means fully opening yourself to your present reality—acknowledging how it is [...] Right here and now" (Harris 2007, 58).

Chapter 6

Practice What You Preach

———◆———

"Behind everything you do is a thought. Every behavior is motivated by a belief, and any action is prompted by an attitude."

Rick Warren

Chapter 6

Practice What You Preach

———◆◆◆———

Any lessons you take from this book or any other self-help manuscript will lack credibility if you preach them without practicing them. You must turn your positive thoughts into action because learning won't truly happen until you put your lessons into practice. Positive thinking will not take place—your positive thoughts, plans, and commitments will not acquire real value—unless your thoughts and actions are constantly in motion. "Our worth is always determined by our deeds, not by our good intentions, however noble [or well proposed they may be]," says Og Mandino (Mandino 1991, 8). The first requirement for practicing what you preach is to apply any advice, coaching, or teaching to your own life.

How can you promote solidarity and commitment to others if you are not performing it in your own life? You cannot give things you that don't possess. Loving yourself and your neighbor can be a difficult test, one that challenges your attitude, passion, talents, and commitments. You will gain real glory when you become a doer and not just a thinker. The way to do this is by determining a practical daily approach to follow your dreams. Assume the responsibility of your duties and act according to a plan of action. Maintain an open mind so you can learn, develop flexibility so you can evaluate, and keep a commitment to practice everything that you teach.

The difference between a winner and a loser is not just the victory or the dimension of the accomplishments. The difference lies in the strong commitment a winner makes to put what they preach into action. A winner pursues his/her vision regardless of the obstacles that may stand in the way. Winners try to improve their skills every day. If they achieve a very good result, they still feel they can do better and advance from good to great. Winners know they must always strive to improve. On the other hand, the defeated have two choices. They can keep crying and blame others for their failures or learn from their experiences, concentrate on their strengths, and better utilize any new opportunity as a chance to succeed.

To practice what you preach means you must move your mind from an analytical overview of events and circumstances to the practical mind-set that lets you become the actor of your own destiny. Pierce Charles Sanders stated this when he said, "There is no distinction of meaning so fine as to consist in anything but a possible difference of practice. It means to pass from the theoretical and rhetorical state of mind to the frame of mind of actions and executions." His point is that we must act according to our ethical, spiritual, and philosophical precepts, and we must help others understand theirs. But we must *act*. Keep in mind that the first person you need to confront is yourself. It is your soul—your internal receptor—that needs to constantly question the way you act and think. Your soul is the internal voice you hear as you practice any action. It is a voice that speaks up when you apply a self-talking strategy. It is the voice you might hear after you have done something wrong and you start blaming yourself for the bad attitude, feelings of regret, or poor performance that come as a consequence.

Parents, teachers, and other authority figures learn that the best way to get people to make commitments is to demonstrate with personal examples and practice whatever they advocate. When you advise people about the way they should act, you will get better results if they can follow your actions and not merely listen to you talk about it. When you practice your teachings by demonstrating concrete examples, you make what you say more meaningful. The teaching process becomes more significant. If you are already teaching by example, I recommend that you do not simply assume that others understand this. True communication happens when you know that your listener not only hears but also understands. Make sure you share your thoughts with others, but also make sure that you explain the basic cognitive stages they will need to acquire knowledge: the "what," the "why," and the "how" so they can see, express, and practice true change.

The "what" is the statement you need to provide to create the incentives to change or modify a current attitude. The "why" includes the rationale for a transformation. "How" translates the strategy you derived through your powers of intuition to promote change. The best practices come when you exercise your teachings. Whether your life is already wonderful or you're seeking to rise above disasters, it is always necessary to remember that you must have harmony if you want to make the spiritual and emotional correlations that motivate you to think and act properly.

"Spiritual experience has to do with your connection to other people and the world, and your spiritual practice has to do with your service to other people and to your community," says George Lakoff (Lakoff 2004, 103). The way you make that personal connection is important. People can express such strong feelings with their facial expressions, tones of voice, and gestures that sometimes it becomes difficult to move beyond a first impression. That's probably what Ralph Waldo Emerson was alluding to when he said, "What you are [tend to be] expressed so strongly that I cannot even hear what is being just said" (Canfield & Hansen, 112). The connection you make through preaching can be a powerful stimulus to motivate spirit, intellect, and emotions to think and speak proactively. More important, it can spur souls and move bodies to take ongoing action. So practice what you preach as you maintain positive thinking and exceptional things will happen.

Positive Thinking, a Key Element in Facing Challenges

The way you face obstacles or challenges determines whether you can resolve differences and prevent conflicts from escalating. Your behavior will help you find alternative solutions for any given incident before it escalates into a calamity. You can find ways to end disagreements by maintaining connections with other people and creating relationships of mutual respect. There are two distinctive approaches to any controversy. One is to respond appropriately and honestly by listening to other people and respecting their views. The other is to ignite antagonism by refusing to think outside your own frame of reference. The outcome of any situation depends on how you respond or react to it. You have the choice of either reacting on impulse or taking a meditative, rational approach.

Sometimes the issue itself is not the real problem; our unwillingness to listen and respect other views is. That can be a result of accumulated resentment or unhealed confrontations from the past. At all times we must be very careful to avoid overreaction or becoming engaged in arguments when we don't understand the facts. Don't drag in old unresolved episodes, either consciously or unconsciously. When you have a positive-thinking mind-set, you can transform any difficulty into an opportunity to see and enjoy the true gift of life. Remember, "Joy does not come from avoiding a problem or having someone else deal with it. Joy comes from overcoming a problem or simply learning to live with it while being joyful" (Stovall 2006, 67).

The fundamental principle is that you must respect and understand different viewpoints and respect people's opinions and personalities in any conversation or negotiation. Arguments can arise for different reasons, including miscommunication, disrespect, or unrelated circumstances. Be prepared to confront any such issues by remaining calm and seeking different options. Control your emotions rationally as you deal with conflict or challenges. Never react or express your opinions when under the influence of anger, distress, or other strong emotions. Never let the moment's grievances prevent you from measuring the consequences of your actions. Relax, take it easy, and explore in silence the outcome of your words and deeds. Always remember that a word once said cannot be taken back, so think before you speak. Even if you are not in charge or if you are not the person who starts the conflict, your attitude still matters. You need at least two people for an argument. It has been said that "there are no winners in any conflict," so it is best to avoid disputes. As you confront difficult situations, try to prevent conflict, keep a problem from escalating, and always consider any incident as an opportunity for growth.

If you do not have anything positive to add, remain silent and be conciliatory. Even after a conflict becomes resolved the environment will never be quite the same. "One of the most appreciated gifts of maintaining silence is caution," says Silvia Bolet; "it is interpreted as prudence" (Bolet 2001, 168). I realize that it can be very difficult to control our emotions and our words, but our listening abilities and negotiation skills are important tools for maintaining relationships of mutual respect.

One of the principles of the art of negotiation and a good method of conflict resolution is to arrive at a "mutual concession" or "business deal." This is a type of consensus that you achieve when everyone has an equal chance to be heard, and therefore the discussion reaches a point of mutual satisfaction. Stephen Covey asserts that the art of mutual consent transforms the decision-making process into a fair and efficient alternative (Covey 1989, 274). Two wise suggestions that everyone should keep in mind for dealing with interpersonal relationships are to maintain auto-emotional control and use common sense to measure how we act and what we say to others. Our actions and our speech are interconnected and the wise use of both is important for creating and maintaining relationships of mutual respect.

The first recommendation, auto-emotional control, means you should assume responsibility for your emotional responses. You can do that in two ways: positive or negative. Obviously you should use positive thinking even in difficult or challenging times. A positive approach won't avoid trials or difficulties, but it will control impulsive actions. On other hand, negative emotions generate anger and bitterness and can give rise to unexpected reactions that can damage or destroy relationships. As Silvia Bolet says, we cannot avoid our emotions but we can control and take responsibility for them (Bolet 2001, 117).

The second recommendation is to measure the consequences of your actions. This relates to the necessity of thinking before acting. It also encompasses what we say and how we say it. Words can wound more than objects because a physical force hits our body while an emotional one punches our soul. The way that we respond is more important than how we answer. Respect is not weakness; authority does not mean unlimited power; kindness is not cowardice; firmness does not mean tyranny.

When you dream and have a firm intention to accomplish goals, you should have at least three basic things in mind if you want to maintain positive thinking and prevent negativism. Those three things are the significance of planning; the way of dealing with challenges, and the importance of preventing conflicts by measuring what you do and how you express it. My humble advice is to take the initiative and control the circumstances whatever they may be by keeping calm, seeing different options, accepting things are they are, and recognizing a situation as a temporary condition so you can learn from it without compromising your commitments. Mishandling a situation can create irreconcilable differences and allow anger to have a negative impact.

The main thing is to see any given event from different perspectives. Consider alternative options that may not have been explored sufficiently. Remember that the initial difficulty might not be the real problem; how you handle it could be. Decide how you will respond to an event. You can be angry or pleased; it is your own will that determines that.

We all report to someone or are accountable to someone. That includes parents, teachers, bosses, leaders, ministers, stockholders, friends, significant others, or God. On the other hand, we also have people that we take care of or who need our compassion, advice, company, or experience. We are all interdependent and we need one another if we want meaningful and happy lives. One of the things that can interfere with our ability to deal positively with others is that we sometimes forget what we are, where we come from, and where are we going. As Wally Amos mentioned, sometimes we are so concerned with today and the little obstacles that we face that we lose sight of what we are becoming. It is important to remember that the present is just one step away from becoming the future (Amos & Amos 1988, 186).

We have the free will to choose a balanced way of living, one in which you don't take things too lightly or too seriously. How you choose is something that lies within yourself and in the life you choose. That is my understanding of why our creator gave us free will, so we have the power and responsibility to enjoy our accomplishments and learn from our challenges. That is why people should develop their talents, explore their options, and utilize their preferences. And that means you must accept the responsibility for what you do without blaming somebody for the outcomes of our own actions.

Positive thinking is a powerful tool for overcoming challenges. Not only is it important to practice, you should also constantly monitor the relationship between what you do and what you say you do. Practice what you preach, and let those practices reveal ways you can contribute to society, leave your mark, and make a difference to others. It is our responsibility to build a legacy for future generations. According to an old saying, "The real context of heroism is found in ordinary work, made on daily basis and in an extraordinary way." Creating a legacy comes from a real intention to contribute, not from self-centered or egotistic schemes.

It is not my intention to strive for self-recognition when creating a legacy, but to act with the sincere objective of finding satisfaction and pride by aiding social justice in my private and public affairs. You will not find solidarity, healthy relationships, and happiness by seeking earthly recognition. As an old adage I've mentioned before says, "Those who truly deserve a monument do not really need it." The real monuments exist, constructed by the hearts and the fortitude of those who practice what they preach in terms of positive thinking.

One way to create a legacy and spark fundamental change is by exercising the kind of leadership that helps you gain confidence in yourself and earn the respect of others. Great leaders earn trust, allegiance, and even love from those with whom they work. When you receive the trust of those you lead, you can feel the positive impact on the entire group. Proactive thinking and the power of optimism derives from the authority of the leader and the power of his/her influence. However, the essential test of your leadership comes after you leave your position. That is when you will really be recognized for the outcomes of your actions as well as the greatness of your legacy.

In many cases it is only after people leave a position of authority that they can measure their true influence, the loyalty of their team, and the friendship of those they worked with. True friends remain even after a leader no longer has power or influence. That is when you can determine the true essence of feelings and emotions. When people remain friends even when power has passed, that confirms your true leadership ability and your capacity to create relationships of mutual respect. Those relationships do not depend on status, category, title, or a fleeting social, economic, or political stature. Situational leadership is ephemeral. Its greatest moments come when former leaders find that they still have sincere friends, instead of acquaintances who only honored them because of their former authority.

The main consideration of true leadership is that you are in charge and therefore responsible for the consequences of your choices. Leaders must have the capacity to learn from any experiences and use them to release tension, seek solutions, and, hopefully, bring pleasure. You also have the option to express uncontrolled negative emotions and express resentment. How you respond lies in your hands. It is all in the power of your choices.

We can all think positively and resolve our challenges by addressing them. Deal with one issue at a time so you can avoid becoming trapped in the misfortunes of the past or anxieties of the future. Sometimes solving a conflict may appear impossible, but once you do find a solution the experience will contribute to the creation of more happiness. The harder the game, the sweeter the victory! The triumph feels even better when our adversaries did not simply give up, because the constant striving helps us realize our maximum potential. Finally, keep in mind that "Problems may only be avoided by exercising a great judgment. Good judgment may only be gained by experiencing life's problems [And challenges]" (Stovall 2006, 59).

The Circular, Linear, and Dimensional Approaches in Dealing With Challenges

You should not consider a problem or obstacle to be a setback. When you are filled with positive thinking, you should instead look at any barrier as an opportunity to learn, a chance to grow, and a step that will take you higher. There are at least three basic ways of looking and dealing with problems and concerns: a circular or redundant approach to the primary issue; the linear or direct-to-the point approach; and the multidimensional tactic that means you face obstacles from different angles and perspectives.

The circular tendency surfaces when you focus exclusively on the cause of the problem by going up and down and all around the issue without actually looking for solutions. Sometimes people who use the circular tendency to handle problems end up addressing external influences that may not even be related to the initial issue. This kind of scenario typically plays out by focusing attention on troubles and concerns instead of strengths and solutions. You need to focus on the latter elements if you want to discover alternative responses to the problem.

The second way to confront a problem, the linear, manifests itself when people focus on an event by examining its effects or what they expect will be its immediate consequences. This approach focuses on outcomes by looking at immediate results, but avoids dwelling on any positive effects. The issue and its immediate solution become the only thing that matters, with the intention of only solving the problem in limited time. The mentality of the linear feels that if something happens today it should be resolved today, right here and right now! The linear way of thinking is a closed approach that doesn't consider the causes, but only the effects and consequent solutions.

I do understand that some obstacles need be solved right away. Nonetheless, there is always time to think about and reach mediated solutions. Giving ourselves time to balance our decisions and find a peaceful space to meditate about our alternatives is an important part of positive thinking. That approach may be one of the reasons why Goethe said, "Talent is nurtured in solitude; character is formed in the stormy billows of the world." Goethe was absolutely right. A meditated decision so often leads to self-analysis of cause and consequences and a proper approach to predictable circumstances. That is why a moment of silence is so often necessary. It gives us time to self-reflect and utilize our internal strengths when we deal with both expected and unexpected events along life's pathway.

When you lead with obfuscated thinking or manage through anger or by consistently introducing upset, the end result may be bitterness, resentment, and confusion that escalate into unresolved conflict. Avoid such results by making a careful examination of your options. If necessary, reframe your point of view and bring creative and contemplative responses to the fore. Such reframing is an essential element of creativity. It encourages critical thinking and helps you develop innovative solutions as you begin to see issues from different perspectives. It will help you find your way out of the trap of blaming others or even ourselves for our initial failures. Instead, it will show you how to recognize your talents and utilize them in your favor instead of against you.

One way to do that is by applying critical thinking. Focus your attention on strengths and positive factors that you discover within an unexpected problem or concern. After you highlight your strengths, make an effort to identify your weaknesses and find ways to improve them. Look at the positive side instead of concentrating on the negative. "The more we focus on unpleasant thoughts and feelings, the more we disconnect from the present moment," advises Russ Harris. "This particularity tends to happen with depression and anxiety" (Harris 2007, 131). It does not matter how you resolve conflicts or how comfortable you are in dealing with them. What really matters is the attitude, habits, and behaviors you use when addressing them.

The consequences of our actions arise from our choices, and our choices are affected by the waves of positive or negative influences we receive from our environment and our acquaintances. We want to make the best choices possible. One way to ensure that is by facing one problem at a time. Prioritize your concerns and address those that really matter first. Take your time to exercise your intuition, plan ahead, and visualize yourself solving your problems and conquering your fears and uncertainties.

Keep in mind that deep problems can arise when your thinking interferes with your performance. Don't let your conscious and unconscious get in the way by dwelling on errors. Instead, learn to recognize the opportunities that often spring from the same sources as our grumbling. As I've said before, consider any challenge to be an opportunity. Focus your time on understanding causes and finding solutions. Use your gifts, exercise your talents, and practice what you preach. That is the essence of rational judgment, emotional intelligence, and social competence.

The third way to analyze problems is what I call the "multidimensional concern approach." It utilizes four parameters for analyzing a problem. The first one is the "height" or altitude. It asks how "big" the impact or effects will be and what positive results we can get from it. The second is "width." This focuses on how many people will be affected and how many activities will gain an advantage from the decision. The third parameter is the "length" of the problem. Here we consider how much time it will take and whether or not it is urgent enough to require an immediate response. Using these parameters, you can measure and analyze any problem by focusing on its different aspects.

The fourth element of the dimensional approach is the "volume" or size of the problem. It also takes into consideration the event's essence. The circumstances are, of course, totally different if the event involves a life-threatening issue or a business transaction that could impact your retirement, reputation, or public credibility. If, on the other hand, the problem requires a different logistic approach or different perception or a circumstantial inference, then it does not require as much consideration, just intuition and an informed decision. In such situations it might help to consider Og Mandino's advice: "Search for the seed of good [that usually is hidden] in every adversity [...] those who never made a mistake have never known the thrill of turning apparent loss in gain" (Mandino 1991, 120).

In summary, the best predisposition to positive thinking comes from a willingness to accept any situation as only a temporary reality. Problems are part of human existence. In some cases they can be prevented, but they cannot be completely eliminated. We might see obstacles and barriers as enemies of success, but it is better to think of them as elements that will eventually bring pleasure once we overcome them. Remember that "acceptance breaks the vicious circle of struggle and frees you to invest your time and energy in life-enhancing activities" (Harris 2007, 96).

It is my recommendation that whatever challenges you face, you should welcome and confront them in a positive manner. Assume a problem is just a temporary barrier. More importantly, acknowledge that once you overcome a concern and reach your planned objective, you have moved forward on the pathway toward finding meaning, purpose, and pleasure in life. As Eckhart Tolle says, "Failure lies concealed in every success and success in every failure [...] All forms are impermanent" (Tolle 2004, 184).

The Importance of Praising People Instead of Merely Criticizing Them

If we want to pursue a meaningful and purposeful life we require two basic things: knowledge and healthy relationships. Knowledge can be formal or informal. It comes from schools and from the wisdom we pick up through the experience of life. Relationships with other people are necessary for those times when we need help. Sometimes we strike up relationships through business networking, which can prove helpful in our professional lives. In short, we need the knowledge to make practical, informed decisions and effective social interactions if we want to confront life's challenges in a proactive and successful manner.

One of the main principles for maintaining strong relationships is to show love and sincere appreciation for other people. The art of collaboration comes into play when we can recognize people's virtues instead of merely criticizing them. If we want to win people's support for our personal or community-oriented tasks, we must first conquer their hearts, then get the intellectual cooperation from their minds, and finally gain their pledge to action. An old adage says that the key component in social and ethical interactions is to "love people and use things, not love things and use people."

Sometimes we delay the acquisition of our objectives because we are being our own worst enemy. There are times when we allow the opinions of others to influence us in a negative way; in effect we hang ourselves without a trial. In those cases we continuously devalue our self-image, values, and expertise. Sometimes it's an unconscious act and we're not even aware of what we're doing. It is behavior we can recognize and change. As Og Mandino says, "Nothing external can have any power over you unless you permit it. Your time is too precious to be sacrificed in wasted days combating the menial forces of hate, jealousy, and envy" (Mandino 1991, 114).

One symptom of a negative self-image is when we begin to neglect our own possibilities. That can show up in conversation when you fall into a habit of justifying yourself when you express something different. At those times you pepper your conversation with words like "try," "but," and "if." Remove those words from your daily vocabulary. They reduce positive thinking. They have an unconscious negative implication that can deter you from moving ahead and promoting positive thinking. Instead of saying "I try," say "I will." Dale Carnegie recommends that we replace the word "but" with "and" to transform a negative statement into a positive one (Carnegie 1981, 198). His reasoning is that when you recognize a person with encouragement and praise and follow with the word "but," you take away from the commendation. For example, if you say to your son, "Good job, boy! You have ten As! But why did you get two Bs?" where do you think you are placing the emphasis, in the positive or in the negative? It is why praise followed by the word "and" will carry more meaning and provide a stronger affirmative recognition.

Anytime you use these words, pay attention to the context and be alert for any inconsistency in your statements. Are you aware that negative statements often come packaged as contradictory assertions? In those cases the end result is that we deny praise and focus on shortcomings instead, even if your initial intention was to offer congratulations. Make it a point to offer positive reinforced statements so your intentions don't get lost. Make sure that you are really praising people instead of offering criticism in the guise of a positive statement.

Praise stimulates our self-esteem. It inspires and motivates people and helps them develop empathy and pride. On the other hand, if we dwell on mistakes instead of accomplishments, we are using destructive techniques instead of productive ones. Constructive criticism should be a tool that emphasizes actions to make corrections, instead of simply condemning behavior. As Rudolph and Kathleen Verderber say, "Constructive criticism is not based on judgment, but empathy" (Verderber & Verderber 2005, 161). Praise coupled with censure or appreciation linked to disapproval will not reinforce positive thinking. Such dual ways of thinking prevent direct communication with others.

You need a healthy and balanced diet to feed your body, just as you require self-encouragement to nurture your mind and nourish your spirit. You need positive reinforcement to create what Goethe called "the power of commitment." One of the best ways to deter negativity and create positive thinking is to embrace self-reliance and transmit enthusiasm in any activity you take on. More importantly, when you do it, transmit your positive feelings to others. Maybe it is one of the reasons why people often don't say what they mean or mean what they say. Remember, life is a constant process of problem solving and every problem you encounter includes an opportunity for growth. It is your responsibility to utilize your talents, synchronize your mind, control your emotions, and use your limitless spiritual resources to live your life in a proper manner.

Success usually comes from little battles and small victories that we accumulate on our pathway to achievement. Success can lie hidden within those challenges that you are afraid to confront. I am not saying that you should pursue problems. I mean that you should analyze all obstacles—those that seem easy to overcome as well as those that are hard—to discover the true meaning of happiness. "What we obtain too cheap, we esteem too lightly," said Thomas Paine; "it is dearness only that gives every thing its value."

In conclusion, my advice is that you should incorporate real willingness to achieve into everything you do. Attack any opportunity as if it were your last chance to reach your goal. You will see that the positive way of thinking brings gains, not just for your own benefit, but for those who surround you as well. More importantly, approach your tasks with patience, humility, and a willingness to accept the views of others. Remember that sometimes the best opportunities come disguised as misfortunes. So learn from them and get the experience and expertise you need to confront life's challenges. As Aldous Huxley said, "Experience is not what happens to a man; it is what a man does with what happen to him" (Canfield & Hansen 1995, 234).

Consistency and Determination: Skills Needed to Achieve

Consistency is the keystone of commitment and the root of determination. It provides the foundation for affirmative thinking and is a key element for maintaining a positive attitude. Consistency requires self-discipline. It is a product of confidence. Determination is all about practicing what you preach. Consistency is a promise to yourself that you will maintain your objectives, while determination is about redirecting all your efforts so you can achieve your goals and succeed in life. Success is not just a decision; it is a determination. Consistency is based on faith, trust, conviction, and self-confidence. Determination is a commitment to pursue a goal despite any failures, fatigue, struggles, mistakes, or disadvantages.

Consistency means you must persist and maintain your ideals without losing perspective of your final goal or mission. Consistency promotes decisions and a sense of continuity while determination advocates courage and commitment. Consistency means to keep going. Determination gets you to the goal line. Just because it is not easy to keep going does not give you justification to abandon a goal, even under the most trying circumstances. Those who know where they are going should not stop to discuss their dream with those who have not even thought about a destination.

Consistency means you keep going without allowing internal doubts or external warnings to alter your expectations. As Jose Ingenieros said, "Those who are walking to the light cannot see what happens in the darkness." You cannot achieve simply by trying. Success comes to those who truly believe and have the self-reliance to pursue their dreams, whatever the cost may be. Some people trap themselves within their own procrastination and weaken their ability to thrive. Those who give up their dreams through an inability to persist and maintain consistency lack the basic motivation to keep from losing. When you have motivation you have the self-confidence to keep your dreams alive; consistency is all about having the confidence to succeed and not merely settle for "trying."

Persistence means you have the confidence and ability to do the right thing when you follow plans and strategies, whether they are long- or short-term projects. Remember, you cannot reach perfection without effort. A commitment to hard work is one key for maintaining consistency. Another tool is to visualize your final dream, which helps you remain determined. When you take action with confidence and use a mental model of visualization you will be well on your way to success. Avoid fears and worries that are no more than self-imposed barriers that can affect your behavior. Of course, there are times when past episodes can interfere with a resilient mind-set. As John Gardner says, "Most of us carry in our head a tremendous catalogue of things we have no intention of trying because we tried them once and failed."

Yet we have the power of decision and the willingness to take risk to solve problems and initiate new adventures. One reason why people fail is that they settle for "trying." "Trying" is only intention. "Willing" is a commitment. Remember also that actions and reactions are not the same thing. Action is a matter of decision making and provides a pathway to change. Reaction is an emotional response you make on impulse. That is why informed, intuitive, and creative assessments are fundamental for preventing reactions and promoting effective and efficient actions.

Action combines rational and emotional approaches. Action results from strong will, while reactions are feelings and sensations that arise from our emotions. "Action seems to follow feeling, but really action and feeling go together," said scientist William James; "and by regulating the action, which is under the more direct control of the will, we can indirectly regulate the feeling, which is not" (Carnegie 1981, 357). What you want is a balance between will and feelings; an equilibrium between persistence and strengths; and harmony between mind and heart. Positive thinking is an asset that allows a sensitive attitude to carefully measure, balance, and analyze the process of decision making.

When people really desire to do something, no obstacle can stand in the way. You must confront uncertainties that can become barriers by affirming constancy and reaffirming persistence. Fears can become unseen powerful enemies that will gnaw at your predisposition to think positively. Worrying destroys your ability to think and act, while fear prevents you from making your own decisions. Avoid fear by not letting presumptions of the past and uncertainties of the future interfere with a determined plan and a proactive assumption of predictable occurrences. It is normal to be afraid or harbor doubts, and it is natural to feel discomfort when you make changes. But do not allow fears, uncertainties, or lack of commitment lead to inactivity or a continuation of the status quo. Positive thinking will let you acknowledge fears and reservations without accepting them as barriers. As Jean Turner says, "We learn the rope of the life by untying its knots." It is by untying the knots and overcoming barriers that we uncover our potential and reinforce our strengths.

Fears, anxiety, and depression are bullets that hurt the soul instead of the body. That is why you must accept circumstances as they come, analyze your options and resources, use your instincts, and move to meditated and conscious rational action. Do that without wasting your energies on events that have already happened and are thus beyond change. Everything starts with the power of your thoughts and the energy that they radiate. "Thoughts become things," says Mike Dooley. Rhonda Byrne adds to that when she says, "Your thoughts are the primary cause of everything [...] and that includes your feelings: the cause is always your thoughts" (Byrne 2006, 30).

It is a good habit to acknowledge and accept reality as it is, instead of superficially rejecting it. Confront your fears. "Acceptance of what has happened is the first step in overcoming the consequences of any misfortune," as William James said (Carnegie 1981, 261). Acceptance does not mean you agree with it, but that you acknowledge its occurrence. Acknowledgment is something you should apply to any circumstance. It is a tactic that allows us to dedicate our efforts to potential solutions instead of lamenting things we cannot change.

The next time that you experience an unexpected event, remain calm and confront it as a transitory condition. At such times people need a great flow of consistency. That requires effort because it may force you to change habits and mind-sets. "Being tenacious requires that you give 100 percent—not more, but certainly not less," says John Maxwell. "If you give your all, you afford yourself every opportunity possible for success" (Maxwell 2002, 145).

Consistency is the key to achievement, the essence of fidelity, and the foundation of commitment. Perseverance is an inner value that lets us expect more from ourselves than from others. It is about thinking that anything we conceive is possible. "The difference between history's boldest accomplishments and its most staggering failures is often, simply, the diligent will to persevere," said Abraham Lincoln. Therefore, forget the past, leave former worries behind, and enjoy your present while preparing for your future with the ability to do what you want and, more importantly, enjoy and love what you already have.

When we are born we have a natural ability to learn. As we grow we earn the privilege to learn. When we reproduce and contribute to the continuity of life we also get the responsibility and pleasure to share. Finally, when we die we have the obligation to give back whatever was granted to us. In the spiritual point of view, "When we live we die and when we die we really live."

Humility to Understand Differences

---

*"People with humility don't think less of themselves;
they just think of themselves less."*
Ken Blanchard and Norman Vincent Peale

Chapter 7

Humility to Understand Differences

———◆—◆—◆———

Our world is a very diverse one. It's full of different personalities, cultural traditions, and languages. It offers a wide variety of spiritual, physical, and mental challenges. It includes different approaches to things such as philosophy and politics. People come from different social-economic statuses and have individual abilities and disabilities. All this influences the way we treat other people, the assumptions we make about them, and the way we respond to them. The way we think may fluctuate according to our relationships and our perspectives about moral, ethical, philosophical, and spiritual standards. Yet even though we are all different, we also must all contribute to this global village we share, even if we approach life's purpose from myriad directions.

You need an open mind to accept differences. An open mind will let you give people the latitude to be themselves without worrying about being judged because of their appearance or ethnicity. It is a person's character that matters. We are all unique in one way or another. We all have different roles and assignments in life as well as diverse attitudes and aptitudes for contributing to the whole. It is not a matter of having others judge you as "bad" or "good." It is a question of having the freedom to be yourself, free of reservations or preconceived prejudices.

In Chapter 2 I used an example to clarify the variables of positive and critical thinking. I also mentioned that you should include a willingness to embrace diversity, not just through your rationality but in your emotional responses as well. This is necessary to make sure your intentions align with your frame of reference. Otherwise it does not matter how hard we try; the result may not be what we desire because the intention (awareness and understanding) does not match with our frame of reference (internalized judgments). Awareness and a way of thinking must work together if we are to really acknowledge and accept people's differences.

If we want to foster acceptance in our social interactions, we should periodically inspect our frames of reference and avoid dogmas and fundamentalist doctrines that can block a positive way of thinking. Maybe that is why René Descartes developed his famous "moralist theory" as a way to challenge his own knowledge and philosophical convictions. His goal was to discover what he called "transcendent truth" (Ordóñez 1989, 39).

We need to find our own transcendent truths so we know who we are. Just as an incorrect map or wrong directions can send us to the wrong place, an absolute or rigid frame of reference can compel us to take up unconscious segregation of people who are different from us. That is what we do whenever we make discriminations based on social and economic status or judge our fellow human beings based on differences in age, affiliation, spirituality, or religious affinity. We can also make the same kinds of unconscious discriminations when we deal with people with different physical or mental abilities. Consciously we may believe that we dutifully follow all laws and regulations that allow equal access to all without being aware that we still discriminate by allowing lack of access or by not implementing friendly environments that welcome everyone.

Respecting and accepting differences means more than just acknowledging official regulations or work-environment policies. A personal commitment to diversity is a holistic predisposition that must come from the bottom of your heart. It needs to be rooted in your intelligence and impregnated within the structure of your rationality. Most people are not even conscious of the hidden privileges that some portions of the community receive and others do not. That is why government regulation is sometimes necessary to ensure that everyone receives freedom, equality, and justice as well as full human rights for everyone.

If our mind-set (our internal subconscious approach) remains filled with past prejudices, predetermined resentment, and inflexible ways of thinking based on past episodes, then it will be very difficult to change unless the decision comes from both mind and heart. Even if you publicly declare your toleration you may still be unconsciously stereotyping and discriminating against those who seem different. It all depends on your internal preconception or the auto-imposed thoughts and inflexible postures that affect attitude, behavior, and ways of thinking.

You can truly accept differences when you respect your own freedom as well as the freedom of others. "Freedom is the pursuing of our own good in our own way, so long as we do not attempt to deprive others of theirs," said John Stewart Mill. If we extend Mill's comment to take into consideration the concept of diversity and the ideal of creating responsible citizens, we can say that an environment of diversity exists once people can exercise their authenticity without limiting their individuality to public demands. I think that John Oliver Killens found one of the best ways to express this. "We are not fighting for the right to be like you," Killens said. "We respect ourselves too much for that. When we fight for freedom, we mean freedom for us to be black, or brown, and you to be white, and yet live together in a free and equal society. This is the only way that integration can bring dignity for both of us" (Mazel 1998, 107).

THE CREATIVE ENERGY OF POSITIVE THINKING

When we concentrate on the value of diversity and individual freedom we must acknowledge the unique contribution of all members of our society, even as we consider the accomplishments of the whole. "We require individualism which does not wall man off from the community," said Arthur J. Schlesinger; "we require community which sustains but does not suffocate the individual." This is why a positive-thinking mind-set must include an open mind willing not only to accept differences but also to respect and acknowledge that the differences that apparently separate us tend actually to complement our abilities to fulfill our needs. Positive thinking requires a peaceful relationship with ourselves and with those who are around us.

Embracing diversity can teach us to explore new experiences and points of view. A mind open to diversity offers the opportunity to see the greatness of creation and the diversity of its species. It offers the chance to enjoy a more colorful and pleasant life. By embracing diversity we can implement change and transform our society. Keep in mind, though, that any such transformation starts through a change in our inner self. It is our responsibility to evaluate and revise our perspectives so that our mind is in tune with our perceptions and our views embrace the greatness of inclusion. It is through understanding differences that we can understand the value of the diverse composition of the fullness of the creation. As Graham Hetrick says, "What a sorry world it would be, if all flowers were yellow or all trees were pine."

Understanding diversity helps us grapple with the sensitive topic of poverty. It is a complex problem, but one that we must understand if we want to produce a better society. Acceptance of differences also means people can clearly express their views whether they are white or black, tall or short, thin or fat, man or woman. Appreciating differences means you should be friendly with people from different statuses, origins, and backgrounds. The greatness of our authenticity and ability to perform based on what we really are stems from our awareness of the importance of the whole and the significance of individual uniqueness. Humility to understand differences will help us accept our differences as an asset to society and a magnificent opportunity to embrace everyone as individuals.

On the other hand, the absence of understanding, awareness, and sensitivity leads to repression, segregation, and discrimination. It creates the conditions necessary for hate, intolerance, incomprehension, fatalism, and negativism. To avoid these pitfalls we need a sensitive approach so we can develop respect and grant a sense of acceptance in any community. Acceptance is a higher level of understanding, one that is fundamental to avoid discrimination and prejudice. The sad fact is that we can find insensitivity all around the world. It is so common that it has created what Eckhart Tolle calls "collective manifestation of insanity" (Tolle 2005, 11). This collective dysfunction and self-applied destructive impulse threatens the divinity and extraordinary composition of humankind. It creates violence, hatred, and self-destruction that arise from our lack of awareness and understanding. In order to appreciate differences, you must be willing and able to practice not just tolerance, but acceptance. There is a significant difference between tolerance and acceptance, and the difference boils down to whether you include or exclude. "Acceptance does not mean putting up with or resigning yourself to anything," says Russ Harris. "Acceptance is about embracing life [...] It means fully opening yourself to your present reality—acknowledging how it is [...] Right here and now" (Harris 2007, 58).

The first step for preventing xenophobia, hatred, and discrimination is to ensure that you acknowledge and accept that we all have unique individual characteristics and personalities. Over the past centuries, the most tenacious discriminations are racial ones, which arise from our resistance to acknowledge diverse ethnic composition and color differences. In fact, racial profiles have driven people and governments to segregate and create assumptions based solely on clothing that reflects an ethnic origin. The fact is, we usually ascribe greater differences among ourselves than really exist.

It would be better if we started recognizing the much greater similarities that we all share.

For instance, from the genetic and biological point of view we are not so different from one another—no more than 2 percent of our entire composition. In other words, we share 98 percent of our genetic code. Then why do we permit so much division by race, color, language, or economic class, all of which are just incidental occurrences of life? On the other hand, that little portion of genetic difference keeps us unique and lets us contribute in different ways to society. It is another demonstration that what we become is not merely what we inherit, but what we learn, experience, and develop during our time on earth.

The fact is that we reveal differences and share similarities all the time. "Personal identity and racial identity are inextricably linked," say Marci Hanson and Eleanor Lynch. "Even though race is not scientifically relevant, it is very socially [and economically] relevant" (Hanson & Lynch 2004, 19). The real issue is obviously not material differences but rather the perceived variances manufactured in the cauldron of ethnocentricity and political power. Our diverse color composition represents just tiny difference between the people that make up the whole masterpiece of the human race.

Racial supremacist movements focus on dissimilarities and assume preeminence for one group or another. The concept of a race's "purity" or the exclusivity of an ethnic group is an absurd one, founded on narcissistic or egoistic premises. It is one of the most disastrous forms of exclusion and one that creates intolerance, societal conflicts, disparities, and social inequity. The conception of an "unmixed race" is an extreme view that merely promotes controversy and exclusion. Sometimes these views arise from a lack of social skills or an absence of trustful spirituality. (As I have mentioned, spirituality is not the same as religion, which in many cases has helped foster negative assumptions, prejudice, and hatred.)

In the past much hatred has risen from an inability to comprehend human distinctiveness. The concept of tolerance is just the first step on a pathway toward recognizing societal obligations and equal rights. Tolerance alone is not enough, not even in developed countries such as the United States or those of the European Union. The norms of the past have become obsolete in a world of instant communications, when events that occur on one side of the planet are known everywhere almost instantly.

Tolerance alone is not sufficient because it does not represent a holistic recognition of human dignity nor the inalienable rights that belong to all human beings. Nevertheless, some sensitive areas of the world have a chronic lack of even basic tolerance, thanks to pseudo national security policies or geopolitical strategies. For instance, in recent years, immigrant communities have become the target for hostility all around the world, particularly in the United States and some European countries. That kind of hostile reaction denies the important need to understand differences, and it demonstrates a lack of sensitivity to the concept of global integration.

Fueling anger and hatred between people due exclusively to their differences initially affects the people who feel and suffer the hardships of discrimination and exclusion firsthand. In the end, though, the people who promote hatred will be even more affected by it. As an old adage says, "Envy is like an acid; it corrodes the items that hold it." Similarly, hatred affects the receiver as well as the supplier. So why should we waste our time promoting segregation and highlighting distinctions of color, language, place of origin, religion, or sexual orientation? Why do we focus more on the superficial than on the essence and pay more attention to the appearance instead of the fundamental nature of an individual?

We can make some progress on this matter by incorporating policies of inclusion. Furthermore, we should also reaffirm the importance of diversity in the framework of our moral and ethical values and support it by respecting and recognizing the inalienable dignity of all humankind. If we can remember the horror of the genocidal confrontations from the past and, in some parts of the world, the present, we can agree on the importance to end discrimination. The first step is to bypass the old-fashioned notion of tolerance and pay deference to its upgraded version, acceptance.

Tolerance means to simply continue on your way without really considering the viewpoints of others. Acceptance includes understanding, which is an intellectual recognition of different cultures, perspectives, customs, and values. When we commit ourselves to understanding differences, we can expand our thinking and discover the virtues, talents, strengths, and contributions that others make. More importantly, a perspective of diversity and inclusion, love and compassion, and kindness and solidarity helps us reframe our ways of thinking. Many principles, such as patriotism and respect, never result from compulsory measures but only from free-will determination. The same should be true of the principles of authenticity and inclusion.

Tolerance indicates only knowledge of dissimilarities while acceptance implies an acceptance of and respect for differences. Tolerance means we recognize that people are different. Acceptance means we are willing to explore and assimilate a spirit of receptiveness. That does not mean we should deny our differences, but that we should respect and accept them even as we focus our attention on our similarities. More importantly, an acceptance of differences is imperative if we want to maintain a solid community structure without interfering in the personal views of the people that make it up.

In the European Union an alternative and positive word used to describe assimilation or acculturation is integration. The meaning of integration includes an inclusive and proactive way to promote people's talents, where assimilation implies an absorption process that removes individual components or cultural characteristics and makes everything part of a single structure. Assimilation doesn't take into consideration the value of differences and can lose different views and perspectives. It is a process that moves from generation to generation.

In brief, acculturation, assimilation, or adjustments are all examples of internal and external oppressions that people face in any region where a dominant group prevails. For this reason, the openness and sensitivity of the dominant group, as well as the flexibility of other societal components, can lead to a better and more peaceful world where different values, customs, beliefs, and ways of thinking can coexist. Getting there will require understanding of people's differences and creating more opportunities for peace, fellowship, fraternity, and solidarity.

Our main responsibility in respecting the dignity of all human beings is not just to be aware of these principles, but also to acknowledge the practices that advance them and work effectively in an inclusive cross-cultural environment. Our main intention is to understand, appreciate, and recognize the benefits we derive from a diverse population. Differences arise from different factors; it is not related solely to opening or closing borders, changing immigration policies, advocating for the purity of ethno-racial classes, or conserving the predominance of a specific lineage, language, or religion.

The basic root of Caucasoid, Mongoloid, Negroid, and Australoid "races" comes from an initial ethnic distinction that predominated in ancient times. Since then these "races" have been refined by a constant intermixing that overlaps geographical, cultural, and language boundaries. It has been happening progressively, but is more visible today as intermarriage has become more common, creating the multicultural, multiethnic, and multilingual environment around the world. These multicultural identities do not fit a single set of traditions or behaviors, but follow a diverse group of patterns.

Strengths and weaknesses are components of any community. The differences in quality of life are determined by the contributions of each individual, especially those who have a real sense of belonging to a specific group and maintain tight relationships with their pasts. All persons bring their own experiences and develop their ways of thinking based on past episodes, present influences, and future expectations. The great asset that diversity brings to the community springs from both the similarities and the dissimilar approaches that each individual brings. Antonio Karantonis discusses this in his book, *Perspectives of an Iconoclast*, by saying,

> Every citizen of a country has a clear conscience of their country, their national pride, and their cultural identity [...]. [We cannot define these concepts without interfering with the diverse view points of other cultures and sub-cultures [because] cultural and national identity is truly in the eye of the beholder. Within a culture there are varying political and philosophical norms; some of those norms are located at opposite poles of one another [then,] one cannot deny the unique influence that diverse ethnic groups have in adding their significant contributions to a society's cultural makeup as a whole (Karantonis 2005, 13).

Karantonis's view reconfirms the value of people as individuals and in a group. A diverse composition broadens a community and also reaffirms the concept that we have all become citizens of the world. In this situation, positive thinking supports the idea and clarifies the conviction that this permanent mixture of ethnicities, cultures, languages, and customs offers us more opportunities to grow, both as individuals and as a society. More important, diversity brings authenticity and permits us the free interchange of traditions that opens avenues of learning and sharing so we can respect, different viewpoints and adjust our traditional ways of thinking.

Positive thinking encourages an open mind that respects and accepts the advantages of differences. It helps us appreciate the things that make us unique. Before we can do that, though, we must know and appreciate ourselves. Being aware of your own assets and the things that make you different will help you understand otherness. Keep in mind that real peace is not just the absence of violence, but the presence of trust, respect, and confidence within us as well as others.

In brief, tolerance is the first step for the elimination of hatred and racism. An appreciation of differences represents a sensitive approach to understanding diversity and creating awareness. Tolerance deters hate but it does not guarantee inclusion. On the contrary, it perpetuates segregation. Acceptance is the higher level of understanding that guarantees inclusion and the value of differences. It helps to avoid prejudice and exclusion. You can reach your maximum level of acceptance through the process of receptivity, which means not just objective acceptance, but a respectful consent to the positive-thinking approach of seeing the same thoughts and objects from different perspectives. Receptiveness recognizes and affirms the extraordinary value of human dignity.

It is when people feel free to be who they really are that the spirit of true acceptance and diversity flourishes. Just remember that the most marvelous episodes of life come mainly through our differences, so understanding and accepting differences becomes an advantage in any system. Acceptance, however, is possible only if you develop a predisposition for receptiveness, which is an unconscious way to reinforce sensitivity. Acceptance is a conscious, objective, and rational way to understand differences. It does not necessarily mean agreement, but respect. Receptiveness tends to be more subjective because it embraces the emotions and sentiments that arise from personality. The combination of acceptance and receptiveness leads to a higher level of understanding differences and a wider spectrum for promoting cultural competence.

A culturally competent environment provides the ideal scenario for promoting a system that works effectively and efficiently in cross-cultural settings and addresses all the common roadblocks we often find on the road to cultural sensitivity. Knowing and understanding cultural diversity and the differences that spring from social and economic classes boosts positive thinking. Understanding diversity will help you accept the different ways that people interact with others.

Understanding diversity and the culture of acknowledging differences is a process you should implement and sustain in all areas at all times. For instance, in the workforce you need to develop proactive initiatives if you want to recruit, orient, retain, and promote people from all constituent groups. That includes, but it is not limited to, respecting cultural and ethnic differences, viewpoints, and diverse opinions. All organizations need this mind-set in place from the top to the bottom to prevent the stereotypes that so often destroy relationships and create an unbalanced access to services and a disproportionate administration of justice.

Stereotypes or prejudices are typical attitudes toward others based on conjectures and/or preconceived assumptions about a group. It is a quick and automatic determination, fed mainly by accumulated misinformation and/or internalized oppression. It leads us to judge, consciously or unconsciously, people whom we consider different from us. Remember, it helps us discover our own authenticity and perform according to the way we really are when we become aware of the importance of individual uniqueness.

Positive thinking and the pursuit of happiness are intrinsically linked with the need to understand differences. One of the best ways to maintain proactive approaches and develop better ways to communicate is by paying attention and respecting other people's perspectives and concerns. The humility it takes to understand differences implies a commitment to become aware of and sensitive to the diverse composition of our society. It implies awareness, acknowledgement, and acceptance of different customs, values, opinions, and traditions.

Understanding and Accepting Diversity

Pascal Zachary says in his book, *The Diversity Advantage*, that diversity helps define the health and wealth of nations because competitive, political, cultural, and economic power relies on the racial mixture that any community can experience in a world with more than 5,000 ethnic groups and at least 600 active languages. We are such a diverse people that any community has uncountable ways to see and understand the miracles of life.

The theory of human evolution has generated controversy and creates difficulties in our understanding of human differences and therefore the acceptance of diversity. One of the concerns natural selection creates is the growth and development of racism and the assumption that some ethnicities are superior to others. This is one reason why it becomes even more important to accept diversity and the prevalence of elemental human rights, which recognizes the dignity and contributions of all human beings. We were all created equal. That does not mean we are the same. It means that we have equal access to all our rights, a principle behind the Declaration of the Universal Human Rights of 1948. This document considers all human rights as universal, inviolable, unrestrictive, and interdependent. It recognizes people are free to express their individuality and exercise their authenticity.

The state of human rights in the United States has changed dramatically over the past 50 years. The Civil Rights, Voting Rights, and Age Discrimination Acts of the 1960s helped identify and eliminate—at least legally—widespread discrimination. In the 1970s and 1980s, the Affirmative Action principle allowed people of color access to the same opportunities in the workforce. In the 1990s and up through the present we have begun understanding diversity in a broader and more affirmative way. Sometimes it took a single person, a Rosa Parks or a Martin Luther King, Jr., to challenge the system or defy the status quo so everyone could enjoy basic rights without consideration of social, cultural, or economic status. The election of Barack Obama as the first African-American president of the United States marked a landmark example of the possibilities of overcoming institutional racism. The nomination and confirmation of Sonia Sotomayor as the first Latina named to the U.S. Supreme Court is another example of the opportunities that have opened up for future generations. Nevertheless, we have not reached the point where equal rights and opportunities are available to all. Over the course of human history human rights have never been granted, but demanded. Future progress remains an individual and collective responsibility.

The main idea behind diversity is to ensure that all cultural backgrounds can become integrated into society without being denied cultural, philosophical, or religious identity. It also allows them to adopt the best practices from their original or adopted cultures so they can identify who they really are. In the words of Jack Lannom, "Diversity, rather than being a source of comparison and competition, should be a source of wonder and admiration" (Lannom 1998, 71). It should be a cause of pride and not shame. Nobody loses by accepting diversity. In fact, it helps people discover their strengths and accept their weaknesses. Diversity lets people retain their sense of individuality and allows them to contribute different perspectives to society as a whole.

Joseph Campbell wrote, "The privilege of a lifetime is being who you are." That's the goal for a society with a free interaction of cultures, customs, and traditions, when people can exercise their principles and select their choices instead of having them imposed on them. It is for these reasons that people have been developing a new way of looking at the process of assimilation. Instead of the old "melting pot" theory, we now have the "fruit salad" concept. In the melting pot, everyone lost some individual identity for the benefit of the whole. With the fruit salad concept, each part of the whole retains its identity and flavor and yet contributes to the excellence of the final product. In this concept people can keep individual identity and special characteristics. The resulting blend of diverse groups injects new cultures and traditions into society without necessarily changing them. It opens minds to the advantages of transnational citizenship, as has taken place with the European Union. Pascal Zachary cites one example in novelist Amin Maalout, who was born in Lebanon and spent almost half of his life in France. Asked if he feels more Lebanese or more French, Maalout answered, "Identity can't be compartmentalized. You can't divide it up into halves or thirds or any other separate segments. I haven't got several identities. I've just one, made up of many components in a mixture that is unique to me, just as other people's identity is unique to them as individuals" (Zachary 2003, 6).

Since positive thinking focuses primarily in addressing people's strengths and only later on individual concerns, the acceptance of diversity similarly focuses attention on the advantages, talents, abilities, and strengths of people before addressing disadvantages, limitations, and weaknesses. In this era of globalization, the increasingly multiethnic society and the spread of interracial marriage generates a constant recreation of identity. That makes it all the more important for a diverse society to accept differences with sensitivity and allow its members free expression of their own authenticity.

Whether a country receives immigrants or sees its own citizens leaving for other lands, it has the potential to win or lose something. Countries can benefit from the advantage of becoming more diverse, or suffer when new arrivals raise undue concerns about ethnic conservation or cultural dissemination. Tensions can rise in countries where people feel that new arrivals are taking their jobs. This book is not intended to debate the advantages or disadvantages of immigration policies. My sole purpose is to demonstrate the importance of accepting diversity and the benefits it gives to any society.

The fact of the matter is that the mixture of talent, ingenuity, creativity, and innovative views that fresh waves of immigrants bring with them have helped sustain policies that welcome new arrivals, at least those who come from pre-selected countries. In the world today we must accept the diverse composition of our society. Immigration and a consequent increase in diversity has been a fact of life throughout history. As Pascal Zachary says, "Sociologically, biologically, historically, we are all from somewhere else, outsiders to one degree or another." As American writer Fae Myenne observes, "We all have an immigrant ancestor, one who believed in America; one who, daring or duped, took sail [to pursue the promised land, the American dream, or the land of freedom]" (Zachary 2003, 43). It is not a lack of patriotism that drove people to leave their native lands to accept new soil as home. The need to retain a feeling for one's origins did not spring from an absence of respect for a new country. It came from a deep conviction of the importance of diversity and the need to respect the authenticity of the individual without affecting the harmony of the nation as a whole.

We cannot divide ourselves based on origin or color. We are all residents of some country, with guaranteed sacred rights. That is even more significant in the United States, a country created and reshaped by immigrants. In the European Union, new citizens find that they are legally and constitutionally part of this concept of social and economic integration. It is another way to provide social and ethnic interrelationships with the invaluable benefit of cross-cultural interactions.

Nationalism can unify a country if we keep the clear understanding that we are also diverse. The imposition of assimilation does not make a country strong. It may look solid, but it will be weak in its internal composition. True patriotism does not derive from law books, but from the civic commitment of its citizens. Nationalism is not endowed at birth, but is a sentiment that people develop over the years through their courage, character, and loyalty.

With that in mind, I would like to share the following quote that I read at one of the exhibits at the National Civil War Museum in Harrisburg, Pennsylvania. It was written by an Irish-born private who fought for the Union in the conflict that threatened to tear the country apart. He wrote, "This is my country as much as a man who was born on the soil [...] I have as much interest in the integrity of the nation as any other man." So why do we assign difference between those who were born here and those who have just arrived? Why do we allow segregation and discrimination and harbor unconscious stereotypes and conscious prejudices that divide and separate us?

Stereotypes are common assumptions we make about characteristics or behaviors of different groups. They usually originate due to the ignorance or an inability to acknowledge different people and diverse cultural backgrounds. Stereotypes can also be reinforced by a resistance to accept the existence of the essential nature of individual and community differences. Prejudice, on the other hand, is a "rigid attitude that [...] predisposes an individual to feel, think, or act in a negative way toward another person or group" (Verderber & Verderber 2005, 39).

A commitment to maintain positive thinking involves, at minimum, an agreement to improve our knowledge, understanding and, hopefully, acceptance of the world's diverse composition. If any of you readers are recently descended from immigrants, as is the situation with so many in the United States, my humble advice is to analyze your viewpoints, challenge your way of thinking, and develop informed responses before judging or stereotyping others.

Sensitivity is a key component when we want to have meditated and rationalized approaches to diversity. When we seek a true commitment to diversity, we should start by asking for policies and procedures that freely permit community engagement, shared responsibilities, and equal benefits. This way of thinking offers an opportunity for us to open the closed mind-set of isolation and affirm a conviction to see a wider spectrum of possibility. For those who are forced to deal with intolerance and cultural rejection, I offer the thinking of Eleanor Roosevelt, who said, "Remember, no one can make you feel inferior without your consent" (Theibert 1997, 143).

So celebrate diversity, enjoy your fortune, share your wealth, and enjoy life. That is how you can bring synergy to your diverse community and truly understand the strength we derive from our differences. In fact, the context of synergy is a little more than just comparing cultures, weighting values, or testing principles. The need to find common values and share similar principles is as important as the necessity of accepting differences and allowing everyone their authenticity. It is really a fundamental asset for finding common ground and generating the synergy we need to face present and future challenges. "Synergy means that the relationship which the parts have to each other is a part in and of itself," writes Stephen Covey. "The essence of synergy is to value differences [,]—to respect them, to build on strengths, [and] to compensate for weaknesses" (Covey 1989, 263).

Additionally, understanding diversity and applying synergy is not something that we can simply plan to do. It is something we must actively promote. The presence of diversity is a fact; by understanding it we will see it correctly as an asset and not wrongly as a disadvantage. As Pascal Zachary has discussed, the diverse composition of our communities has allowed the creation of a hybrid society that tacitly expresses the dynamic of people's differences. This ongoing process of acculturation is what I prefer to call "cross-cultural interactions." Zachary calls it a "hybrid modern civilization" (Zachary 2003, 110).

We must understand diversity and accept differences if we want to prevent rancor, reduce negative assumptions, and balance perceptions so we can truly understand the world's realities. It is also a necessity if we want to maintain each individual's dignity, freedom, and equality. In order to grow as a society, we must understand, respect, and accept our differences as well as our similarities. Equality does not mean we have to create the same models, patterns, or ideals. Equality means we all have access to equivalent rules and opportunities. At the same time, equity means we must create the rules, norms, laws, and policies that ensure we will address disparities, stop discrimination, and eliminate segregation.

Finally, an inability to understand differences can easily advance from an initial divergence of opinion when confronting multinational and multiethnic issues to an unconscious frame of reference that insists on segregating people. This can happen when you begin labeling some portions of the population by class, affiliation, or inclination. One of the worst ways of segregating people is by social condition or economic status. Consequently, the acceptance of diversity, as well as an understanding of poverty, becomes crucial as you develop creative strategies to maintain positive thinking and generate more enjoyment as you pursue happiness.

Understanding Poverty

Dr. Ruby Payne defines poverty as "the extension to which an individual does without resources" (Payne 1996, 176). Payne makes it clear that poverty springs from the lack of basic resources, not just the absence of money. We can measure poverty by noting people's access to elemental assets that include, but are not limited to, mental, spiritual, physical, and emotional assistance.

Poverty is relative. As Dr. Payne says, "Poverty or wealth only exists in relationship to known quantities or expectations" (Payne 1996, 2). You can find it in all groups of people and in all countries. Because poverty is the lack of access to basic needs you can measure it by quantifying the availability of these resources. There are two forms of poverty, generational and situational. To paraphrase Dr. Payne, generational poverty exists when a situation has lasted for more than two generations. Situational poverty is a lack of assets due to extenuating circumstances or temporary conditions.

Poverty has been associated exclusively with the lack of material assets. Nevertheless, an insight into poverty demonstrates that it includes a little more than just the lack of financial resources. In fact, there are ten basic resources involved with the culture of poverty. Dr. Payne mentions nine of them: financial, emotional, mental, spiritual, physical, support systems, relationships, the knowledge of hidden rules, and copying strategies (Payne 1996, 11). In addition, I believe that education is a tenth resource and its lack plays an important role in the increase of poverty. Education is an asset that, once granted, cannot be taken away from you.

The ability to leave a state of poverty depends more on the accessibility of factors beyond the financial ones. Of course, money will inevitably be a fundamental factor for alleviating severe poverty. A permanent source of income can secure productivity and stability but it is not enough to maintain sustainability. For instance, when we can satisfy our needs and aspirations, rationally and emotionally, monetary resources merely extend the pleasure we derive from other factors that are fundamental for our pursuit of better ways to enjoy life. Monetary resources represent just one of several factors that can address poverty, self-sufficiency, sustainability, and happiness. As James Nicholas says, "We certainly need money to satisfy our necessities; otherwise, we would be unhappy. But once our basic needs are met, further increments of money do not lead to further increments of happiness, except marginally" (Nicholas 2008, 25).

I have addressed most of the nine basic resources Dr. Payne identifies in different chapters. For instance, financial resources are income streams we need for reasonable access to supplies and services. Those resources usually come from a good career, the right marketing of talents and skills, entrepreneurial initiatives, a faithful commitment to succeed, and so forth. That usually requires access to formal and informal education, organizational skills, positive relationships, connections, and the intuition to discover and utilize opportunities.

Positive mental abilities come from the appropriate use of moderated behaviors, intelligent responses, proactive thinking, and intellectual approaches to the challenges of daily life. We also have emotional possessions—feelings, motivations, and ways of behaving. We assume that everyone has access to basic emotional resources, but often people mired in poverty remain unaware of them. They also need to develop the ability to calm down, reflect, create alternatives, and make critical and balanced decisions as they confront their difficulties. Such approaches allow people to control their emotions and balance them with the logic of their rationality.

One source of support, which I have already addressed, is spirituality, which represents our faith and beliefs. Spirituality is an invaluable asset, especially when you remember that the ultimate purpose of human existence is to find the power that inner peace brings. Spirituality, found in our deepest convictions and exercised in the holistic conception of our body, brings meaning and purpose to our lives and makes us better people. As Eckhart Tolle says, "You do not become good by trying to be good, but by finding the goodness that is already in you, and allowing that goodness to emerge" (Tolle 2008, 164). Another valuable resource is our physical assets, which include the gifts we receive as well as the responsibility of taking care of them appropriately. Acknowledging that your body is your temple is essential to care for it rationally, feed and release it emotionally, and treat it respectfully.

Having a healthy mind and a vigorous body will let you mentally, emotionally and spiritually balance your human necessities without overriding your unique purpose and mission in life. Your physical resources are those possessions that belong to you, including body, intellect, feelings, and spirit. You find a sincere approach to the true concept of happiness and the mitigation of poverty when you experience the special sensations created and enjoyed by your body, prized by your heart, appreciated by your mind, and treasured by your soul.

By recognizing and identifying the direction of your life you develop the motivation to develop the social skills you need to escape from generational poverty. There is a difference between those who are trapped by poor self-esteem and negativism as they confront life's challenges, and those who find themselves temporarily bound by the inequalities of economic differences due to situational adversity. In both cases there are two important assets that can help: access to social support systems and the ability to navigate societal relations. The first asset, social support systems, is linked to the basic resources that government, institutions, and organizations offer the community in the form of economic assistance, human services, charitable programs, tax credits, social programs, grants, and so forth. Of course, these resources are more available in economically and industrially developed countries.

The second factor is significant relationships, which are fundamental assets for getting ahead and climbing the ladder of social and economic classes. By creating healthy relationships and investing in social interaction you gain access to positive role models who can provide advice to help you create a better vision of your purpose in life. Teachers, social workers, and human service providers play an important role in this. Money is important, but in some ways the most valuable tools for leaving poverty come from education, talent and life skills, and accessibility to positive and healthy relationships.

A personal vision or intrinsic goal will help too. This will give you a sense of purpose. Education and skills prepare you for both expected and unexpected opportunities. In addition, healthy relationships with positive role models can provide connections with people who can help you rise. These positive relationships offer practical ways to induce strategic and systematic change. They might also help you understand what Dr. Ruby Payne calls the "hidden rules of the economic classes." To paraphrase Dr. Payne, these hidden rules are implicit habits of a group or patterns of behavior that everyone brings in relationship to a specific environment (Payne 1996, 37). When people understand of the patterns of behavior within the economic classes, they have a better sense of how to confront difficult situations, respect opinions, and understand different points of view. You should not use these rules to make assumptions about individual behavior, but understanding the hidden rules of the economic classes will help you promote relationships of mutual respect because the patterns of behavior in each economic class lead to different viewpoints of life, time, space, and commitment.

For instance, according to Dr. Payne's research, the driving forces in the poverty culture are survival, relationships, and entertainment. The forces that drive the middle classes, by comparison, are work and achievement. The priority here is job stability and education. In the wealthy class, the driving forces are financial, political, and social connections (Payne 1996, 42-43).

Understanding these patterns of behavior will help you comprehend some challenges that other people face in their daily lives.

Education, awareness of current conditions, self-control, and information are important when we face challenges like poverty. "The price of education [formal and informal] is paid only once," says Jack Lannom; "the cost of ignorance must be paid forever" (Lannom 1998, 120). Understanding cause and effect is a vital part of recognizing your power of choice. When you don't measure your actions, you tend to react impulsively so you will not have the resources you need to act the way you should under unpredictable circumstances. Sometimes you can ruin your entire life over a quick and unexpected overreaction. "Fully half the cases in our criminal courts originate in little things," says Frank S. Hogan, a former district attorney from New York. "Barroom bravado, domestic wrangling, an insulting remark, a disparaging word, a rude action—those are the little things that lead to assault and murder" (Carnegie 1981, 310).

Proactive decisions come from both rational and sensitive approaches. Reactive responses, on the other hand, arise from emotional inclinations rather than rational thinking. Before we move on, let's first confirm that intellect has nothing to do with poverty. There is no evidence to support the assumption that being poor means to be ignorant or lack intelligence. In fact, an aspiration for education and the virtue of acquiring information are important for any economical group. The real distinction is the way that people from different classes perceive schooling.

For example, in situations of generational poverty, education often seems to be an abstract concept instead of a concrete one. Education requires planning and involves the future, considerations that are secondary for people who live permanently in a survival mode. It is not my intention to judge patterns of behavior here. My primary purpose is to make you understand that we all have problems. However, we cannot be naïve by pretending we all have the same resources and opportunities. Many people are limited by extreme social and economic differences in a society where different classes have a disproportionate level of access to opportunity.

To truly understand poverty we need to perceive its patterns. These patterns, however, are not absolute, but relative. All models of behavior have exceptions. All poor people do not behave the same way so we cannot stereotype or create prejudices by assuming ways of behavior. But in order to concentrate our thinking on creating a permanent generation of positive thinkers, we must understand those who may differ from our social, economic, spiritual, or political views. This is why communication skills play such an important role in social interactions. By communication I mean the process of sharing meaning, a process determined by our level of attention, environment, and social context. When we do communicate we must be careful how we express our ideas. What we say as well as how we pronounce and emphasize our words have significant importance to the people with whom we interact. Furthermore, the style, tone, and gestures that we use have an impact on whether we can create relationships of mutual respect.

Poverty is a society-wide problem and addressing it is not the sole responsibility of either individuals or government. It is an all-inclusive, shared responsibility for everyone. Any potential solution to poverty must come from a collaborative effort that employs fundamental values of solidarity centered on a strong base, a focus on solutions, and an approach to the best modeling practices.

One other thing to consider when discussing poverty is the perception of time and the way it differs among economic classes. For those in poverty, the present time is always the most important, so they make decisions based on the feelings of the moment. That differs from the perspective of the middle class, where decisions are based on future ramifications. My humble advice to all of us is that we invest our time wisely and use it appropriately.

A lack of planning and organization is also a typical pattern for people in generational poverty. Often the poverty-stricken lack the resources necessary for organizing not only any material assets they may have, but their spiritual and mental resources as well. As I said earlier, personal organizational skills are important for the planning process, so this is an issue that must be addressed if we want to alleviate generational poverty. Of course, I do not want to imply that a lack of planning and organization is an exclusive characteristic of people in poverty.

Keep in mind that I am talking about overall patterns. While it is clear that lack of organizational skills exists in all socio-economic classes and cultures, my main point is that people's ability to organize themselves is typically a transcultural asset and an extraordinary resource for those who want to leave poverty. It helps people maintain order, clarify their views, and advance toward their desired future. Living in poverty has been described as the "oppression of the moment" or the "tyranny of the urgent." Both descriptions underline how the subjugation of the immediate present traps people in a desperate cycle of dependency, usually without plans or strategies for the future.

Since my basic goal is to highlight the value and dignity of all human beings, I think it's important that I provide ways to ensure the self-determination, proactive approaches, and confidence needed to create productive citizens. One approach is to create an environment where people are aware of economic differences and make an effort to allow equal access to services and opportunities through collaboration instead of competition. The main idea is to create self-reliant people who value themselves. To reach this point, we need to open the window to collaboration by understanding the diverse components of our society. In addition to maintaining sensitivity to the composition of our already fragmented communities, positive thinking will help generate informed, rational, and innovative decisions instead of emotional or circumstantial assumptions. Poverty alone does not equate with dysfunctional behaviors. Those behaviors exist in all economic classes. However, the lack or complete nonexistence of resources among the poverty stricken will negatively impact people's perspectives.

As I mentioned, the intent of this book is to create awareness in the self-help discipline as well as in the spheres of personal and social responsibility. If we want to have a mission and purpose that leads us to a meaningful life, we must maintain equilibrium in both thought and action. Self-help is possible when we keep in mind the principle of giving back to others and the core value of solidarity. As the scriptures say, "I know the Lord maintains the cause of the needy, and executes justice for the poor" (Psalm 140:12). The message there is that we must make all efforts to find solutions to poverty, inequity, and injustice.

Understanding poverty requires us to look at the problem from different perspectives and analyze it instead of just expressing emotional negative assumptions. Yes, there are times when resources are lacking. I also understand that financial struggles can limit people's abilities to take action. It can also thwart their best intentions and decrease their ability to find positive approach to solving problems.

I recommend addressing just one concern at a time. Tackle problems one by one and little by little. Try to see every struggle as just one more barrier to overcome. It is also true that sometimes our problems hit us simultaneously, no matter what your economic environment might be. In those cases, the presence of the four basic internal and external personal resources becomes even more important to help you deal with stressful situations.

Proactive thinking becomes a key component when you're addressing fundamental issues such as material poverty and spiritual indigence. You can discourage negativity and focus your attention on your strengths by identifying and clarifying your concerns. Seek creative and alternative solutions instead of merely denying that the current situation exists. Even in the culture of poverty, the concept of imaginary visualization or the use of mental models are tools that can help you translate your thinking from the abstract or theoretical model to a concrete form of problem-solving.

The issue of poverty should concern all members of the community. I find it embarrassing that some people can live among abundance while others remain trapped in the most incomprehensible misery. In his book *La Persona y el Bien Común* (*The Person and the Common Well*) Jacques Maritain said that the contents of every community's common well must be distributed equally and replenished (Maritain 1988, 57). In other words, the duties of the entire society rest with us all.

Social responsibility is linked to positive thinking. Our society requires prevention as well as intervention. It has a critical need for both leaders and followers to use their minds and their hands to serve others. All of us should accept our duties as a social responsibility instead of living cloistered in our own self-sufficiency, comforted by the egoistic satisfaction of individual accomplishments or the selfish refuge of self-isolation. It is not right for us to refuse support of the more elemental human needs or excuse ourselves instead of extending our hand to those who need assistance.

As I mentioned before, we can do this through compassion, although the holistic and proactive approach of serving others above self is better defined through the concept of solidarity. Compassion means to be aware of the suffering of others. It helps us understand and feel sympathy for their struggles. Solidarity goes beyond compassion. It means we both acknowledge and intervene when others are suffering. It means we apply our resilience and empathy to alleviate their discomfort. Intervention forms the basis of compassion while involvement is an elemental component of solidarity. Solidarity means a commitment to deliver material, sociological, psychological, or spiritual aid above and beyond the informal contractual obligation to society that every individual owes. If there is something more detestable than poverty itself, it is the maintenance of the status quo or inaction that allows the spread of material, mental, and spiritual poverty.

In my view, the true poor are those who suffer penury in their hearts and poverty in their spirits, who have eyes yet cannot see the amazing wealth that exists inside them. In short, poverty is a matter of individual attitude. Diseases of the body kill thousands of people every day, yet there are also diseases that fatally hurt our sense of worth and infect us with the sad conformism of spirit. A lack of self-control, self-esteem, purpose, and meaning in our life creates what could be called the euthanasia of positive thinking. James Shengold describes it as "terminal thinking" (Garbarino 2000, 118) and described it as a condition were positive attitude and progressive purpose do not exist. Terminal thinking is one of the worst diseases because it affects our mind, hurts our soul, and pollutes our spirit.

The fight against poverty is a task for us all. Nevertheless, the main initiative must come from each individual's predisposition to change and a strong conviction to alter the status quo. The highest expression of self-confidence comes from our inner self; it is one of the most important assets in the battle against adversity. The pleasant moments we experience form a bridge that allows us to reach the pathway of happiness. However, something even more important than happiness is the attainment of love, wisdom, and peace of mind. These are things beyond price.

We measure our satisfaction by our level of achievement. Contentment is a stream of emotional wealth, and pleasure a flow of rational and physical comfort. "It is not how much we have, but how much of it we enjoy that determines our happiness," says James Nicholas (Nicholas 2008, 12). Possessions, culture, color, language, or spirituality may come to us by accident. We build the substance of life in the development of character, integrity, and values. In my view, everything depends on your commitment to think positively, your conviction to act accordingly, and your decision to live and enjoy the full flavor of life.

The struggles that cause stress, pain, and suffering do not necessarily come from a lack of money, but from a scarcity of mental, emotional, and spiritual resources. As Howard Cutler explains, there is a substantial difference between pain and suffering. Pain is a physical condition; it is mainly a physiological process. Suffering is a mental and emotional state; it is essentially a psychological response or reaction to the pain (Cutler 1998, 206-211). Most of the time, our attitude determines the degree of pain and the extent of suffering that any circumstance can cause us.

However, pain and suffering are not necessarily tragic. For one thing, they are usually temporary conditions. Sometimes they even aid growth. "When confronted honestly, pain can bear fruits of great importance. [...] It is a harsh reminder of what is essential. It can connect us to others. Yes suffering can harden us or make us more cynical, but it can also make us kinder" (Ferrucci 2006, 89). We can overcome the pathology of sadness by maintaining positive thinking and remaining aware of our assets. Don't let a crisis or temporary discomfort panic you. It could open up an opportunity for success. Nor should you let failure alarm you, because that too can lead to opportunity. Our main focus should not be to avoid suffering, but to accept it as a part of life and as a temporary condition along the road to happiness. Remember the words of an anonymous saying: "Beneath the presence of challenges, lies also the presence of unexpected hidden opportunities."

The predisposition to accept whatever we confront in life will bring us alternative choices to success. Remain conscious of the true factors of joy, the harmony of faith, richness of peace, abundance of love, and presence of meaning. Problems and difficulties will always exist on earth, to paraphrase Howard Cutler, but change for the better is always possible. It happens any time that you decide to be optimistic and apply positive thinking to all your actions (Cutler 2003, 33).

In conclusion, we can better understand poverty if we open our minds and accept that we can lose anything but confidence, faith, and hope. We may have limits on our material needs, but our thoughts and emotions will remain unlimited once positive thinking fills our minds with pragmatism, our hearts with enthusiasm, and our spirits with deep faith and self-assurance. Everything we do is not necessarily about today, but tomorrow. Every generation has the social and collective responsibility to create a legacy for the generation to come.

Chapter 8

Solidarity to Share

"For the measure with which you measure will in return be measured out you."

Luke 6:38 NAB

Chapter 8

Solidarity to Share

———◦•◦———

Solidarity is a humanitarian responsibility that includes, but it is not limited to, personal obligation, moral approach, and social attitude. It is a personal and collective duty where the sincerity of our actions transforms mandatory social accountability into a voluntary public commitment. Human commonality takes place when we convert community responsibility into the duty to help one another, respect each other's rights, exercise our private talents, and freely enjoy common assets.

One advantage to practicing solidarity is the law of reciprocity, which means that whatever we do to others tends to reflect back on us. That is why the effects of giving, especially spiritually and psychologically, are greater for the giver than the receiver. When you apply solidarity and practice the virtue of giving and sharing with others, you develop a deeper communication with yourself and develop a holistic interaction with all facets of your personhood. It may also help you achieve a higher level of understanding so you can become conscious of the inequities of our social structure.

Solidarity is a sincere commitment to others. It is the art of giving not just material goods, but also appreciation and companionship. Solidarity is a virtue, one that promotes world peace, public harmony, social cohesion, and sense of community. It also implies more than simple charity or pity. Effective social cohesion, occurs when every individual contributes to the benefit of society as a whole by helping those who are less fortunate and can't enjoy the resources and opportunities that should be available to all.

It is through individual and collective effort that we can find the root of solidarity and pursue the cooperative endeavor of local communities to create a renewed cultural, social, and economic order. This is in line with the thinking of Pope John XXIII, who emphasized the collective responsibility for building a sense of community in any society. He said, "Solidarity requires a *firm and persevering determination* to commit oneself to the *common good*; that is to say to the good of *all* and of each individual, because we are all really responsible for *all*" (*Sollicitudo Rei Socialis*, 1988, 38, 5-6).

The use of the power of positive thinking implies the inclusion of solidarity by making us conscious of the good fortune and unlimited wealth granted to only a few while the majority get an unjust share. Consequently, positive thinking asks us to observe the extreme disproportion in the distribution of wealth and advocate for the opportunity for everyone to enjoy basic human rights. Solidarity means we practice our commitment to accept our blessings with gratitude and share our good fortune, instruct others in self-sufficiency, and help reduce the disparities that affect villages, states, and countries.

One beauty of life is the ability to share your dreams, commitments, desires, and passion with others. That is why we need one another if we want to enjoy life or seek comfort from the temporary influence of misfortune. Have you ever dined in a wonderful five-star restaurant by yourself? Have you gone by yourself on a vacation trip? Have you ever been alone and discovered the misery of having no one with you? In these cases I am not talking about solitude, but loneliness.

The fact is that we need companionship. We need other people if we want to really understand and value material, emotional, and spiritual resources. We need family, friends, coworkers, and neighbors so we can share successes and challenges. The real value of humankind is to serve, give, share, provide, and gain friendship. Human beings should not live in isolation, but in association.

Fortunately, happiness is available and accessible. Happiness and the opportunity to express solidarity knock on our doors almost every day. However, if we want to utilize the benefits from all our natural, emotional, and spiritual resources, we must open the door. Express your initial gesture of solidarity to yourself and then transmit it to those around you. However, real solidarity means you also serve those who are far away.

Solidarity should be expressed in a sincere and disinterested way without any expectation that you will get something directly in return. One way to express solidarity is by assuming conscious responsibility for your community. Any individual can create pleasure and happiness, but the underlying message of solidarity is that you should share your blessings with others, especially those in need. In order to start that process, you should approach all individuals with respect, understanding, and compassion and treat them with dignity, kindness, and deepest empathy.

Therefore, if you feel pleased with the blessings of your life, then share them with those who have not yet discovered their gifts and talents. If you cannot give money or material goods, at least you can offer understanding, appreciation, and kindness. It could be as easy as delivering a sincere smile or providing genuine empathy or a conscious acceptance of people's differences. Our world has become accustomed to so much insensitivity that it has created what Eckhart Tolle calls "collective manifestation of insanity" (Tolle 2005, 11). This is a type of collective dysfunction that eats away at the divinity and extraordinary composition of humankind.

Violence, hatred, discrimination, and self-destruction often originate from a lack of information, awareness, and understanding, a tendency that stems from an absence of love and solidarity. We can also blame a lack of sensitivity, which is a self-imposed inability to differentiate facts from opinion, evidence from theories, perceptions from misinterpretations, and judgments from realities. Remember that even if you feel you are not getting anything back, you should still keep giving. You might not feel that you are getting a return for your efforts, but you will surely gain emotional and spiritual benefits from your kindness.

So, share! Donate or contribute to a cause even if you lack some resources. If you can't contribute money, donate your talents or share your knowledge. In the end you will receive as much as you give. In effect, as Jesus Christ said, you should practice solidarity with everyone without considering who the beneficiary may be. Practice solidarity with your neighbor, which means anyone who lives, works, or is around you. The Book of Matthew shows the basic principle of solidarity when the prophet describes the encounter between the Lord and a righteous man, who was going to be judged by his mission on earth. God glorifies the wise man by saying:

"For I was hungry and you gave Me food; I was thirsty and you gave Me drink; I was a stranger and you took Me in; I was naked and you clothed Me; I was sick and you visited Me; I was in prison and you came to Me." Then the righteous [man] will answer Him, saying, "Lord, when did we see You hungry and feed You, or thirsty and give You drink? When did we see You a stranger and take You in, or naked and clothe You? Or When did we see You sick, or in prison, and come to You?" And the King will answer and say to them, "Assuredly, I say to you inasmuch as you did it to one of the least of these My brethren you did it to Me." (Mathew 25: 35-40)

Genuine solidarity means to do good selflessly, regardless of the benefits. The difference between those who seek personal compensation and those who share their blessings with the less fortunate is an understanding that life on earth does not last forever. I recognize that in this often unjust world, the segregation of economic classes contributes to the spread of poverty. Never forget that giving brings more benefit to the giver than to the receiver. Perhaps you will be surprised to discover that you are already receiving back whatever you have contributed in the past. "It is truly in giving that we receive." That is the law of reciprocity and a hidden strength of giving.

Of course, sometimes you may not receive a gift from the same person you helped, but you may already be receiving prayers, blessings, and services from somebody else. Giving and receiving work together. When something is sincerely given, it is proportionally received. Deepak Chopra's *Seven Spiritual Laws of Success* highlights the natural law of cause and effect, which says that any action provokes energy that comes back to us in the same proportion (Chopra 1995, 37).

The point is that no matter your religious or spiritual background, what you give is small in comparison with what you get in return. Giving and receiving creates a flow of positive energy. If you want love, appreciation, and peace, you should deliver them, openly and sincerely. The key element in living a pleasurable life is to redistribute your blessings by serving others. As Victor Cousin, a French philosopher from the eighteenth century said, "You can only govern men by serving them." The Bible supports that thought by saying, "He who oppresses the poor reproaches his Maker, but he who honors Him has mercy on the needy" (Proverbs 14:31 NKJV).

Every year millions of our fellow human beings die from preventable diseases and the lack of food and water. Solidarity supports the belief that we must use our resources appropriately instead of wasting the abundance we have been granted. If we do not value our blessings, if we fail to recognize the dignity all human beings, if we do not foster understanding, goodwill, and peace all over the world, then we become tools of injustice.

Giving and sharing are effective ways to generate a proactive approach to the struggles of life. Meaningful intervention occurs through the power of giving and in the act of solidarity. Many humanitarian organizations, such as Rotary, Lions Clubs, and Kiwanis, prioritize community service as one of their principles. However, financial aid and community service may lose their impact when we give without empowering communities and fail in transforming the old notion of charity into the concept of solidarity.

For instance, Rotary, a private worldwide community service organization, bases its principles on a commitment to serve above self. This humanitarian approach is based on what Rotarians call "The Four Ways Test." These four principles, created by Herbert J. Taylor, establish a fundamental code for social interaction. The first asks, "Is it true?" and promotes the need for honesty and integrity. The second asks, "Is it fair to all concerned?" and raises the question of civil, social, and economic justice for everyone. The third principle asks, "Will it build goodwill and better friendships?" which assures the development of fellowship on local and international levels. Finally, the last test asks, "Will it be beneficial to all concerned?" This is another basic principle of solidarity, one that promotes our responsibility to take care of one another and make sure that the benefits for the individual will be also shared by the whole.

We can summarize these Rotarian principles as the supremacy of offering service above self and the exercise of servant leadership. Communities today suffer from a lack of true servant leaders. A servant leader is truly a guide, coach, manager, and chief who exercises solidarity and the power of giving. Leaders need followers, and followers need leaders. A servant leader is both, especially if his/her main commitment implies "service above self." "The servant is a giver and not a taker," says Jack Lannom. "He sows the seeds of self-sacrifice in order to reap a great harvest of good for others" (Lannom 1998, 18).

Solidarity and the power of giving can help alleviate the intolerable fact that millions of people lack access to water, food, health, and shelter. Are you doing something about it? Our fellow human beings need you; they need all of us. People in generational and situational poverty need our commitment to reduce the wide disparities that confront our social, economic, and political order.

When you do give, it should come without preconceived conditions or obligations. It should be given with love. That is the essence of genuine giving. Anything given without love is not really conferred, but merely delivered. Solidarity is an expression of genuine love. It is a virtue that you can implement, and when you do, you will find that the return on investment is priceless. According to Alasdair MacIntyre, the seeding of virtue is a matter of character. As a consequence, virtue becomes a high-merit endeavor that leads to meaning, coherence, and purpose (Haidt 2006, 166). An act of solidarity without true love is like praying for money without work or getting a promotion without deserving it.

Jack Lannom interprets true love as "a mental attitude of commitment, not an unstable, whimsical feeling. [...] [Additionally], loving people is not just the right thing to do; it is the only way to live" (Lannom 1998, 23-79). Consequently, when you give earnestly, it should come from your heart, not merely from your wallet. Prophet Joel reaffirms that by saying God summons us to "Rend your hearts, not your garments" (Joel 2:12-18). If you cannot give financial resources or material goods, give your time, deliver advice, provide mentoring, embark on missionary trips, or collaborate with humanitarian foundations. There are many ways of serving, sharing, and collaborating.

One of the worse psychological diseases comes from a lack of love and affection. There can be pain even in a family environment. It may come from divorce, lack of parenting skills, lack of respect and compassion, a rejection of the elderly, or a shortage of solidarity. On a larger scale, these kinds of behaviors hurt the entire world. That is why we must first seek change in our inner selves before we can look for change in others. Peace, love, compassion, gratitude, and solidarity are some of the different pathways that will help us find happiness. We will always need positive thinking and self-determination if we want to transform our world. It is possible, and we can do it if we start with ourselves. You can make a difference by giving and promoting joyfulness, solidarity, and love.

A well-known rule for achieving positive results is to maintain equanimity in times of triumphs and serenity in times of challenge. That is why peace of mind tends to have more meaning than happiness. The art of life is to use your time and resources wisely while enjoying any second of peace that comes along. Do that by generating unending positive energy, smiling always, laughing often, and offering love. Exercise peace of mind and enjoy happiness by becoming involved and giving back to your community.

There is a big difference between becoming involved with others and merely being interested in their issues. In this world at least a billion people suffer from severe poverty and public neglect. This is not tolerable. Those who have been blessed with abundance should share it with those who lack almost everything. The first step is to take an interest and become aware of the facts. Get involved and support people's efforts to become better. Interest alone will not be enough. It is an incomplete approach, taken by people who merely pretend to resolve our current problems without taking an active role. The mandatory code of human responsibility and the ethical policy of social solidarity require involvement and participation. We must act and become involved to create positive change in our communities.

Sometimes, just a commitment to change and find self-reliance is not enough. Sharing resources or investing monetary capital may not prove sufficient either. The essence of productive change comes through the seeding, bridging, and bonding of social capital and self-determination instead of the exclusive practice of charity and pity. Becoming interested is a good thing, but it is not a great or primary step. Being interested means you feel pity and compassion. Being committed means you become part of the quest for justice and solidarity. Becoming involved offers you thousands of opportunities to experience the pleasure of solidarity and give your voice to those who do not have one.

The following tale is a concrete example of the difference between being interested and being involved:

Once upon a time, a chicken and a pig were good friends. They lived in a town with widespread poverty where many people went hungry every day. The animals wanted to help. The chicken said, "I have an idea of how you and I can help these poor people. I could give the eggs I lay and you could make some of your big body into ham so we could give the people a breakfast of ham and eggs." "I understand your concern," the pig answered. "But what is just a donation for you is a total commitment for me." This is the different between being interested and being involved.

Solidarity is not just the pleasure of giving, but also the gratification of sharing. Solidarity involves the application of the rule to "Love one to another," a rule that is valued in almost all religions and practiced by Christians, Jews, and Muslims. Some spiritual beliefs, such as Buddhism, Zoroastrianism, and Hinduism, base their principles on this elemental commitment to take care of one another. Where the Christian Bible teaches, "Treat others the way you would have them treat you" (Matthew 7:12), the Jewish Talmud Shabbat 3id expresses as, "What is hateful to you, do not do your fellow man." In Islam, the Sunnah says, "No one of you is a believer until he desires for his brother that which he desires for himself." Other spiritual orientations also promote the elemental requirement of solidarity. For instance, the Udana-Varga 5, 18, states that "Hurt not others in ways that you yourself would find hurtful." The Hindu Mahabhrata 5, 1517, expresses a similar principle by saying, "This is the sum of duty: do naught unto others which would cause you pain if done to you."

Solidarity is a requirement but also a benefit. One of the ways you can gain from practicing solidarity is through spiritual and emotional development. Such personal growth is more important than simply seeking happiness or accomplishing your goals. Wisdom and self-development leads to maturity and an awareness of the links between life, time, action, and purpose. It is by continuing the process of growth that people get the experience to succeed and the ability to overcome whatever barriers they may confront. As Jack Lannom says:

> If we are not growing, we are shrinking! If we're not improving, we are repressing! If we're not living, we're dying! Our life's focus should be on health and growth. If we are not moving forward, then we are slipping back. The only way to move forward is to challenge the limits we've always known and to embrace the improvements that will help us to hurdle those barriers [and defy those things that are hidden or unknown to us] (Lannom 1998, 102).

We are not expressing solidarity if we are not genuine about it in all our ways of acting and thinking. Our thoughts and attitude reflect the authenticity of our inner self. In other words, the prism through which we assimilate our perceptions plays a fundamental role in expressing who we really are. A frank analysis of our thoughts is necessary to sustain the continuity of solidarity. That is why we must maintain a permanent communication between our physical aspects and the internal equivalent of our soul. This kind of self-awareness moves us beyond the physical capacity of our senses and allows the intelligent, emotional, and spiritual intervention into our thoughts.

For instance, we may see ourselves in a mirror and contemplate the material aspect of our body. If we look closely we may see the essence of our self reflected in our face, although it is transmitted from our spirit. It is the true reflection of our soul and our inner self. You experience life completely when you connect your interior with your exterior, your spiritual action with your faithful commitments, and your rationality with your emotional counterpart. Find awareness of your inside and outside worlds and you will see what you are and what you would like to be.

Authenticity provides the real connection between you and the world inside yourself. Solidarity is the correlation between you and the world outside. Both worlds are intrinsically connected and related to your ways of thinking. Spirituality, beliefs, and faith are means of finding the true essence of your self, although some people may develop alternative methods to find themselves. Sometimes your responses may express your convictions in ways that cannot always be seen, touched, or even felt. This type of self-assessment involves holding up the mirror to your own soul so you can rediscover who you truly are and analyze how you are doing.

There will always be ways to release the creativity, motivation, and stimulation from your internal, interconnected self. Sometimes the connection between mind and spirit occurs in simple events such as listening to people, understanding their concerns, offering a smile, or being sincere in your kindness and appreciation. Solidarity is not the exclusive delivery of material needs, but the fundamental action of giving from your heart instead of merely from your mind. Sometimes a hug, a smile, or good advice is not enough, but it can at least reestablish someone's belief in the power of choice, confidence in the explosive energy of life, and trust in the value of positive thinking.

Real solidarity means helping others without expecting to be compensated for the assistance, but keeping an invaluable reward from enjoying your actions. The application of solidarity does not mean we lose our possessions, but merely that we give freely. When we help others, we help ourselves. That is the precious value of solidarity. The sharing process helps us exercise compassion and express love. Henrietta Mears wrote that people who are busy helping those who are less fortunate usually don't have time to envy those who are more fortunate (Maxwell 1998, 60). Solidarity is a commitment on the personal and societal levels. The heart of social justice comes from allowing people to test their abilities and enjoy equal participation in the benefits granted to the whole and not merely to the few.

Therefore, it is not right to condescend to those who are worse off than us. We must use kindness and sensitivity even with those who are imprisoned, suffer from behavioral challenges, or face situations of psychological desperation. James Garbarino says that the approach of any human services agency or detention center should be "gentle but firm, always kind [...] [and proactive instead of] the old rules where the outlook was to oppress, deprive, isolate and punish" (Garbarino 2000, 220). In these places positivism is fundamental to reduce recidivism and to ensure the prevalence of the positive thinking.

We need solidarity in this world of challenges. The aid you provide can be financial or it can be a food donation. Whatever it is, your way of giving back to the community will always be appreciated if your intention to help others comes from your heart and not just from your pocket. Give with the firm intention of creating independence and opportunities to produce individual self-sufficiency and community self-support. It is one of the great ways of creating relationships of lasting value and creating healthy social interactions.

C h a p t e r   9

Positive Relationships

———◆———

*"Many people will walk in and out of your life, but only true friends
will leave footprints in your heart."*

Anonymous

Chapter 9

Positive Relationships

Positive relationships develop the social skills we need to succeed in life. They also promote capabilities that can help us start climbing the socioeconomic ladder and chase success. It is to our advantage when we can interact in a diverse socio-economical environment. That capability allows for more encounters with success and a sense of realization.

Rational and emotional health, as well as social and public competence, are fed by two basic streams: formal/informal education and social/business networking. The combination of education and connections will help accomplish your mission and achieve your purpose in life. You do it by utilizing a positive-thinking approach where you perceive any action or occurrence as an opportunity for growth. "Opportunities are never lost," according to an old saying; "those that you do not use, somebody else will get them." Relationships are important; but they can be positive or negative. Positive relationships will help you advance and become aware of the difficulties you will face as you pursue your objectives. Negative influences will diminish and even annihilate you. As Jean-Paul Sartre said, "Both hell and heaven may come across in our interaction with other people" (Haidt 2006, 133).

Positive and negative relationships influence our societal interactions. Some interactions help us succeed; others hold us back. Some things, such as lack of education, social exclusion, racism, religion intolerance, and economic differences, will throw up barriers to interaction. For instance, many people are excluded because of differences in economic or social class. These distinctions are so impregnated in our world that discussion is not so much about who is up or down as who is included and who is not. True social inclusion will occur only when a community respects diversity, promotes the unique value of all human beings, and highlights the significant contribution of differences in any society.

However, a substantial and consistent learning process will be necessary before we reach significant relationships of mutual respect. Until then there will be a lack of social interaction as long as one class, group, community, or state predominates and pretends racial dominance over other human beings. In effect, humankind will remain wracked by conflict until it deals with the problems of increased manifestation of delusion, lack of purpose, and absence of the individual and collective mission.

Positive thinking and proactive attitude is possible. The process starts when we accept the differences between individuals and the combined and shared responsibility of the whole. We need this dual interaction to find common ground as we improve our societal dealings. We must start by developing these concepts within ourselves even if that forces us to move outside our accustomed comfort level.

Our relationships provide a fundamental base for the development of our social capital and economic development. Cultivating and maintaining positive relationships is a personal decision. It starts with the interactions within your own family and the development of close fellowship. It becomes a social practice of selecting partners, associates, friends, colleagues, coworkers, and companionship through common activities, shared goals, and societal commitments. Openness to relationships of mutual respect is fundamental if we want to accomplish our life mission and practice our learning experiences.

Networking remains one of the main means of navigating in the current world system. For instance, in the United States and other developed countries, networking is a necessity if you want to become visible, create contacts, and make connections. You can be a genius with extraordinary abilities but that doesn't mean you can enclose yourself in a comfort zone of self-imposed mental fences or introverted personality styles. By remaining self-enclosed you hide yourself away from the thousand of opportunities that arise in social networking settings.

Interactive social relationships provide the basis for networking, which is an ongoing way of connecting people with each other. Networking is a continuous interaction of giving and receiving. It is a channel in which we can exercise solidarity. As Frishman and Lublin state, "Implicit in networking is the understanding that there will be a giving, an exchange" (Frishman & Lublin 2004, 6). The wisdom of networking comes by finding mutual benefits, but its true essence lies in the art of giving, sharing, and connecting to others.

Networking is primarily a form of business communication in which you interact with others and promote the resources that you bring for reciprocal relationships. Networking is an interchange of culture, voices, information, experiences, and best practices in gaining expertise and making informed and worthy choices. Networking transmits information so people know who you know.

One of the basic rules of networking is that you should not limit yourself to a restricted circle. You must expose yourself to others who can open avenues of opportunity. You must also dedicate yourself to the permanent task of developing your social skills. Use your social and economic interactions to form associations and develop potential partnerships.

Networking is a subject that most schools do not teach. The middle and upper classes tend to look on networking as something we understand automatically, but it is not automatic in the lower economic levels or where education is lacking. People can say they know the importance of investing in relationships, but a failure to understand the real value can limit their ability to develop available resources. Some people feel that participation in events, fundraisers, cocktail parties, and business gatherings is a waste of time. In fact, such activities offer access to a pool of potential friends, mentors, and role models. They can help open up a previously close-minded frame of reference.

At the beginning of my career I was only superficially aware of the importance of relationships. I lacked a clear understanding of the advantages of being exposed to different social and economic spectrums. Later I learned the importance of creating connections and relationships of mutual respect so I could build a pool of future allies and prospective partners who could help me in private and public affairs. On the other hand, even the meaning of networking changes in relationship to socio-economic levels. For instance, those in lower economic levels typically see networking as mere relationships or ways to relate to one another. The middle class perceives networking as a way to engage and negotiate or associate, while the higher economic levels see it as an opportunity to connect and link to others.

We all should expand our circle of influence and increase our access to positive connections, influential mentors, and proactive role models. Understand that creating a relationship of mutual respect is a two-way street and you can better appreciate the importance of having a positive-thinking frame of reference. When you accept the influence of positive thinking, you know that change starts with yourself, that anything is possible, that you can ignite your thoughts with proactive approaches. You can use this awareness as an invaluable tool for cultivating relationships, feeding your mind, and nurturing your spirituality.

Try it. Give it and yourself the benefit of the doubt. Through the faithful implementation of our values and the exercise of our principles we are constantly exposed to a new range of ideas and perspectives. Use them to awaken the altruism of your spirit and become excited about exploring additional abilities, searching out new contacts, and fostering new acquaintances. These are the interactions that will help you make powerful informed decisions and find the energy and dynamism you need to make network connections.

Remember, it is in the free choices of our decisions and in the connections we make with our interior and exterior world that we find and acknowledge the virtues of our own self. Challenges arise because, so often, we become disconnected with what really matters in life. As Russ Harris says, "Too much of the time, we're so absorbed in our thoughts that we aren't fully engaged in our lives and aren't in touch with the wondrous world around us" (Harris 2007, 124). On the other hand, if we want to connect with others we must first connect with ourselves. Once you do, you become aware that in order to live a life of fulfillment, one with purpose and mission, you need friends and family around you.

Finding true happiness does not usually occur solely because you practice the power of healthy relationships or become a decision-making expert. The real talent you need is the ability to use your rational, emotional, and spiritual resources to engage with and connect to one another. Practice sensitivity and exercise understanding so you can find the discipline and confidence you need to accomplish meaningful purposes.

Communication: An Invaluable Asset to Maintain Healthy Relationships

Communication is an interpersonal ability you need to create, transmit, or share messages. It includes, but is not limited to, the transfer of words and meaning. Communication has two basic components: denotation and connotation. Denotation means the direct nature or definition of words. Connotation represents the feelings that words can evoke. Communication is really a process of sharing, transmitting, and receiving messages, but fundamentally the action of exchanging meaning.

In a typical social environment people transmit message and ideas, engage in dialogues, and perform other interactions. All these situations require attentive listening skills so you can facilitate transmission of meaning and find understanding. Effective communication is possible when the two sides, a communicator and receiver, promote an interchange of information that is clear, trustful, and systematic. These exchanges occur when the sender clearly expresses a message, using both verbal and nonverbal signals, and the receiver correctly processes this message internally in his/her mind.

Real in-depth understanding and communication takes place when the communicators and receivers both understand the basic statement as well as any messages transmitted behind the words. Albert Mehrabian and other researchers have shown that in any given interpersonal communication, 7% of the emotional message is transmitted verbally while 93% is communicated nonverbally. Of this 93%, the tone of voice counts for 38%, while 55% comes from facial expressions or body language. Without respectful, proactive listening skills you may miss much of what is being communicated, or fail to communicate effectively. "No one will listen to you if you don't accord them respect," says George Lakoff. "Listen carefully to them. You may disagree strongly with everything that is being said, but you should know what is being said" (Lakoff 2004, 113).

Social interaction allows people to develop personal contacts, professional connections, and interpersonal relations. The power of sharing and understanding messages builds the foundation of future relationships. Respect for other opinions and viewpoints provides a bridge to awareness and understanding. Respect is a key element in maintaining open communication even if we disagree with some ideas. Keep in mind that communication is an interaction between the transmitter(s) and the listener(s). To generate positive thinking, then, it is vital to accept differences and diverse opinions as a natural outcome of social interaction.

Sometimes misperceptions can cause disputes, which again highlights the importance of active listening skills. They are a gift that we must develop and practice constantly as one of the basic elements of social management skills. Too often the lack of active listening skills leads to miscommunication. Listening is not merely the act of hearing. It also means showing real interest in what you hear and empathy in grasping the content and understanding the feelings behind it. Sometimes you must eliminate bias in your perceptions so you can ensure you are not just hearing, but actively listening. That means paying attention to everything you hear without applying filters, judgments, or assumptions even before the speaker has finished.

"Our divine creator wisely designed us with two ears and one mouth so we can speak one time, but listen twice," according to an old saying. It is a wise observation, because many people do not listen with the intent to understand; they hear with the intention to reply. Consequently, there is no guarantee that a person receives the real underlying message. Often people are supposedly listening when they are really preparing to speak.

A common listening error is lack of attention. People often assume conclusions or rehearse responses before they even hear the whole message. Giving your full attention means maintaining an open mind. It also means you pay attention to the body language of the person you communicate with. In order to grasp the real meaning of what is being transmitted you need to fully understand the feelings, gestures, and facial expressions that are transmitted within the message's content.

Positive thinking requires positive listening. It means you participate in an interactive dialogue that allows acknowledgement, respect, and understanding from both speaker and receiver. It does take self-discipline to offer your full attention without arriving at preconceived conclusions that destroy the principles of active listening. You must practice what Stephen Covey calls "empathic listening," which is a proactive way to accept what is being said without judging, criticizing, or evaluating anything in advance. Empathic listening is more than just active or reflective listening. "The essence of empathic listening is not that you agree with someone," Covey says; "it's that you fully, deeply, understand that person, emotionally as well as intellectually" (Covey 1989, 240).

Another very important aspect of communicating with others is the development of trust and confidence. When developing strong communication skills and healthy relationships, there is no room for gossip or rumors in your frame of reference. Of course, rumor and gossip may enter a conversation without our participation. In those cases try to respond as Socrates did. "Assure it is truth," he said; "confirm that it will not damage anybody; and confirm it will benefit you and/or somebody else." Or, as John Maxwell said, "Great people usually speak about ideas; good persons are those who usually are talking about themselves; while insignificant individuals are those who are constantly just talking about others."

When transmitting a message, make sure that the other person acknowledges the idea. If he/she has not clearly understood it can lead to misinterpretation. One of the lessons I've learned from my experience is that sometimes even when people share the same information they can interpret different meanings. Sometimes that is because someone did not understand the message. Other times, it happens when people were hearing, but not listening. Or maybe they were listening, but did not understand what was being said.

If that can happen when we transmit facts, can you imagine what happens when we spread rumor or gossip? Can you understand the damage we can create by spreading something that we have not even confirmed as credible? Therefore, when communicating with others you must rephrase and reflect what you communicate. Attentive listening skills require that you pay attention to what is being said, reflect on the content, and observe nonverbal signs. You can strengthen attentive listening by asking probing questions and rephrasing what you hear to ensure or clarify meaning. It is always a good idea to clarify specific assignments and duties. It is one of the duties of leadership. Make sure that all direction is clearly dictated, effectively understood, and free of any misinterpretation.

The following example provides a classic case of what can happen if the roles of leadership and responsibility are not clearly identified and understood.

This is the story of four people called Everybody, Somebody, Anybody and Nobody. They had an important job to do. Everybody was asked to pitch in. Everybody was sure Somebody would do it. In fact, Anybody could have done it, but Nobody did it. Somebody got angry with the poor performance because it was Everybody's job. The truth is that Everybody thought that Anybody could do it, but Nobody realized that Everybody wouldn't do it. It ended up that Everybody blamed Somebody when actually Nobody did what Anybody could have done.

We need leadership and communication to delegate tasks and make sure that everybody isn't blaming somebody because nobody did what anybody could do. When we need to establish true communication with others in such situations, we need to use all our resources, including the brain, the physical attribute to hear words and see physical responses. The fact is that whatever medium of communication we use, our actions need to address our reasoning as well as our emotions. We also employ a portion of our mind to analyze the words we hear, and our emotional intelligence comes into play to handle our feelings and sensations. Emotional intelligence plays a fundamental role in transmitting and receiving information and balancing verbal and nonverbal exchanges. Emotional intelligence expresses and describes meaning and intention as well as purpose and sentiments.

Our thoughts come from the convergence of rational, emotional, and spiritual factors. Jonathan Haidt points this out by saying, "We assume that there is one person in each body, but in some ways we are each more like a committee where members have been thrown together to do a job" (Haidt 2006, 5). Consequently, positive thinking requires the balancing of our thoughts through a tuning of our various thinking streams and acknowledgement of further impact that environmental factors might have.

Psychology professor Russ Harris says that the rational portion of our self comes from two basic resources: the thinking self and the observing self (Harris 2007, 63-159). The thinking portion is the intrinsic rational part of our mind (intellectual, emotional, and spiritual rationality). The observing self is the part of us that sees, scrutinizes, and contemplates the thousand of perceptions we get through our senses. We often perform this action without it being addressed by our thinking self.

Understanding this is crucial if we want to become sensitive to the different personalities, styles, cultures, and religions of the people with whom we interact. Effective communication within relationships does not rely exclusively on the capacities to talk, listen, and understand. It requires judiciousness and common sense, which we can acquire when we make internal and external connections. Keep in mind that prudence and good judgment are key elements for character and wisdom. In fact, wisdom is a great ability that cannot be given or transmitted. It arises from a close interaction with our faith, values, highest beliefs, and interaction with our own self. It is the harmonious combination of knowledge, rationality, spirituality, and emotional intelligence. We experience the brightness of intellect, the exquisiteness of wisdom, and the talent of emotional intelligence as we discover the virtues of others through our interactions.

I realize that traditional means of communicating have been changing due to impressive strides in technology that offer us diverse ways to interact and socialize as well as obtain and transmit information. Blogs, on-line videos, social and professional networking sites, virtual interactions, text messages, and so forth have opened up new spectrums of communication. Networking opportunities such as MySpace, Facebook, and Twitter are giving us new ways to interact and get peer-to-peer information, social contacts, casual sharing, and informal feedback. Acknowledging the growing pool of communication skills plays an important role in our social interactions, but we should use these instruments to enhance but not necessarily replace traditional ways of communication. The old ways still remain the best ways to truly engage and relate to one another. At the same time, online chats are an easy way to stay connected and informed.

In conclusion, communication skills are very important tools. True communication occurs in an environment where you can give, share, and receive honest and sincere feedback. Furthermore, communication skills are abilities that you should constantly practice and enhance so you can ensure connections, advancement, and opportunities. Positive thinking gives you the right attitude to interact in your networks, while effective communication provides you the tools you need to relate to others. The trustful relationships you create lead to enhanced social capital in any society.

Relationships of Mutual Respect: An Approach in Creating Healthy Relationships

It's necessary to understand the hidden rules of the economic classes, pointed out originally by Dr. Ruby Payne, if you want to create mutual respect and healthy relationships. This knowledge will help you respect opinions, understand different points of view, and find the right course for confronting difficult situations. Keep in mind that the way people perceive things from within their situation affects how they confront challenges. The fact is that people see life, space, time, and their personal and collective commitments from different angles and expectations. Understanding these differences will help you become sensitive to our diverse communities and enhance your communication skills so you can create and maintain trustful relationships. As Howard Cutler says, "If you just think about your own viewpoints, and you have no willingness to open yourself to opposing viewpoints, there will be no room for worth and improvement" (Cutler 2003, 73).

When developing a relationship of mutual respect you must recognize the behaviors that come from different economic and social perspectives, but you must also consider an individual's private patterns of behavior. The unique characteristics of personality and identity play an important role in social interactions, both with individuals and in groups. Any person or culture represents a combination of strengths and weaknesses, abilities and deficiencies. Keep in mind that identity reaffirms harmony and diversity synthesizes values, so the combination of individual talents and the collective virtue of the whole is what makes identity a cultural treasure and diversity an invaluable asset.

Every community should know the advantages of maximizing its unique potential instead of reacting to a fear of lost purity by denying the authentic evolution of the human race. Cultural identity is to a group what personality is an individual. It is not just one set of rules, but a wide spectrum of diverse norms that shape the group's distinctiveness. Therefore, it is not the singular characteristic of an individual that defines behavior or social interaction, but the mixture of individual qualities. In his book, *Untapped Potential,* Jack Lannom writes about one mixture of qualities in a concept called TEAM, which stands for "Thinker, Energizer, Achiever, and Mediator." Lannom calls these the four faces of personhood (Lannom 1998, 77-94).

Whatever your traits, it helps to understand basic personality styles. That information will help you work with people from different backgrounds and create the relationships you need to reach common goals and institutional objectives. The knowledge of your own pattern of behaviors is important, too. The things that happen between individuals also occur in community settings. The difference is that in the societal environment we do not deal just with internal characteristics but with external aspects as well. A community is a conglomerate of talents, skills, abilities, and thoughts contributed by people from diverse backgrounds. By mastering your skills of social competence in such complicated settings you will find a great avenue of opportunity by developing better relationships and proactive networking connections. This is why I emphasize the importance of social skills.

The republican tendencies of the classical Greek and Rome populations, even given the social differences of those times, actually supported the essential concepts of communal life. These ancient communities made it clear, "We exist in community, not as autonomous individuals, but independent constant integrators who complement one another in the communal necessities of the whole." Every individual had a moral and ethical duty to contribute to the common good. Those principles are echoed, to some extent, in the United States Constitution and in the constitutions of other democratic states.

In fact, the United States' legal framework establishes that the main purpose of the nation is freedom and the pursuit of happiness, which can be guaranteed only when a common cause prevails and social justice is applied to everyone. This is the kind of thinking that made John D. Rockefeller say, "I believe that the law was made for a man not man for the law; that government is the servant of the people and not their master." As the great theories of the past become practical methods in the present, it remains our mutual task as individuals to find the energy and the common purpose of life that unifies us. This social and cultural sensitivity will help us rediscover our assets, highlight our similarities, and celebrate our differences so we can create empathy and implant synergy in our communities.

This is why the concept of "service above self" is so important if we want fair benefits for all. It is why Jack Lannom asks all groups, associations, organizations, or communities to rediscover their own internal assets and look for common values that will create synergy, which means "the maximization of collective potential" (Lannom 1998, 95). A real sense of community occurs when every part of the whole participates equally in the redistribution of wealth and all components are recognized for their merits and their unique and valuable contributions to the entire society.

Thus, constitutional rights should be complemented with solidarity, or the premise that the welfare of the whole requires societal privileges for everyone within the community. Two assets that individuals and communities enjoy is the access to power and a chance to participate in the decision-making process. While solidarity embraces temporary aid, it also promotes long-term productivity and self-sufficiency. Therefore, when you empower relationships you make an investment in the future by helping people and communities grow and take personal and collective responsibility of their choices. In fact, the ultimate goal of social intelligence and effective collective management should be empowering individuals and communities. That is why the power should move from the base to the top, while empowerment should move from top to bottom.

Investing in personal and social skills and developing social competence are good investments for your social transactions. In addition, education and social skills are key components for human development and provide lasting benefits to the individual and the community. Dedicating your time and efforts to develop self-awareness and manage relationships will transform the investment of intellectual strengths and networking skills into social capital.

Additionally, solidarity and positive relationships become factors that help solve current challenges and prepare for our desired future. For instance, James Garbarino states that values and positive relationships play an important role in preventing violence and negative influences. More importantly, they also help create a roadmap to protect our children from "the influences of social toxicity, negative peer groups, and the crass materialism of our culture" (Garbarino 2000, 150). As I mentioned before, those who make the best impression on our children are the people who will become their role models. Children tend to model their behaviors after their parents or primary caregivers; it has been said that the first five years of a child's life determines what that child will become. If we do not provide positive role models, our children will learn instead from whoever makes them feel accepted.

Therefore, make sure your children's future is in your hands, not the hands of somebody else. If you agree with that—and who doesn't?—then now is the time to act. Assume your responsibilities and start changing the status quo. Change starts with you, and therefore inside yourself. You need a trustful relationship to support any transformations and programmatic change. In addition, we all need exposure to proactive environments if we want to share our experiences, learn from others, and acquire positive influence. It is by acquiring social skills and getting access to positive networking settings that we enhance our private abilities, societal competence, and social intelligence.

The art of social participation starts at home because the foundation of any community rests on its families. The seeds of self-sufficiency, self-appreciation, and self-discipline are planted in the early years. Children's behaviors are reaffirmed during their school years. Children seek love and appreciation, a sense of belonging and being accepted. If they do not find them it can lead to major problems such as delinquency, substance abuse, criminal tendencies, gangs, and so forth. Of course, I have to accept that behaviors do not develop exclusively from the behavior of parents and individuals. Government, economic structures, institutions, and community organizations have an impact as well.

All of us at some time have been exposed to bad influences, negative stereotypes, and the spread of negative energy and pessimism. Nurturing relationships of mutual respect are unfortunately not available to all, thanks to factors that create segregation and discrimination in our local communities and all around the world. Access to networks and opportunities to interact with different classes are necessary if we want to generate wider social interaction. Of course, everything from education to political inclinations may work to prevent people from participating in such social interactions. As

Konrad Adenahuer says, "We all live under the same sky. But we don't all have the same horizon" (Maxwell 2003, 61).

Those of us who are fortunate in having so many gifts and access to so many resources are the ones who need to start implementing solidarity and social justice in our local communities and social networks. We can spark true change in our lives and in our communities by opening ourselves to healthy relationships and allowing others to be part of mutually beneficial interaction. You can also assume the responsibility of sharing this information with others so that everyone knows there are choices to make, alternatives to select, and dreams to pursue. This will also benefit you personally because it will demonstrate that you care for others and at the same time help you market yourself as a positive, proactive, and effective person. You will keep yourself visible and actively involved in developing your connections in networks and social interactions. As Rick Frishman and Jill Lublin says, "If you simply sit around and expect to be discovered [...] you may have an awfully, lonely wait" (Frishman & Lublin 2004, 23).

Of course there are exceptions. Some people have done fine without investing in social interactions. Some gained opportunities by default or through unexpected circumstances. There are people without a formal education who have succeeded tremendously in life. Nevertheless, these are only exceptions. In most situations, finding good luck and opportunity usually requires action on our part, coupled with an attitude to pursue formal and informal learning as well as social and networking connections.

The art of relationships is a balance between developing talent and meeting remarkable people. The main idea is to build a friendship circle with those who are an important part of your life. Establish honest and reciprocal relationships with those who can help you make connections and develop expertise. Interact with the best people in every discipline. That does not mean you should exclude or segregate everybody else, because everyone counts in networking. Sara Michel discourages segregation or exclusion in networking because, as Frishman and Lublin point out, we may become "network drive-bys." Always be open to listening and understanding everyone. You never know with whom you might be interacting. A positive-thinking networking approach means to be aware that every person contributes something to networking settings.

The essential philosophy of networking is to create an environment of mutual respect, which forms the basis for trusting relationships, the foundation of solidarity, and the elemental structure of communal life. Relationships of mutual respect and trustful networking approaches are linked to the mind-set of positive thinking. It is wise to be open and willing to learn about one another without focusing on differences, but strengths. Remember, trust and respect are two of the best characteristics of worthy social interactions. One of the best ways to build trust and credibility is to practice what you preach; do what you say you will execute; and to do it by the time you say you will.

The key to moving things forward in a consistent and communal way, says John Maxwell, is to take "relational approaches instead positional styles." Relational interactions focus on developing relationships, where positional styles concentrate on title, authority, or circumstantial positions or labels. Relationships provide diverse levels of interaction. One difference is that relational interactions are usually moved by influence while positional associations are generally moved by persuasion.

On the other hand, there is a big difference between networking and social relationships. Networking is mainly a business matter while social relationships are more personally oriented, although the two may overlap. In any case, it is always best to use your instincts, expertise, good faith, and sincerity when building relationships of mutual respect and reciprocal benefit. Remember that any time or place can provide an opportunity to establish social and business connections. As Keith Wyche points out, "Social encounters provide a dynamic opportunity to network, show a more socially ongoing side of your personality, and allow you to gather information that may not be disclosed in a more formal setting" (Wyche 2008, 88).

The fact is that in both networking and social relationships it is not enough to be clever or courteous or to rely on monetary resources or social skills alone. The art of positive thinking in creating networks and positive relationships means to get something and share something with the group. This is why you should practice networking without thinking exclusively of personal agendas, but with an open mind that lets you honestly absorb the benefits of social interaction. You are expected to reinvest networking gains, primarily in your original circle of contacts and later with the other connections you make.

The ability to network is an extraordinary capability that gives people visibility and exposure in a wider environment. Much as monetary resources generate revenue and economic development in the marketplace, social investments bring social capital to the group and ultimately to the community.

Networking is an exceptional tool but only if you put it into practice. "You cannot teach people a virtue by requiring them to read books about it," says Louis Menand. "You can only teach a virtue by calling upon people to exercise it. Virtue is not an innate property of character; it is an attribute of behavior" (Tatum 2007, 51).

When you use your talents and emotional abilities, you can help transform this world, little by little. It is a task for you, for me, and for everybody. It is a private, public, personal, and collective responsibility. The good news is that we have a lot of thinkers and dreamers, but we still need practical doers. It is possible; it is necessary; it is fundamental and vital for happiness and for the continuation of the human species. I admit that we are very diverse and that it is difficult to find a fit for all the different personalities, styles, traditions, beliefs, and ways of living. However, we need one another and we depend on one another.

To live in isolation is impractical. We all need companionship. Therefore, differentiate facts from opinions and people from ideas. When you interact, focus on debating processes instead of discussing personal issues or personality traits. Networking and positive relationships will offer you a way to project your values and talents and promote your visibility. It will also help you market yourself and enhance your opportunities to accomplish your dreams and life objectives.

Remember, people value you more for your care than your knowledge. Consequently, your commitment to serve will return to serve you and your network. By utilizing kindness, solidarity, trust, and respect, you will multiply the return of your social investments. Serving others is crucial to enrich people's confidence; it should not be done to increase their own power, but to share their remarkable potential, increase their social capital, and enhance their growth. Positive relationships and servant leadership are fundamental ways to connect your thoughts with your actions and your values with your purpose in life.

Intelligence and emotions are interconnected in the brain. Therefore, it is not in the isolated individualities of our sources that we build social capital, but in the combined interactions of our internal and external resources. In other words, balance the pathways of your thinking where you can create a philosophy to promote acceptance and a doctrine to create solidarity both from the individual perception and from the collective perspective.

Emotional Investment: A Key to Maintain Loyal and Healthy Relationships

Emotions play an important role in building relationships. Stephen Covey refers to the interpersonal bank account or mutual interactive emotional transaction. If you make too many withdrawals, you will go broke. On the other hand, if you invest in understanding, respect, and kindness, then you will earn the gains of true and healthy relationships in which you can invest and endow to ensure long-term proceeds.

A solid emotional intelligence will give you a range of possibilities to link the rationality of your choices and the emotional sensation of achievement. As Jonathan Haidt says, "Human rationality depends critically on sophisticated emotionality. [...] Reason and emotion must both work together to create intelligent behavior, but emotion does most of the work" (Haidt 2006, 13). The main principle behind a healthy relationship is to maintain a positive balance with our emotional resources by making deposits and avoiding withdrawals.

Consequently, the primary responsibility of you as an individual is to learn to stand on your own and to take care of yourself, which is the magic of self-reliance. You create positive emotional stability when you ask for favors only when you need them and after you have made your best effort to get what you need by yourself. The principle is that you must give something in order to receive something. In other words, you should invest if you want to get returns. In his book, *El Zahir*, Paolo Coelho called this the "favor's bank." It uses the same criteria you use to manage a bank account but it deals with favors, facilitations, volunteerism, generous donations, philanthropy, and so forth (Coelho 2003, 22).

One hidden rule of social networking is to ask for help or favors exclusively when you need them. At the same time, it is important that you help out promptly when others need you and without consideration of race or social or economic status. When you help somebody you should not expect that the initial favor will return to you. The objective is to make several investments in your "bank" by helping people without waiting for an immediate reward.

The next step in "favor banking" transactions is to convert the initial goodwill into a real concept of solidarity. Helping others is a human asset that we can develop as soon as we understand the rewards of giving. It might not be easy. For instance, some of you may think, "I do not have anything. How can I give what I do not have?" Keep in mind that we all have multiple gifts and assets that we can share. Highlight your gifts, talents, and blessings and share them without neglecting your assets. As you do so, remember that you invest in the "favor's stock" any time you give something back to your institution, community, or country.

Making positive emotional investments is another tool to reshape your attitude and understand the true concept of happiness. There are many ways to share, so assign yourself the task to evaluate your strengths and resources. Share your assets, not just material goods or financial resources. One way that many servant leaders help is through the power of volunteerism, which helps create equality, equity, and social justice by giving time and services to those in need.

Whatever you give back to your community contributes to the enhancement of others as well as yourself. You have the choice to invest your assets in any way, but you should try to invest in areas that give you the satisfaction and gratification your spirit needs to master the internal necessities of your soul. Extending efforts to serve those in need is a civic responsibility of our leaders, but also a mandatory task of any human being.

Servant leadership recognizes the value of individual contribution but that the final result of whatever we do as a group, organization, or community relies on a collective effort. The essence of responsibility comes primarily from the individual and secondly in the group. That is why I stress individual responsibility for giving back to the community. Those who have been blessed by fortune and endowment have the moral responsibility to give something back. In the end it will increase your pleasure and wholeness.

Community service, giving back, and solidarity also promote and support change. There is so much you can give. You can offer accessibility to physical, mental, emotional, and spiritual resources, or you can promote volunteerism, mentoring, coaching, training, or advising. The point is that all of us should give back and help others follow our footsteps or inspire them with our leadership abilities. In all cases you require a strong devotion to your values and a willingness to follow your core principles if you want to ensure total commitment from your mind as well as your heart.

Remember, reciprocity helps maintain relationships. There is always something to give and always pleasure in receiving. Relationships and networking will help you identify opportunities and pursue your dreams. For example, my dear friend Graham Hetrick examined how emotional investment created options and opportunities. He found that it is important to create "doors," gates or avenues of opportunities in order to follow a dream or way of life. The process includes both formal and informal learning as you develop skills, talents, abilities, aptitude, and attitude to succeed in life.

The concept of "doors" is a mental model that helps you build opportunities and raise future expectations. The idea is to generate a series of alternatives and give people access to a pool of options so they can exercise the power of choice. Being short of alternatives can slow your predisposition to reach your dreams. In addition, having choices helps people avoid becoming trapped by the necessity of reacting to unexpected circumstances that can suddenly change or destroy their lives. A wide array of doors does not guarantee success, but it does provide alternative solutions so you can make selective and informed decisions. Gary Thorp furthers the concept by saying, "You can make a commitment to being either inside or outside of something larger than yourself [...] Doors are more than wood or metal. [...] They are places that can become turning points-either you pass through them, or they block your path" (Thorp 2000, 12).

Let me explain it with an example. For instance, if you are a teenager who quits school and gets a job, you have limited options. Your only door would be the skills you have acquired for work. If you decide to remain in school and also get a job then you have built two doors; skills from your current job and formal information. Perhaps you also decide to join a school club, play a sport, or participate in your church or community. Each of these choices would give you access to more doors.

You can develop leadership abilities, administrative skills, and interpersonal communication and you can expect that you will get a new set of experiences from the time you invest in self-improvement. You create even more doors to opportunity by making new relationships and contacts and developing more skills. You are also investing in your personal education and in the emotional savings account of interpersonal relations.

Sometimes, you need to make some withdrawals in order to get new contacts. When you do, make new investments to keep a positive balance as you make your way up the ladder to success. The goal is to maintain a positive balance and open new doors so you can increase your options. The concept of doors relies on your mind, but the lock is in your heart. You can create physical doors to get opportunities and satisfaction and mental doors to access to life enrichment and genuine happiness.

Can you image the number of doors you can create and how much positive emotional balance you can acquire over several years? What you are really creating is called "social equity," an investment in social capital that you should strive for during your lifetime. On the other hand, what happens if you have a negative balance in your emotional account? What takes place when you meet somebody and immediately ask for help? In this example of a networking scenario, it's hard to predict how the long-term relationship will play out because you have not set the boundaries of trustful relationships. These will be determined later depending on the emotional investor with whom you are dealing (partner, coworker, or guest) and the social skills that every person brings to the table of mutual relationships.

Be careful about withdrawing emotional resources. There is nothing wrong with making occasional withdrawals but if you do not have enough balance you can make yourself emotionally bankrupt. In addition, favors are granted tacitly once a trustful relationship has been established, which is why it's important to make deposits and build doors if you want to fully utilize the reciprocal benefits of networking. And do it now because you are in charge of your own future. Start investing in yourself and do it by helping others. Forget bad experiences from the past. Live in the present and open the doors that you create for your future. "Life can be understood by looking to the past," said Soren Kierkegaard; "nevertheless, it may be lived by seeing to the future." Looking to the past means thinking and reflecting. Seeing to the future means transforming what you are into what you would like to become. A good life is the effective idealization of your thoughts so you can find pleasure and affirm your character.

Networking provides an environment where we can actively make emotional transactions, both deposits of kindness or withdrawals of favors. These relationships can bring pleasure as well anguish; it is within your free will to pursue those that fit your values and abandon any that compromise your principles. As you make these decisions, remember that all outcomes are intrinsically related to your way of thinking and whether you see things from an optimistic or pessimistic point of view. Emotional investment has a strong connection to seeing things as opportunities to grow. The fact is that any event or circumstance has a positive side and things to teach us. Everything in life is relative. Keep this in mind as you cultivate an open mind to see things from different angles, but without confusing reality with illusion. An opportunity can open a door to suffering or a door to satisfaction. It all depends on the power of your mind and the quality of your thoughts. As Howard Cutler says, "Unhappiness is ultimately caused by the gap between appearance and reality, the gap between how we perceive things and how things really are" (Cutler 2003, 9).

This is why Jonathan Haidt sees every action as an opportunity to create what he calls "vital engagement," which is the connection between our interior and exterior worlds. "Vital engagement does not reside [exclusively] in the person or in the environment," says Haidt; "it exists in the relationship between the two" (Haidt 2006, 225). It is a commitment a person makes with the environment, as well as with himself, so it reaffirms the necessity of acquiring internal confidence and external social abilities to create an enjoyable and meaningful life.

Of course, social and business networking meetings are good environments to live these experiences, apply intercommunication skills and develop interpersonal relationships of mutual respect. This is how you develop influence and find the perfect scenario to make contacts. Networking is the best place to apply the "door" concept because it is where you expose your human and social capital and measure your emotional balance. The key is that you seed first and harvest later.

Financial resources are important and even necessary in this world. In fact, monetary rewards can play an important role in the exploration of pleasure and circumstantial comfort. Nevertheless, it does not guarantee success or happiness. Do not focus your life purpose and networking intentions on the accumulation of material goods. Good wages do not guarantee that others will value you or that you even value yourself. Appreciation and thankfulness are not measured by money.

Character, however, is a priceless value. It's something you recognize through your own conscious and the accomplishments of your values. People who believe that money or power will bring everlasting happiness are totally wrong. Money can supply our needs but not necessarily our wants. Financial resources are just one component of satisfaction but income alone does not guarantee happiness, peace of mind, or enlightenment. I am not saying that material possessions are good or bad. I am saying that extremes can cause discomfort, suffering, and unhappiness.

You can find things of great value through the constant use of phrases of affection, respect, encouragement, courtesy, and kindness. People are hungry for social recognition. While financial resources are necessary, emotional and spiritual sources are also essential for an enjoyable life. People need kindness, love, friendship, and trust. Consequently, we need to practice solidarity. Of course, that requires decision, determination, and choices.

From time to time you need to invest your resources in order to create contacts that may help you in the long term. Such investment does not necessarily mean exclusively money; it can also mean affection and friendliness. However, all emotional transactions come with risk, as happens with any other investment portfolio. For instance, financial investments usually focus on strategies to maintain your principal and increase returns. Likewise, emotional investments and positive relationships require trusting spiritual approaches that are covered by love, friendship, kindness, and appreciation. Sometimes you may become nervous when some investments do not give you any return for a long time. However, that may not be the case at all, as you may discover when a self-evaluation of your thoughts makes you aware of the positive or negative inclination of your ideas.

The best way to evaluate the thoughts that you send to your subconscious is to ask yourself if they are helping you in the present or creating a desired future. As psychologist Russ Harris says, "If it is helpful pay attention, if it is not, defuse it" (Harris 2007, 46). If we feel confident that our thoughts and ideas are right, then we must stay on course even if so doing will temporarily challenge or dishearten us. The fact is that any relationship of mutual respect is a win-win situation with reciprocal benefits. For example, both participants gain from a mentoring relationship.

Positive relationships and interaction with optimistic people are healthy associations and assets for making connections and social and economic advancement. Of course, in any relationship, keep an eye on your values and your goals. Values give us meaning; goals give us purpose. Together they should create a harmonious balance.

According to an old saying, "It is not the level or place that really matters; it is the direction that you should care about. Destination is the key." Getting there requires the strength of mind granted by our consciousness. It is like an imaginary companion, a self-reflection of our determination. While positive thought is good, achieving greatness requires action. Good is not enough; we must reach for greatness and significance, which requires positive thinking. "It is not enough to just be good!" says Keith Wyche. "Good will keep you employed. Good may even garner you a raise or two. But if your goals are higher than just being mediocre, then you must be willing to make sacrifices necessary to reach the top [...]" (Wyche 2008, 23). Any moment without action is a waste of the short time we are granted.

Therefore, open your mind to the little details that make life matter. Unfasten your heart and give your soul more opportunities for friendship and encounters with love, peace, and happiness. You have been granted just one life, at least on earth or in our current form. Perhaps you perceive life and relationships from a different perspective. Still you must agree that each lifetime is unique, so live yours holistically and intensely. Life is whatever we create in our mind, so we can become whatever we conceive in our dreams.

In order to value and appreciate relationships, always be positive. Utilize proactive responses, offer encouragement, and praise people's contributions. Keep in mind that thoughts are driven by feelings, so stimulus and motivation are necessary to inspire and maintain positive thinking. "Act the way you want to feel" and you will surely become the person that you would like to be. It is all in your attitude.

In conclusion, it is our primary duty is to enhance our communication skills and invest in relationships of mutual respect. This includes, but it is not limited to, opening your mind to new ideas and challenges, balancing your emotions, and bringing in humor and fun as you manage your objectives, vision, mission, and purpose of life. A positive outlook will generate a soulful connection with your highest beliefs and a correlation with your deepest emotional cravings. Whatever is the purpose of your life, it should have at least three elements: it should make sense; it should not interfere with your right to enjoy it; and it should include a physical, rational, emotional, and spiritual balance of your resources. Happiness and sadness are just mental conditions whose attributes cannot be ruled or imposed on you because they depend on the individual power of choice.

Chapter 10

A Genuine Approach to the Pursuit of Happiness

"The primary cause of happiness is never the situation but your thoughts about it."

Eckhart Tolle

293

Chapter 10

A Genuine Approach to the Pursuit of Happiness

———•◦•———

Happiness is subjective. We all experience it differently. However, there is something about happiness with which we must all agree—happiness is not a destiny, but a journey. Even when you think you've acquired happiness, it's just a temporary condition, one that can change from day to day. Happiness is not a permanent condition, but neither is sadness. Happiness is a situational attitude that you can experience in the simplest things or by tackling a difficult task. You can measure happiness from different perspectives and through different lenses, regardless of the resources you possess or the enjoyable hours you spend. Happiness depends on you.

The pursuit of happiness is a journey. The attainment of it provides a moment of instantaneous satisfaction, but its duration and effect depends on the person experiencing it. The fulfillment of happiness does not necessarily happen in great triumphs; sometimes it is hidden in tiny details. Thus you should enjoy every single moment of the present without losing sight of your next adventure, plan, or commitment during your temporary journey on earth. The capacity for joy is inside us. It is a sensation we take from our inner self and freely expose to the outside world. For instance, we create pleasure when we allow our spirit to become aware of our nature's infinite potential. "We go for the outer things thinking they're going to bring us happiness, but it's backward," says Marci Shimoff. "You need to go for the inner joy, the inner peace, the inner vision first, and then all of the outer things appear" (Byrne 2006, 110).

A predisposition to change and enjoy every second of interaction with others will increase our contentment. So we should always be sure that we are making the best use of our time, developing a willingness to share, and finding opportunities to serve. All are indispensable if we want to maintain a positive attitude and get pleasure and satisfaction. They create an energy transfiguration in the mind-set of those who trust the command of their thoughts. The power of positive thinking relies on the rational and emotional conviction that what we think is what we become and that we can achieve the greatest sensation of happiness through loving concern, critical judgment, and supportive spirit.

Any time that you experience a manifestation of your spirit and a commitment from your emotions, you may discover what Tom Jablonski calls the ability to rise above self and transcend our common nature. As I've said before, the secret to happiness is to follow your dreams without losing perspective of the present while enjoying your journey to your desired future.

The legend of the Alchemist includes a description of the concept of happiness. It tells the story of a young boy and his efforts to discover the meaning of happiness. The story says that the young man's father told him that only a wealthy and wise man, who lived in the wilderness, could answer his questions about happiness. The boy went to the desert seeking the wise man. After several days of searching, the boy found the old man in a palace and finally asked his question: "How can I discover the secret of happiness?"

The wise man listened attentively [...] *but told the boy he didn't have time just then to explain the secret of happiness. He suggested the boy look around the palace and return in two hours. "Meanwhile, I want to ask you to do something," said the wise man, handing the boy a teaspoon that held two drops of oil. "As you wander around, carry this spoon with you without allowing the oil to spill." The boy began climbing and descending the many stairways of the palace, keeping his eyes fixed upon the spoon. After two hours he returned to the room where the wise man was. [The boy told the wise man that his task was done. The oil was still in the spoon and now he wanted to learn the secret of happiness.]*

"Well," asked the wise man, "did you see the Persian tapestries? [...] *Did you see the garden that it took the master ten years to create? Did you notice the beautiful parchments in my library?"*

The boy was embarrassed and confessed that he had observed nothing. His only concern had been not to spill the oil that the wise man had entrusted to him. "Then go back and observe the marvels of my world," said the wise man. "You cannot trust a man if you don't know his house." Relieved, the boy picked up the spoon and returned to his exploration, this time observing all of works of art and the ceilings and walls [He has been taught that in order to succeed in life, people should finish their task completely and in timely manner]. He saw the gardens, the mountains all around him, the beauty of the flowers and the taste with which everything has been selected.

Upon returning to the wise man, he related in detail everything he had seen. "But where are the drops of oil I entrusted to you?" asked the wise man. Looking down at the spoon, the boy saw that the oil was gone. "Well, there is only one piece of advice I can give you," said the wisest of men. "The secret of happiness is to see all the marvels of the world, and never to forget the drops of oil on the spoon" (Coelho 1998, 31-32).

Happiness is a condition that we acquire during our journey to crystallize our dreams; happiness is also an ongoing adventure that we may discover and rediscover in the passion, joy, and efforts we find along the way. Happiness is not the solitary accomplishment of a task or an exclusive fantasy of contemplating the marvels of nature. Happiness hardly exists if we don't link the tasks, joy, and our mission of life. The main purpose of life is to live each second intensely by maximizing our capacity to fulfill our dreams while enjoying the satisfaction of the small victories as well as great accomplishments. The secret of happiness is to follow your dreams and transform them into plans, goals, and objectives while enjoying the journey you make to achieve them.

If you want to find happiness, do not ignore your dreams and never forget to enjoy your journey on your way to conquer them. That is what happiness is all about. As Jonathan Haidt points out, "When it comes to goal pursuit, it really is the journey that counts, not the destinations" (Haidt 2006, 84). Live your own dreams from beginning to end and value every moment in between. Bad times as well as good ones provide opportunities to learn, enjoy, and live in genuine happiness.

Sometimes it takes some physical or psychological pain before we can discover and appreciate our strengths and become prepared to confront challenges. "People need adversity, setbacks, and perhaps even trauma to reach the highest levels of strength, fulfillment, and personal development," says Jonathan Haidt (Haidt 2006, 136). Such cases should not be interpreted as a masochistic approach or self-imposed penance for gaining re-silience, but as tools we use to assume change and take responsibility for our acts. It is not my intention to celebrate suffering, but to encourage you to face challenges with dignity and confront adversity with a positive-thinking attitude.

The greatest teachings have demonstrated that, as Haidt says, "Adverse fortune is [at the end] more beneficial than good fortune; the latter only makes men greedy for more but adversity makes them strong" (Haidt 2006, 25). Happiness means being conscious of what happens around us, in good times and bad. Pleasant moments allow us to enjoy the beauty of life and explore the magnificence of happiness. However, as Russ Harris says, "Don't get too attached to pleasant feelings. Don't center your life on chasing [exclusively] them. Pleasant feelings will come up and go. Just like every other feeling. [...] So enjoy them and appreciate them when they visit, but don't cling to them! Just let them come and go as they please" (Harris 2007, 201).

Sometimes pain and frustration provide the best motivation to search for opportunity. The difficulty may arise from an idea that has been dis-proved, a battle that has been lost, or a dream that seems unreachable. As the saying goes, "What losers call adversity, winners call opportunity." Pain and sadness can help increase your strength as you prepare to succeed in a new battle. "No condition is ever permanent." Do not become frightened when life compels you to confront challenges that will help you acquire experience you need to better understand the beauty of life. You can use bad times to discover new ways of overcoming difficulties if you remember that every event offers a new opportunity to succeed.

We can have constant encounters with pleasure and we can find marvels all around us in the present, in our memories of our past, and in the mental visualization of our future. Contentment becomes even more accessible when we focus our efforts and rely on faith. To be happy requires paying attention to details, mental and spiritual sensations as well as emotional ones. As Dale

Carnegie said, "We are dreaming of some magical rose garden over the horizon instead of enjoying the roses that are blooming outside our windows today" (Carnegie 1981, 254).

In order to find a meaningful approach to anything we think or do, we must make the connections among body, mind, emotions, and spirit and find harmony in the balance of our thoughts, the equilibrium of the environment, and the positivity of our actions. We find the essence of happiness in the journey of doing what we love and in the pleasure of loving what we do. It all stems from the power of attitude because the root of most problems does not lie in the struggle, but in the attitude with which we confront adversity.

Two different people can confront a similar situation but approach it from different angles, from a good perspective or from a bad one. With a positive frame of reference, a person's attitude will remain upbeat. A negative viewpoint may lead to reactions, conflict, and defensiveness. Whatever the case, the difference comes from the mental lenses you use to view life and the attitude with which you confront life struggles. As Dale Carnegie says, "Two men looked out from prison bars; one saw the mud, the other saw the stars" (Carnegie 1981, 395).

No matter what our situation we should always find time to reflect, accept, and enjoy whatever we have chosen. It is up to us. The ability to maintain positive thinking makes the difference between a life of great accomplishment and a real mess. Everything starts and ends with the power of your thoughts and happiness must be enjoyed and lived in the present. It is why Seneca said, "True happiness is to enjoy the present, without anxious dependence upon future, not to amuse ourselves with either hopes or fears but to rest satisfied with what we have, which is sufficient, for he that is so wants nothing" (Mandino 1991, 112).

There is no exclusive shape for happiness. There is no stepladder, private bridge, or pathway to reach it. You will find no universal recipes, but only widespread principles and holistic and comprehensive guidelines. Happiness is personal, a unique circumstance that people see from different angles and perspectives, depending on attitude. One way to pursue happiness is by allowing your dreams an opportunity to become objectives. Then you must write down your plan, highlight your goals, and place them into practice without losing sight of reality.

The main point is that we should give all wishes, desires, visions, and aspirations an opportunity to succeed. All dreams deserve consideration. Some dreams will never cross the border that separates fantasy from reality and you will have to decide whether to keep trying or to desist. That's why it's important to first determine if your project is a feasible goal or merely a wish and why you must base your dreams on measurable outcomes that you can accomplish in a reasonable time.

In other words, give your dreams a chance. Establish goals based on informed decisions and determined outcomes. As a basic principle, we can accomplish any dream, as long as we follow a wise axiom that instructs us, "Act as if it were impossible to fail." Nevertheless, there are rules, policies, and procedures that you should follow to make informed decisions based on knowledge, experience, and instinct. This is what people with great talent do when they pursue their dreams. Many people who ended up transforming lives with their inventions and discoveries were first considered insane because they challenged the status quo.

Remember that Galileo was imprisoned for denying that the earth was the center of the universe, which was considered a blasphemy in his time. Louis Pasteur was ridiculed when he said tiny organisms that we now call germs caused disease. Dr. Robert Goddard was considered crazy when he said rockets could one day propel people into space. These examples teach us not to feel discouraged at the first signs of resistance. Keep pushing until you've reached your objective.

My only recommendation is that you keep your dreams separated from fantasies. It does not mean that you must prescreen your dreams; that would go against nature. In fact, as Milton Erickson says, "Anything you can pretend you can master." Everything deserves an opportunity and anything is possible provided it is accompanied by meditated thoughts and planned actions.

On the other hand, people sometimes feel dismay after experiencing failure and refuse to try again. This is a terrible mistake. As Jose Ingenieros said, "Those who are afraid of failure do not deserve to get the crop of tomorrow; the cowards do not collect roses for their fear of the spines." Once you have made an informed decision, you need attitude, enthusiasm, confidence, and commitment to pursue your dreams. As Paolo Coelho has pointed out, there are two main reasons that people are usually afraid of following their dreams, "Because they feel that they don't deserve them or that they'll be unable to achieve them" (Coelho 2000, 131).

Keep in mind that meaningful change, inventions, or transformations happen when people harmoniously use the power of imagination, their convictions, and the power of visualization to challenge the status quo. Positive attitude allows emotion to interact with rationality, an interaction that has served as a template for the social transformation of humankind. A commitment to action is the price required to transform thoughts into realities. We have to give something in order to get something and success requires dedication, sacrifice, and self-discipline. There is no perfection without effort.

You should not limit your dreams. In other words, dream big. Too many people become happy with domestic triumphs or satisfy themselves with little accomplishments. We lose the chance for real happiness and long-term satisfaction when we limit our own capabilities.

Keep in mind that happiness is not eternal, but circumstantial. You can experience significant moments of enlightenment at one moment and encounter sadness or difficulty just a few minutes later. Experts call this "the polarity shift of the opposites," a concept Eckhart Tolle described by saying, "The same condition that was good yesterday or last year has suddenly or gradually turned into bad. [...] The same condition that made you happy then makes you unhappy. The prosperity of today becomes the empty consciousness of tomorrow" (Tolle 2004, 185).

So therefore, never complain about what you receive. It may be bad or it may be good. The fact is that so often we find unexpected benefits in anything that happens in our lives. We will have a better chance to find happiness if we develop the wisdom to leave our circle of comfort and pursue dreams despite those who tell us they are impractical or even impossible. Keep your dreams alive without being distracted by pessimism from the past or uncertainties of the future. Stay always in the present and enjoy the marvelous occurrences that occur all around us.

The only limitations to our dreams are the ones we create ourselves. Therefore, do not give up on your talents or abilities you have received. "Live your life as if it would be finished tomorrow and learn something new as if you were going to live forever." Everything is in the power of your thoughts and the supremacy of your imagination. Life is beautiful; your happiness does not require being in a specific social or economic class. Enjoy every moment and live it intensely. Live the present without forgetting to prepare your path for tomorrow.

Extremes are dangerous. We find wisdom in the harmony and balance of our alternatives. That does not mean you should delay the pleasure of enjoying your present, but to do what you must to ensure a joyful tomorrow and a legacy for generations to come. You should balance and measure your present and the preparations for your future, without trapping yourself in the fatality of destiny or pre-assumed luck. Living each day as if it were your last means enjoying every second without diminishing the ability of others to enjoy theirs. All is in the supremacy of your thoughts and the power of you imagination. As Albert Einstein said, "Imagination is everything. It's the preview of life's coming attractions" (Byrne 2006, 91).

The main objective of this book is to create the conditions necessary to maintain positive thinking. I am certain that our thinking offers us our greatest assets and the ways to discover pathways of possibilities for finding contentment, satisfaction and happiness. Just remember that your actions can be damaging, but your thoughts hurt only yourself because what you think directly affects how you feel. You must pay special attention to the relationship between rationality and emotions, which influence emotional change and consequently can create uneven moods and feelings. This is why a positive-thinking mind-set attracts contentment. It utilizes emotional shifts that make you aware of wishes, memories, and facts. This framework makes you more knowledgeable of your mood, attentive to the direction of your thoughts, and alert to the tune of your thinking. When you express your feelings you find a monitor that recalls awareness of your thoughts and consequently your predisposition to contentment.

Kelly Wilson and Tobias Lundgren list four areas that connect our values with a meaningful and purposeful life: Relationships, work/education, leisure, and personal growth/health (Harris 2007, 173). By living our values and linking them to our goals we can feel pleasure even before achieving them. In the same way, positive thinking predisposes us to happiness at all times.

In summary, it is clear that everything starts with confidence, commitment, and a trustful relationship with your inner self. There are no undisclosed rules or commandments for achieving happiness, but it does require a harmonious balance of our assets and equilibrium between our internal and external assets. If there were anything that could be called the "secret" to positive thinking and happiness, it would be the acknowledgment of what Rhonda Byrne calls the power of attraction. It is based in the premise that what we think is what we attract. In effect, Ms. Byrne says, "What we think about most or focus on the most, is what will appear as your life [...] your thoughts are seeds and the harvest you reap will depend on the seeds you plant" (Byrne 2006, 17).

Living for today means maximizing your physical and spiritual resources so you can enjoy a life in peace with yourself and others. In order to realize your ideas and goals, you must utilize each day as a resource and any opportunity as a possibility to achieve. Today is another opportunity to live and enjoy, one more time, the beauty of the universe. On the other hand, tomorrow is the future, an undecided event that may or may not occur. The only thing that exists now is the present. You and I are so fortunate to be here today, so let us use and enjoy our lives fully and completely.

The present allows us to utilize what we have now instead of waiting for the perfect time to enjoy life. The present is a continuous sequence of opportunities and you must use all your capacity to fulfill them. Tomorrow is hypothetical, but its outcome will depend on your ways of thinking and your approach to life. Our frame of reference dictates the mood and attitude we have toward everything. Use them all as assets to achieve your dreams and goals. Without a proper balance, we may lose wonderful opportunities and marvelous occurrences that constantly surround us. Therefore, enjoy what you can today and do not wait until tomorrow.

The secret of happiness is to transform your dreams into goals and objectives and to conquer them today, in pieces or as a whole. The option is yours; it depends on your stimulus and the priority you establish to achieve them. Your pleasure will be even greater if you have already enjoyed your journey and find happiness at every single station where the train of your life has stopped. Pleasure is a temporary momentum that we feel physically through our body, intellectually by our mind, emotionally by our heart, and spiritually by our soul.

We can find the taste of happiness anywhere because it is part of any pathway or destiny you choose. You should live and enjoy the glorious times of achievement with the same intensity as experience your smallest victories. The same principle of breaking down a problem into little pieces is one you can apply to enjoying pleasure as you pursue your goals. It is a tactic that can help you digest the greatness of pleasure before you reach the real context of happiness when your plans become realized. Contentment may not be full expression of happiness, but it is a clear sense of satisfaction. As the Dalai Lama says, "If you have a strong sense of contentment, it doesn't matter whether you obtain the object or not, either way, you are still content" (Cutler 1998, 29).

Make a commitment to get pleasure from life and live purposefully, without regret. This is another way to prepare your way and plan your objectives. Today we have life; we can laugh, smile, and bring peace to others. Today we seed; tomorrow we harvest. If tomorrow does not happen, we have already enjoyed our time. It is wise to use every second of your life learning enthusiastically to do what you love and love what you have freely decided to do.

Living today does not mean to become irresponsible and forget that you have a mission to accomplish and a purpose to fulfill. Living today also means to keep a balance as you prepare your path for the next day. My point is to live and enjoy the present without forgetting to plan for tomorrow. If the miracles of life allow us to live one more day, then we will take this new chance with more intensity and accomplish our dreams.

Happiness is an attitude. It is all related to the confidence of our thoughts, so it makes sense to follow meaningful thoughts instead of wasting your energy on insignificant ones, difficult as that may be. "It's impossible to monitor every thought we have," says Rhonda Byrne. "In fact, researchers tell us that we have sixty thousand thoughts a day hitting and passing by around our mind" (Byrne 2006, 29). Some thoughts are just transitory; others make an impact. The serious thoughts are the ones we analyze and assimilate physically, rationally, emotionally, and spiritually.

Happiness is a predisposition to enjoy the journey toward greatness, even in the face of possible failure, because every experience can offer enjoyment if we accept them as learning experiences. Learn to laugh at your mistakes while correcting your errors and perfecting your talents. Attitude plays a significant role in our conception of happiness. A positive-thinking mind-set relies in the power of our thoughts and the commitment of our attitude. We attract what we think about most and we turn into what we intentionally choose. What we think is what we create and what we do is what we become.

Share your contentment and enjoyment with friends, relatives, and loved ones. Use any chance you have to give, share, and receive the energy of love and the splendor of peace. Enjoy every second of your life so when your final moment on earth arrives you can say, "I have not lived in vain. I have enjoyed every second of my life and did my best to accomplish my mission and enjoyed my life accordingly." Love your friends and forgive your enemies. Understand differences, accept diverse opinions, promote change, understand those in need, and practice what you preach. You will be surprised by the amazing wealth and source of happiness that lies inside each one of us.

Happiness varies from one individual to another. Buddha defined happiness as "the end of suffering." Some people find happiness by finding success. Many think that happiness is inconceivable without the aid of illusion and fantasy. Others assert that happiness is not the accumulation of material possessions, but spiritual assets. Happiness is not simply the enjoyment of good health or the accumulation of wealth and position. Many people with extraordinary monetary resources have totally empty souls. Some of them may suffer even more than those who have no financial assets.

On the other hand, there are a lot of talented people in the world. Some of them are educated and some are not; some have physical resources and some lack all material assets. Nevertheless, even those who lack resources can have hearts filled with the pleasures of joy, love, and compassion. As Eckhart Tolle says, "Joy does not come from what you do, it flows into what you do thus into this world from deep within you. [...] What you are enjoying is not really the outward action but the inner dimension of consciousness that flows into the action" (Tolle 2005, 299).

On the other hand I have seen healthy young people dying from a lack of love and attention and even people with many descendents who beg for love and cry for understanding. Happiness is not a unique recipe that works for everyone, but happiness is inside every person. It all relies on your attitude. Your attitude can create an easy or a hard pathway as you confront simple or complex life trials. Your attitude is fundamental; it determines your inward and outward reactions to daily concerns.

We can learn from successful people and explore the best practices outline in self-help books, some of which I used in the preparation of this book. For instance, Lyubomirsky, Sheldon, Schkade, and Seligman developed what they called "The happiness formula," or $H = S+C+V$.

S represents the genetic biological influence; C represents the influence of love, work, knowledge, and relationships; and V means the voluntary activities that you do (Haidt 2006, 91).

You can test this formula's practicality by yourself. If it works, play by its rules and enjoy its outcomes. If it does not work, remember that it's just one approach. Use whatever matches your talent, ability, and desire in achieving your goals and purpose of life.

Success has different definitions depending on different perspectives. What you consider success is a reflection of your life vision. It varies depending on personality as well as an individual's life mission. The definition of success varies from one to another because of differences in values and principles.

In order to apply positive thinking and find more happiness, you should explore the world from the outside as well as the inside. You won't find the true purpose of your life exclusively in its outward level, represented by the finite things of the universe's materialistic composition. Most times, it is in the inward level, characterized by the unlimited essence of your spirituality, where you find true purpose. The outside universe stands for doing or having. Inner space stands for being.

As a result, you won't find genuine purpose in the context of doing, but in the essence of living, where you discover the harmony of an inner connection between your thoughts and your predisposition to awareness. In other words, happiness is an internal disposition that comes basically from stimulus or motivation from our rationality, feelings, spirituality, and the responses that these actions reflect on us. We can encourage the approach of happiness by filling the space between the stimulus, incentives, or motivations that we receive in our daily interactions and the consequent responses we transmit in our social dealings.

On the other hand, there are two different kinds of situations that affect our search for success and/or happiness, and these situations are determined mainly by the external conditions of your life and choices that you make voluntarily. Keep in mind that everything in life has a price. The price that we are willing to pay for acquiring pleasure is just the foundation for understanding contentment and the importance of capturing the real sense of joyfulness. As Stephen Covey says, pleasure is "the fruit of the desire and ability to sacrifice what we want now for what we want eventually" (Covey 1989, 48).

Happiness is related to time and space. The only time we can be happy is the present. However, the future is an ongoing process that we are constantly preparing and evaluating in the present. What we are, think, and do is what we become. Positive thinking and a predisposition to happiness will help us attain a holistic connection with ourselves so we can assume the responsibility of living wisely and in accordance with our values, faith, and principles. Whatever the term "eternal life" may mean to you, it can help you create a balance between what you are and what you become, as well as what you get and what you leave for others during your presence on earth.

As we advance into the maturity of life, we have an increased knowledge and a sense of respecting, investing, and valuing the way we spend our life. As John Maxwell says, citing the poet Victor Hugo, "Our life is already short;

however, we may make it even shorter if we continuously waste the invaluable time that is gifted to us every day" (Maxwell 1998, 124-129).

Wherever you find happiness, you will find the presence of love. For this reason, positive thinking must address the fundamental role that love and moral values play in people's interactions. Recall the religious view of the context of love from one of the epistles of the Apostle Paul to the Romans, which says, "Neither death nor life, nor angels nor principalities nor powers, nor things present nor things to come, nor height nor depth, nor any other created thing, shall be able to separate us from the love of God which is in Christ Jesus our Lord" (Romans 8:38-39).

The transcendence of moral values brings an environment of conscious self-acceptance, peace of mind, and self-confidence to pursue happiness. Moral values are those norms that become fundamental habits of human behavior and are fundamental for reaching healthy social and cross-cultural interaction. Consequently, it is through moral values that people can identify themselves with the true essence of human nature to "Love the beauty, seek the goodness, search the truth [...] [And pursue happiness]" (Aragunde 1998, 32).

Happiness and success in life are not measured by material accumulation or lifespan. Neither is even permanent. Those who have everything are not necessarily as happy as those who lack everything. Happiness derives from the ability to ensure the balance of natural laws and individual governance. In other words, as symmetry is required to use the four basic elements of nature—land, water, sun, and air—similarly, equilibrium is mandatory for the interconnection of body, mind, heart, and soul. In fact, it is through equilibrium that we can find maximum enlightenment, which Eckhart Tolle defines as the "state of wholeness of being 'at one' and therefore at peace" (Tolle 2004, 15).

When there is peace there is joy; where there is joy there is love; where there is love there is solidarity; and where there is solidarity there is peace.

That is the cycle of life enlightenment and the true essence of realization that so often becomes the real meaning of life. Remember, "At the end, a person is just known by the impact that he or she makes in others." That is why I have insisted that people should concentrate more on what they already have instead of on what they lack. We must pay more attention to what we are than to what we would like to become, and see things as they are instead of as they should be.

In the positive-thinking mind-set, the most important thing is to discover your own identity so you can enjoy the little things in life. Of course, we will have great and sad moments. The real virtue is to get something of value from them. We even need crises and difficulties from time to time. They are just part of the challenges of life and we can use them as opportunities to highlight our blessings. As Albert Einstein said, "Without crisis, there is no challenge. Without crisis, there is no merit."

In addition, overcoming struggle can help us tap our creativity, develop our talents, and rediscover our inner self. It is just another way to figure out our own concept of happiness. Whatever your dream or desire, the most important thing is to enjoy the journey. "Any challenge that does not defeat us ultimately strengthens us" (Stovall 2006, 61). Consequently, give more conscious attention to the doing than to the result, without forgetting that happiness is not a necessarily a purpose of life, but a means to satisfy the necessities of the body and the aspirations of the soul.

Paying attention to the "doing" is just the first approach to the real concept of happiness, which we find in "being." Doing and being need to be intertwined. If they are not, the influence of suffering can overcome our predisposition to enjoy the gift of life. To transcend and live beyond suffering, we must accept any circumstance as part of the multidimensional presence of life. Seen in a proactive perspective this will help generate the perfect environment to encourage evolution in thinking and salute the challenges of paradigm shifting. This is the state we reach when consciousness and awareness let us value what we have, appreciate the outcomes of the moment, and live happily ever after with whatever has been granted to us.

"Happiness is not a matter to be decided by picking and choosing," said Master Joshu. "It is much more that we learn how to discern" (Thorp 2000, 12). Consequently, in order to live and enjoy life as it is instead of how it should be, our ultimate goal must be the treasure of happiness, which means the privilege of finding serenity, calmness, and peace of mind. By peace of mind I mean the state where wisdom is granted and happiness or suffering accepted. It is where mind, heart, body, and spirit balance aptitude and attitude; science and faith; form and formless; content and essence; tangible and intangible; rationality and emotions; objectivity and subjectivity.

Suffering and happiness themselves are never the problem—your thoughts about them can be. Being at peace by being your true self is one of the more sacred states of happiness. Remember that authentic happiness rises above pleasure and goes beyond contentment and satisfaction. You reach genuine happiness through the conception of stillness and proper peace of mind. It comes through the combination of serenity and a stable state of mental calmness. According to the Dalai Lama, true happiness is "a state of happiness that remains, despite life's ups and downs and normal fluctuations of mood, as part of the very matrix of our being" (Cutler 1998, 36).

Your state of mind plays a significant role in achieving happiness. It may even be the most important factor in fulfillment. Your mind and thoughts determine your mood and attitude. Therefore, worries and concerns, idealism and practices, illusion and reality—all come from your frame of reference. Anxiety or stress as well as calmness or positivism will create the environment that dictates your attitude and predisposition to solve life challenges.

As suffering escalates and difficulties turn into problems it becomes harder to find the potential for happiness that is present in any human activity. Suffering takes place when people become consumed by worries about acquiring things or gaining power. Sometimes suffering also occurs when the end becomes more significant than the journey, or when you can't identify who you are, but merely what you do. These are the kinds of environments where doing misbalances the stability of being.

It is in your thoughts that the reality of dreams, desires, and aspirations is primarily processed, transformed, secured, and achieved. And that is related to your way of thinking and the choices you make when addressing challenges. It is true that we do not always have control over events, but we can control how we deal with things that take place. Indeed, the way we face any circumstance is all in the power of our thoughts and the confidence of our choices. What we do affects our inner self as well as the balance of the energy of those around us. "Every act we perform has some effect on the choices other people make and the world we live in," says Bernie Siegel. "We are part of the great puzzle of life, and without us it is not complete. [Consequently, it does] not matter how dark the future looks, you can make a difference" (Siegel 1998, 96).

So use the power of your thoughts and the strength of your confidence to generate positive thinking, because everything starts and finishes with our personal way of thinking. Any individual can play an important role in our society. That is why it is so important to emphasize the power of visualization and the necessity of balancing present conditions with future aspirations. By balancing our options we may fulfill a wider spectrum of possibilities.

"Success should not be only pursued, but attracted." Everything is within the power of our thought. I would like to close this chapter by paraphrasing a famous prayer by Mahatma Gandhi. It shows a way to connect with your divine confidence, create spiritual peace and fall in love with your own self as well as with humankind. It goes as follows:

If you give me fortune, do not remove happiness. If you give me fortitude, do not take off reasonability. If you give me success, do not get rid of humility. If you give humbleness, do not take away my dignity. Do not allow me to become arrogant in my triumphs or desperate in my failures and remind me that any failure is a special experience that precedes the triumph.

Consequently, if fortune is not allowed, let me keep the power of hope. If success is not on my side, give me the strengths to overcome challenges and the wisdom to be thankful for all the gifts that have been generously granted. Since pardon is the greatest value of the strong while revenge is the visible mark of the weak, then, give me the courage to sincerely apologize for my mistakes and the fortitude to pardon those who may offend me.

Conclusion

———••••———

"To handle yourself, use your head; to handle others, use your heart."

Eleanor Roosevelt

Conclusion

This book contains a different perspective on how to live better, think positively, and constantly enjoy your presence on earth. I intended it to help you explore the treasure of your inner self and discover diverse approaches to assorted pathways of happiness. It has covered theoretical approaches and best-practices skills, which are the tactics needed to move from awareness to acknowledgment, from acknowledgment to understanding, from understanding to acceptance, from acceptance to adaptation, and from adaptation to behavioral and attitudinal change. This last step of the process of acquiring positive thinking is called receptiveness, which is the willingness to consider, explore, and receive new ideas and diverse points of view.

Receptiveness combines acceptance and adaptation and receives its application in the framework of mental and spiritual peace. A positive-thinking setting requires an immersion in the whole context of change. It provides the environment we need to stimulate our senses and balance our responses so we can converge harmoniously on seriousness and cheerfulness, the simple and the transcendent, and the sadness and happiness of living a purposeful life. Everything starts by **Knowing and Respecting Yourself**. If we acknowledge and accept who we are and where we come from, then we can affirm our identity and reaffirm the values of our personality.

It is through the process of self-awareness and self-acceptance that we find the internal compromise with ourselves and the external responsibility with our community that creates **Critical and Creative Thinking**. In order to promote, exercise, and practice positive thinking you must have a **Positive Attitude** and create a proactive environment in your thoughts. There is a close relationship between attitude and the balance between seriousness and cheerfulness, rationality and emotionality, and firmness and gentleness. Consequently, you should make life decisions by considering your purposes and objectives in life. Humor and fun are extraordinary ingredients for creating your destiny and redirecting your intention to have constant moments of happiness.

Humor and laughter are contagious emotional assets that cultivate positive thinking, promote physical mobility, and endorse mental relaxation. Recognize that you have the power to choose moments of contentment by implementing instants of fun. Cultivate these habits to reduce and control stress, diminish feelings of depression, and lessen sensations of helplessness. Humor gives us a sense of confidence while laughter releases emotions and reduces stress. All depends on the power of our attitude, which we develop through emotions and stimulate by character and motivations.

That is why we need a **Predisposition to Change** to keep ourselves positive, open our minds to new viewpoints, and adequately balance our physical, mental, emotional, and spiritual boundaries. We require informed judgment and logical examination of issues to avoid a circle of distress and misjudgments. That is an ability we cannot master without a predisposition to accept the result of our choices. Of course, we can evaluate and redirect our efforts to keep our actions and our personal, professional, and public mission and objectives on the same frequency. Remember, life is what we create in our minds. Happiness originates in our thinking and is reflected in the outcome of our actions.

Along with logic and feelings, spirituality plays a fundamental role in the construction of meaning and destiny. We need **Faith to Believe** that whatever we create in our minds can become possible if we have trust and confidence in our discerning. Faith and conviction allow people to experience the presence of spiritual significance on the pathway to their desires and life-long objectives. The power of faith gives us the energy to transform ideas into realities. In faith we encounter the inexorable forces of peace, love, and passion that give meaning and purpose to life.

Faith requires trust and self-confidence. At times, faith alone is not enough. Self-reliance often requires religious and spiritual practices as well. We can measure our confidence through praying, solitude, or meditation. Praying can grant you the spiritual and emotional comfort you need to confront challenges. Nevertheless, a sincere prayer should lead to action and induce positive change. As an anonymous bit of wisdom says, "Prayer doesn't necessarily change things for you, but it changes you for things." The power of our faith gives our inner self the fortitude to seize resources and circumstances and adapt them to our physical, mental, emotional, and spiritual abilities.

The confidence and certainty of your thoughts and actions let you set a proactive attitude to chase any opportunity and use it to learn, practice, and enhance your mission of life. Seeking excellence is a habit that you should constantly practice and improve. Faith is the substance of life and all things. Indeed, as Aristotle said, "We are what we create in our minds." Therefore, the power of visualization is a great tool that allows people to enjoy psychologically a desired dream even before it becomes reality.

A vision offers a three-dimensional approach to opportunities. It is a shapeless, unconditional, and infinite power for promoting creativity, development, and unlimited achievement. That is why the power of visualization plays such an important role in conceiving greatness, both in the present and the future as well as in the spiritual conception of the afterlife. Visualization means "holding the image of yourself succeeding, visualizing it so vividly that when the desired success comes, it seems to be merely echoing a reality that has already existed in your mind" (Peale 1982, 29).

Therefore, use your knowledge and talents to **Practice What You Preach** and produce the best you can. Remember that a vision should always be inspired by the spark of possibility and enhanced by the exercise of practicing what you preach. The power of your thoughts and the conviction to be aware of what happens above, beyond, outside, and inside of us permits us to become enlightened. More importantly, it also helps us start living peacefully in advance of the promises of an eternal life.

Positive thinking is a significant asset to succeed in life; however, it is not truly accessible if we do not develop the **Humility to Understand Differences** to affirm our similarities and celebrate those things that make us unique. Through a spirit of inclusion and the acceptance of differences people can freely express who they really are and have equal access to enjoy their rights and the beauty of life. The understanding of differences has been a permanent issue in societal evolution as we move from denial to rejection, tolerance to awareness, acknowledgement to understanding, and acceptance to receptiveness.

The basic approach to cultural sensitivity accepts that diversity is a benefit. It is not an obstacle, but an asset. Diversity brings strengths, talents, abilities, and opportunities that complement one another. A different way of thinking brings access to knowledge, information, and the option to see things from different perspectives. A world where we are all the same will exterminate the elements that really matter in life. As William McNeill says, "Only in remote and barbarous lands did ethnic homogeneity prevail. [...] The ideal of national unity, based on ethnic hegemony and assimilation of outsiders into a fixed norm, is an aberration" (Zachary 2003, 73-75).

Demographics are changing around the world. As populations shift we must create a new, all-inclusive setting in any community. We should foster inclusion in any activity as a continued practice for advancement and mutual engagement. We will make the commitment to supporting inclusion, promoting respect, and create understanding once we offer all human beings an environment that is culturally sensitive, linguistically appropriate, and open to all.

When we practice sensitivity and accept diversity we will be more open to being grateful for what has been granted to us. In my view, this is expressed in **Solidarity to Share**, which is a sincere commitment to share our assets with others. Solidarity is the art of giving not just material goods, but appreciation and sensibility to those in need. It is a personal commitment as well as a principle of communal social justice to ensure equal access and opportunities for all.

Solidarity arises from the philosophical principle of giving back to our community and demonstrating gratitude for whatever we have received in life. As Luke in the New Testament reminds us, "To whom much is given, much is required." We need reciprocity in this often despairing and segregated world. That is why solidarity is so important, but sharing and giving does not include only material goods or monetary assets, but emotional and spiritual resources as well. Solidarity comes not just from your wallet, but also from your heart.

Solidarity is a mandatory duty of all human beings. Sharing and giving creates value and equity. When we give of our physical, mental, emotional, and spiritual resources we create positive attitude, change, faith, and hope. It is another way of creating peace, sharing love, and improving relationships. It also aids sensitivity, awareness, understanding, and the acceptance of differences.

One thing society today needs desperately is servant leadership. To paraphrase Robert Greenleaf, we must make sure that those we serve can grow and become able to serve others. One of the easiest ways to demonstrate solidarity is by sharing love. It is an unlimited resource that almost everyone can find within themselves. Positive thinking includes, but it is not limited to, giving, sharing, and receiving energy and the power of affection.

A sincere smile, a true expression of love, and solidarity are priceless pathways to happiness. Positive thinking and the supremacy of love, fellowship, and solidarity are strengths we need to train our minds to stay positive and optimistic. People will also find the maximum human kindness through the power of love. Remember that time is more important than money, love has more significance than thankfulness, relationships are more important than things, and peace of mind is above contentment.

The last two necessities for self-determination in the cycle of positive thinking are healthy relationships and the commitment to pursue happiness. **Positive Relationships** provide the foundation for healthy communication strategies and the growth of emotional intelligence. Relationships allow the circulation of energy and the interchange of ideas. It is why positive thinking starts with you. Even when two opposites join, the best influence wins.

Positive relationships drive us to proactive networks and optimistic settings of fellowship and long-lasting friendships, but the commitment to create networks starts with you. As Emerson says, "The only way to have a friend is to be one" (Zelinski 2001, 97). You have the power and the choice to influence others. "We influence often more than we think," says Piero Ferrucci. "Right in the midst of every day we are given the chance to torch the lives of others and thus change the world" (Ferrucci 2006, 50).

Healthy relationships and a commitment to happiness and mental peace direct us to the last reward of life on earth, the acquisition of a **Genuine Approach to the Pursuit of Happiness**. Positive relationships underscore the vital importance of communication to maintain healthy relationships, which also require emotional control and social competence. We find happiness in the enlightenment granted by peace of mind and the wisdom to perceive the interconnectedness of life. It is clear that the improvement of our positive-thinking mind-set relies on our ability to interact with our own self as well as the ability to connect with our peers.

Interpersonal capabilities and a capacity to network are fundamental parts of social ability, but they require practice if you want to truly utilize them. Talent, ability, intelligence, and informed judgment all sound like great descriptions of people's aptitudes, but they will all go to waste if you cannot use them properly. You need a complete set of communication skills to interact and gain visibility. As Keith Wyche says, "If you don't display them, you may never get an opportunity to display the others. [...] To be effective you need to be sure you communicate in a concise, clear, and articulate manner" (Wyche 2008, 111-112).

Real communication needs to be attentive, reflective, creative, and open-minded. It should include a deep intention to understand and to be understood. Furthermore, true communication goes two ways. Giving and receiving information is internal and external as well as private and public. Effective communication skills require creativity, imagination, auto-motivation, and the balance of our physical, rational, emotional, and spiritual assets. This basic equilibrium is also necessary for social, economic, and intercultural interactions. The balance of these tendencies, supported by our beliefs, creates the equilibrium that lets us pursue happiness.

I accept that there are controversies over the roles of rationality and emotions, religion and spirituality, faith and science, satisfactions and gratification, and the origin and destiny of life. Remember that an imbalance between intellectual approaches and emotional responses, or intelligence and spiritual conclusions, can create the opposite of what human beings are supposed to be. Happiness and peace of mind are elemental for getting pleasure and life satisfaction, so finding pleasure and gratification as you exercise a meaningful and purposeful life is an elemental aspiration for any human being. Happiness is in our minds. It is in the conviction of our thoughts and in the confidence of our decisions. "Nothing is miserable unless you think it so," says Jonathan Haidt, "and on the other hand, nothing brings happiness unless you are content with it" (Haidt 2006, 25).

Happiness is subjective. It is not a destiny, but a journey. Attaining happiness, though, is an instantaneous satisfaction. We interpret pleasure from different perspectives, depending on individual fulfillment, personal realizations, or how you value achievement. Jonathan Haidt makes a clear difference between physical satisfactions and emotional gratifications. "Pleasure beckons people back for more, away from activities that might be better from them in the long run," he says. "But gratifications are different. Gratifications ask more of us then challenge us and make us extend ourselves" (Haidt 2006, 97).

The secret of happiness is not necessarily or exclusively inside or outside. It is something in between. To have more encounters with happiness, we should balance our four basic resources: body, mind, emotions, and spirit. That requires rational and emotional intelligence as well as informed intuition and proactive imagination based on our faith, values, and mission in life. Imagination includes creativity while inspiration connects our holistic sense and develops our inner talents and capacities.

Seek the mission of your life and the purpose of your existence through deep analysis of your creative and critical thinking. Find the sense of awareness where you can find the flavor of happiness. Keep in mind that there is a strong connection between mission, purpose, peace of mind, and the pursuit of happiness. Connect your life mission to critical thinking and strategic planning, while your life purpose is associated with intentional being. The outcomes of our thoughts drive our life mission; life purpose arises from our feelings and the effects of our performance.

The past lives in memory and positive thinking allow us to concentrate on the greatness of our reminiscences. However, forget the sadness of those past times while still learning the lessons of those experiences. Since the present is the only time we truly possess, target your purpose in the present and on your mission to develop the ongoing future. Mission and purpose are interconnected and interrelated.

In closing, I hope I have demonstrated that positive thinking is the best approach to a genuine concept of happiness and a wonderful opportunity to live your life appropriately. Keep in mind that time is a limited resource. Use it wisely or you will lose it. Time cannot be saved, only invested. It cannot be borrowed, but only prudently managed. You cannot replace time. You cannot accumulate it, store it, buy it, or loan it. You must use your time intelligently because it is priceless.

Happiness is a personal journey. The most important thing to remember along the way is that we are what we make ourselves. What we do today is all about tomorrow. So live the present with your mind in the future and remember to enjoy the greatness of every single moment. Get pleasure from what you already have and keep visualizing whatever you aspire to become because there are no limits except for those imposed by your own perceptions and assumptions.

Visualization and positive thinking require time, commitment, character, and a conviction of your purpose in life. Of course, if you have made negativity a habit of life you may encounter disagreement and even distrust. But why not give yourself an opportunity to move ahead through the power of your thoughts and the impact of our choices?

Visualization is an important tool that makes it possible to project the future in your mind and transform it into potential fact. That is why the impact we make on people influences our peers either positively or negatively. The energy we generate affects those who are in contact with us. Consequently, we can influence our interactions by imposing the rhythm of positive thinking, peace, and love. We can do it to inspire change and growth and experience our personal spiritual journey.

We are what we create in our minds. What we think is what we become, through the right actions, informed decisions, and intuitive and balanced procedures. We are physically what we create mentally, emotionally, and spiritually. So utilize the power of visualization or the implementation of auto-suggestion. It will be even better if you also use the power of faith and a positive-thinking perspective.

You can create a successful life when you truly take charge of it and make sure that your choices rely on the harmony of informed decisions and the influence of positive thinking. Any journey starts in your mind. Recognize that and it will help you throw off lethargy, raise your curiosity, and appeal to your sensibility so you can believe in yourself, change your way of living, and start applying positive thinking for the rest of your life. Remember that Epicurus says; "People need virtues to cultivate pleasures" (Haidt 2006, 161).

Use your strengths to illuminate your thoughts, be thankful for all that has been granted to you, and share it with others to fortify minds, hearts, and spirits. Become the seed of an ongoing process of positive thinking. Utilize the power of faith, love, hope, and solidarity to find cheerfulness, inspire change, spark growth, and explore the opportunities of a personal spiritual journey. Spiritual disciplines are habits formed from character and enhanced by faith. Therefore, your greatest wisdom is to reflect how far you have come instead of how far you still have to go.

I cannot understand why people throw away their lives on vanities; rely on unthinking decisions and waste unrecoverable time as they exist in meaningless lives. Balancing the four faces of manhood should also include the harmony of the basic influences of present, past, and future. This equilibrium can help you avoid what Eckhart Tolle calls the "time anxiety gap," which occurs when we are physically in the present, but emotionally in the past or in the future (Tolle 2004, 43).

If you agree with the benefits of having a positive-thinking mind-set, you should develop your predisposition to live deeply and pursue your most valuable desires. You can do it by taking action through your plans, accepting the responsibility of your actions, and getting the best out of your precious time on earth. Do not dwell on presumed deficiencies and needs but concentrate on the unstoppable resources and blessings that surround us.

Human beings have an unlimited reserve of energy. Energy is an internal movement to action whose outcome relies on the power of choice. It is a strong catalyst with an individual or collective power that is a plus to society. However, people sometimes use it for good and sometimes for bad. It is not always dazzling because it can belong to a cycle between solidness and weakness, up and down, fortitude and debility. In fact, sometimes energy works like a piece of charcoal that needs to be consumed in order to become the flame. We have control of positive energy, depending on our decisions.

Accordingly, we need to activate and maintain our energy to generate accomplishments. Sometimes the primary source may be diluted; however, the essence of the intention, the flame, remains strong. That is why we sometimes have to go from sadness to happiness or smiling to crying. Death, too, is an essential part of life. Life is change so there is no ending, only continuity. The next time that you suffer or confront difficulties, do not feel depressed. The sun returns after the rain; light appears after the darkness.

So use the maximum of your capacity without forgetting to enjoy the satisfaction of your temporary accomplishments. We often find the greatest treasures of contentment and happiness in the process of overcoming difficulties. Just remember that you are gifted, brilliant, and capable of recognizing your blessings and accepting your limitations. "Joyfulness is not necessarily settled to those who get more," according to an old saying; "joyfulness is deservedly granted to those who make the best with whatever has been granted to them."

Live the moment. Enjoy the present without dwelling too much on the past or the future. Such an imbalance may make you overlook the transcendence and the wonderful opportunities of the "now." We need a balance because the past tells us where we come from while the future indicates what we will become. "Yesterday is history; tomorrow is a mystery; and today is a gift." In a positive-thinking mind-set, you don't have to see to believe—you have to believe to see. However, it is not easy to believe if you lack the commitment to love what you get and get what you love.

Most of the time what we want is not necessarily what we need. We should concentrate on the immediate needs of humankind: love and internal peace. The primary strategy in reaching internal peace starts with the predisposition to give love instead of waiting to receive it. Love and affection, kindness and understanding, and benevolence and solidarity can overcome hatred, envy, and intolerance. Positive behaviors such as politeness and sociability are undoubtedly beneficial for all because their opposites generate injustice and inequities and also unhappiness.

In closing, whatever the purpose of our lives, it is my understanding that it should have at least three elements. It should make sense, it should not interfere with our right to enjoy the splendor of life, and it must preserve a balance and uphold interconnection between physical, spiritual, emotional, and rational sources. Positive thinking remains the best way to animate autosuggestion and provide an inner exhortation to maintain proactive thinking. More important, it can help generate creative and instinctive techniques of self-motivation, which come from a harmonious interaction of positive thinking, faith, and self-confidence

It is my heartfelt intention that this proactive approach will form the pathway that transports unconscious processes into the conscious realm of physical, rational, emotional, and spiritual responses. That is why I insist on the importance of keeping a balance that relates to the quality of our choices and decisions. To better understand the mysteries of life, try to satisfy your basic needs, live your dreams intensely, and enjoy the satisfaction of accomplishing them.

We are just the replication of our mental deeds. Therefore we have the choice to be the light that guides or the mirror that reflects our blessings. Happiness and enlightenment may not be permanent, either in failure nor success. Nevertheless, a strong predisposition to change and a positive-thinking mind-set will always be assets to help you confront any situation with humility. At the same time, they also help you face difficulties with hope and determination.

I hope this book will help you redirect your destiny. Thanks for investing your most valuable treasure, your time, with these thoughts. It is my prayer that you will be blessed and find the best from life and share it with those around you. Since positive thinking is the source of greatness, let us deter and reduce the influence of negative thinking that can obstruct the divine intention of a purposeful life. Let all individuals be the happiest that they can be so they can make this world a better place.

Love is the primary source to transform lives, so let us share it. Love is a priceless element that we can freely generate from a positive-thinking mind-set and an optimistic attitude. Love is an extraordinary and magnificent asset and a structural part of creation and an irreplaceable factor for peace, order, and happiness. It is in sharing and practicing love that we apply the golden rule of "Do unto others as you would have them do unto you."

Finally, in order to practice love and peace, we should balance the harmony of the cycle of God, life, hope, and faith with our physical, mental, emotional, and spiritual interface and support it through the equilibrium of brain, heart, mind, and body. We must make a fair commitment to love and honor our beliefs, because love manifests God; God generates life; life inspires hope; hope promotes faith; faith materializes God; and God induces love. I hope the wisdom of these final principles will allow you to maintain positive thinking and find your approach to the genuine concept of happiness.

Bibliography

Adams, Kathleen. *Journal to the Self*. New York, NY:
   Warner Books, Inc., 1990.

Amos, Wally. *Be Positive*. Colorado: Blue Mountain Arts, Inc., 2006.

Amos, Gregory, and Wally Amos. *The Power in You*. Canada:
   Donald I. Fine, Inc., 1988.

Andrews, Linda Wasmer. *Emotional Intelligence*. Scholastic Inc., 2004.

Aragunde, Rafael. *Hostos*. Publicaciones Puertorriqueñas, Inc., 1998.

Arredondo, Lani. *How to Overcome Negativity in the Workplace*.
   Overland Park, KS: Career Track, 2005.

Barnet, Sylvan, and Hugo Bedau, eds. *Current Issues and Enduring
   Questions*. Boston: Bedford/St. Martins, 2002.

Batten, Don et al. *Answers to the 4 Big Questions*. Hebron, KY: Answers in
   Genesis, 2005.

Bolet de Fernández, Silvia. *¡Señor Tengo Prisa!* Miami, FL:
   Editorial Unit, 2001.

Breathnach, Sarah. *Something More: Excavating Your Authentic Self*.
   New York: Warner Books, 1998.

Byrne, Rhonda. *The Secret*. Production Limited Liability Company, 2006.

Campolo, Anthony. *Let Me Tell You a History*. Word Publishing, 2002.

Canfield, Jack, and Mark Hansen. *Chocolate Caliente Para el Alma*.
   Editorial Atlanta, 1995.

Carnegie, Dale. *How to Win Friends and Influence People and How to Stop Worrying and Start Living*. New York: Dale Carnegie & Associates, Inc., 1981.

Chopra, Deepak. *Las Siete Layes Espirituales del Éxito*. Cargraphics S.A. Imprelibros, 1995.

Coelho, Paulo. *The Alchemist*. New York: HarperCollins Publishers, 1998.

Coelho, Paulo. *El Peregrino de Compostela*. Barcelona, Spain: Editorial Planeta, 1997.

Coelho, Paulo. *La Quinta Montaña*. Bogota, DC: Editorial Planeta Colombiana. Calle 21 No 69-53, 1997.

Coelho, Paulo. *El Zahir*. Barcelona, Spain: Editorial Planeta, 2003.

Covey, Stephen. *The 7 Habits of Highly Effective People*. New York: Fireside/Simon & Schuster, 1989.

Cutler, Howard. *The Art of Happiness*. New York: Penguin Putnam Inc., 1998.

Cutler, Howard. *The Art of Happiness at Work*. New York: Riverhead Books, 2003.

Ferrucci, Piero. *The Power of Kindness*. New York: Penguin Group, 2006.

Frishman, Rick, and Jill Lublin. *Networking Magic*. Avon, MA: Adams Media, 2004.

Gadsden, Patricia. *African and African-American Treasures of Pledges and Credos*. Pennsylvania: Life Esteem, 2002.

Garbarino, James. *Lost Boys*. Anchor Books, 2000.

Gilbert, Rob. *The Most Inspiring Quotes*. Chicago, IL: Regan's Motivational Resources, 2005.

Goleman, Daniel, Richard Boyatzis, and Annie McKee. *Primal Leadership*. Harvard Business School Publishing, 2002.

González-Balado, Luis. *Mother Teresa in My Own Words*. New York: Gramercy Books, 1997.

Graff, Jim. *A Significant Life*. Colorado: WaterBrook Press, 2006.

Grobman, Gary. *The Pennsylvania Nonprofit Handbook*. Harrisburg, PA: White Hat Communications, 1999.

Haidt, Jonathan. *The Happiness Hypothesis*. New York: Basic Books, 2006.

Hanson, Marci, and Eleanor Lynch. *Understanding Families*. Baltimore, MD: Paul H. Brookes Publishing, 2004.

Harris, Russ. *The Happiness Trap*. Boston: Trumpeter Books, 2007.

Hill, Napoleon. *Think and Grow Rich*. New York: Ballantine Books, 1983.

Hirschberg, Stuart, and Terry Hirschberg. *Every Day, Everywhere*. The McGraw-Hill Companies, 2002.

Jackins, Harvey. *The Human Side of Human Beings*. Seattle, WA: Rational Island Publishers, 1994.

Jackins, Harvey. *The Human Situation*. Seattle, WA: Rational Island Publishers, 1991.

Jones, Charlie. *Books Are Tremendous*. Mechanicsburg, PA: Executive Books, 2004.

Karantonis, Anthony. *Perspectives of an Iconoclast*. Trafford Publishing, 2005.
Kiyosaki, Robert. *Padre Rico-Padre Pobre*. Tech Press Inc., 2003.

Kreps, Gary. *Las Comunicaciones en las Organizaciones*. Addison-Wesley Iberoamericana, 1986.

Lakoff, George. *Don't Think of an Elephant*. Vermont: Chelsea Green Publishing Company, 2004.

Lannom, Jack. *Untapped Potential*. Nashville, TN: Thomas Nelson, Inc., 1998.

Limb, John. *United in Christ*. Portland, OR: OCP, 2007.

Mandino, Og. *A Better Way to Live*. Bantam Books, 1991.

Maritain, Jacques. *La Persona y el Bien Común*. Quito, Ecuador: FESO, 1988.

Maxwell, John. *The 17 Essential Qualities of a Team Player*. Maxwell Motivation Inc., 2002.

Maxwell, John. *The 21 Irrefutable Laws of Leadership*. Nashville, TN: Maxwell Motivation, Inc., 1998.

Maxwell, John. *Developing the Leader Within You*. Georgia: Injoy Inc., 1993.

Maxwell, John. *Líder de 360°*. Nashville, TN: Maxwell Motivation, Inc., 2005.

Maxwell, John. *Thinking for a Change*. New York, NY: Hachette Book Group, 2003.

Mazel, Ella. *And don't call me a racist!* MA: Ella Mazel, 1998.

Meyer, Joyce. *The Power of Simple Prayer*. Hachette Book Group, 2007.

Narramore, Clyde, and Ruth Narramore. *Como Dominar la Tensión Nerviosa*. Editorial Caribe, 1978.

Nelson, Thomas. *The Holy Bible, New King James Version*. Nashville, TN: Thomas Nelson, Inc., 1985.

Nicholas, James. *A Book of Wisdom and Delight*. Bloomington, IN: University Books, 2008.

Olsen, Walter, and William Sommers. *A Trainer's Companion*. Highland, TX: Aha! Process, Inc., 2004.

Ordóñez, Absalon. *Lo Que Pensaron*. Quito, Ecuador: 1989.
Osteen, Joel. *Your Best Life Now*. Hachette Book Group, 2005.

Payne, Ruby. *A Framework for Understanding Poverty*. Highland, TX: Aha! Process, Inc., 1996.

Payne, Ruby. *Understanding Learning: the How, the Why, the What.*
Highland, TX: Aha! Process, Inc., 2002.

Payne, Ruby, and Philip DeVol, and Terie Smith. *Bridges Out of Poverty.*
Highland, TX: Aha! Process, Inc., 2001.

Payne, Ruby et all. *Training Certification - Bridges Out of Poverty.* Highland,
TX: Aha! Process, Inc., 2008.

Peale, Norman. *Enthusiasm Makes the Difference.* Englewood Cliffs, NJ:
Prentice-Hall, Inc., 1967.

Reid, Gregory, and Charlie Jones. *Positive Impact.* Mechanicsburg, PA:
Executive Books, 2006.

Renard, John. *The Handy Religions Answer Book.* Canton, MI:
Visible Ink Press, 2002.

Sanchez, Carlos. *Sangre de Campeón Invencible.* Ediciones Selecta
Diamante, 2003.

Siegel, Bernie. *Amor, Medicina Milagrosa.* Madrid, Spain:
Espasa-Calpe S.A., 1988.

Siegel, Bernie. *Prescriptions for Living.* New York:
HarperCollins Publishers, Inc., 1998.

Siegel, Marc. *False Alarm.* Canada: John Wiley & Sons, Inc., 2005.

Stone-Zander, Rosamund, and Benjamin Zander. *The Art of Possibility.*
Castle Rock Entertainment, 2004.

Stovall, Jim. *The Ultimate Gift.* Colorado Springs, CO:
Cook Communications, 2006.

Stovall, Jim. *El Ultimo Regalo.* Colorado Springs, CO:
Cook Communications, 2001.

Strobel, Lee. *The Case for Faith.* Grand Rapids, MI: Zondervan, 2004.

Tatum, Beverly. *Can We Talk About Race?* Boston, MA: Beacon Press, 2007.

Theibert, Philip. *How to Give a Dam Good Speech*. New York:
First Galahad Books, 2000.

Thompson, John. *The Truth About Change*. Harrisburg, PA: Inner Vision
Training Institute, 2004.

Thorp, Gary. *Sweeping Changes*. Walter Publishing Company, Inc., 2000.

Tisdell, Elizabeth. *Exploring Spirituality and Culture in Adult and Higher
Education*. San Francisco: Jossey-Bass, 2003.

Tolle, Eckhart. *The Power of Now*. Canada: Hamarte Publishing, 1999.

Tolle, Eckhart. *The Power of Now*. New World Library and Namaste
Publishing, 2004.

Urban, Hal. *Life's Greatest Lessons*. New York:
Fireside Rockefeller Center, 2003.

Verderber, Kathleen, and Rudolph Verderber. *Communicate*, 11th Edition.
Thompson Learning, Inc., 2005.

Warren, Rick. *The Purpose Driven Life*. Grand Rapids, MI: Zondervan, 2002.

Weil, Andrew. *Salud con la Edad*. Vintage Español, Random House of
Canada, 2005.

Widener, Chris. *The Art of Influence*. Doubleday Publishing Group, 2008.

Williamson, Marianne. *Enchanted Love*. New York:
Simon & Schuster, 1999.

Wooden, Cindy. "No Government or Religion Can Limit Human Rights."
The Catholic Witness April 25, 2008.

Wyche, Keith. *Good Is Not Enough*. New York: Penguin Group, 2008.

Zachary, Pascal. *The Diversity Advantage*. Boulder, CO:
Westview Press, 2003.

Zelinski, Ernie. *101 cosas que ya sabes, pero siempre olvidas*.
Vision International Publishing. Editorial Amat, 2001.

About the Author

HECTOR RICHARD ORTIZ

Hector is a Community Liaison and Contract Manager in Dauphin County, office of Human Services, in Pennsylvania. He is also a motivational speaker and a consultant in diversity and leadership development as well as in communication, translation, and interpretation services. Hector is very involved in his community and has been privileged to serve in many capacities and been awarded for his service numerous times (see list on next page).

Hector and his wife, Marisol, run a small business that offers consultation in communication, motivational leadership, diversity awareness, cultural sensitivity, and poverty. Their business includes, but is not limited to, natural products distribution, emotional and proactive approach to conflict resolution, and self-help consulting services. Hector and Marisol are foster parents and live in Dauphin County. They have two children: Cristhian Ricardo and Bonnie Zenobia. Hector can be reached at his website: www.hrortiz.com or by email: richie1166@msn.com.

Hector's Education, Associations, Positions, and Awards:

EDUCATION:

- Leadership Harrisburg Area (LHA) graduate, class of 2005
- Bachelors degree in Civil Engineering
- Masters degree in Diplomacy
- Doctorate in International Relations

POSITIONS AND ASSOCIATIONS:

- Founder and former President of Estamos Unidos de Pennsylvania, a grassroots organization created to promote cultural awareness and post-secondary opportunities for kids
- Former President of the Harrisburg Keystone Rotary Club, period 2008-2009.
- Rotary International Assistant Governor, District 7390
- Chair of the Dauphin County Diversity Forum, Advisory Panel
- Chair of the Dauphin County Integrated Service Plan, Cultural Competence Committee
- Coordinator of the monthly Dauphin County Diversity Network Forum and Poverty Forum
- Member of the United Way Latino Services Task Force and Dauphin County Cultural Celebration Task Force
- Board of Trustees of Harrisburg Area Community College (HACC) and Leadership Harrisburg Area Board of Directors
- Associate member of the Diversity Committee of the Association of Community College Trustees

- Member of the Harrisburg Young Professionals

- Co-founder and currently Vice-President of the Latino/Hispanic Professional Association

- One of the founders and Charter President of the Latino Hispanic American Community Center of the Greater Harrisburg Area

- Member of the Capital Region Chamber of Commerce, Business Diversity Council

- Board member of the Pinnacle Health Foundation and Pinnacle Health Annual Gifts Committee

- Serves in the Tri-county Fatherhood Coalition and the Tri-county Emergency Food Management

AWARDS:

- The Estamos Unidos de PA "Our Leaders, Our Community Award," for 2010

- The Nguzo Saba "Ujima" Award for Collective Work & Responsibility, Kwanzaa 2009 Award

- Cornelius Leadership Award: Arms Around Communities, 2009

- Certificate of Recognition from the Latino Hispanic Professional Association, 2009

- Leadership Harrisburg Area: "20 leaders/20 Years" Award, 2006

- Greater Harrisburg Latin Fest Outstanding Service and Dedicated Commitment Award, 2004.